Georgian Feminists

Ten 18th Century Women Ahead of Their Time

Rebecca Wilson

PEN & SWORD HISTORY

AN IMPRINT OF PEN & SWORD BOOKS LTD.
YORKSHIRE – PHILADELPHIA

First published in Great Britain in 2025 by
Pen & Sword History
An imprint of
Pen & Sword Books Ltd
Yorkshire – Philadelphia
Copyright © Rebecca Wilson 2025
ISBN 9781399069250

The right of Rebecca Wilson to be identified as Author of this work has been asserted by her in accordance with the Copyright, Designs and Patents Act 1988.
A CIP catalogue record for this book is
available from the British Library.
All rights reserved. No part of this book may be reproduced or transmitted in any form or by any means, electronic or mechanical including photocopying, recording or by any information storage and retrieval system, without permission from the Publisher in writing.
Set in Aldine 401 13/16.75
Printed and bound in the UK by CPI Group (UK) Ltd., Croydon. CR0 4YY

The Publisher's authorised representative in the EU for product safety is Authorised Rep Compliance Ltd., Ground Floor, 71 Lower Baggot Street, Dublin D02 P593, Ireland.
www.arccompliance.com

For a complete list of Pen & Sword titles please contact
PEN & SWORD BOOKS LIMITED
George House, Beevor Street, Off Pontefract Road, Hoyle Mill, Barnsley, South Yorkshire, England, S71 1HN
E-mail: enquiries@pen-and-sword.co.uk
Website: www.pen-and-sword.co.uk
Or
PEN AND SWORD BOOKS
1950 Lawrence Rd, Havertown, PA 19083, USA
E-mail: Uspen-and-sword@casematepublishers.com
Website: www.penandswordbooks.com

To my wonderful Mam and Dad, who have been through so much over the years but keep going despite it all.

Contents

Introduction	9
Sarah Pennington: Unfortunate Mother	37
Mary Wollstonecraft: First of a New Genus	55
Dido Elizabeth Belle: Spark of the Abolitionist Movement	89
Jane Austen: Hopeful Romantic	112
Hester Stanhope: Non-conformist Adventurer	137
Elizabeth Fry: Angel of Prisoners	150
Mary Fildes: Peterloo Survivor	166
Anne Lister: First Modern Lesbian	182
Mary Anning: Palaeontological Pioneer	204
Ada Lovelace: Enchantress of Number	219
Notes	241
Bibliography	256
Index	262

Introduction

There have always been women who stand out from the crowd, and the Georgian period was no different.

The Georgian period sweeps across many decades from 1714 to 1830, although it is often extended to include the short reign of William IV and end in 1837 with the accession of Queen Victoria. The period is named after the kings of this era: George I, George II, George III and George IV. It was a time of invention, literature, art, music, architecture, fashion, war, and scandal, with many everyday attitudes and daily life changing.

This period saw a remarkable shift in the values and the lives of women, however, in many ways, little had changed since the Tudor period. Women were still expected to defer to the men in their lives and to a great extent remained in the back seat when it came to any decisions that took place outside of their own homes, even regarding their own lives. The realms of politics, business, and finance continued to be dominated by men. The home and all things domestic continued to be the realm of women as it had been for centuries.

We often think of the Georgian period as being that of enlightenment and travel, of literature and learning, and for an elite few, this was indeed the case. But most of the society was trapped in the rigid class system which bound them to remain on their rung of the social ladder, never to be allowed to step up, but always at risk of slipping downwards, into the social abyss. If we think about the novels of Jane Austen, they reflect that rigid social order so strongly linked to this period. Everyone knew their place and fought to climb upwards towards the dizzy heights of the magnificence and opulence of the upper middle classes and aristocracy.

For the poorer working classes, life limped on as it always had. The men went to work long hours in backbreaking jobs, while the women looked after the home and focused on bringing up their growing brood of children. Little had changed for many generations. The best their family could hope for was a day off together to perhaps walk in the park and play games.

The invention of the steam train changed the aspirations of many and its growing popularity led to travel being available to the masses for the first time towards the end of the Georgian period. With the wonderful opportunities this brought, came the criticism and concern about this mode of travel. It was thought by the well-meaning, but grossly misinformed men at the time, that women's uteruses would fly out of their bodies if they were to travel at speed. The bizarre idea that the uterus wanders around the body was a notion that dates from Ancient Greece. It is strange that such an out-of-date view would still be prevalent as late as the Georgian period. It shows a shocking ignorance of the female anatomy and a huge underestimation of women's resilience. The concerned men perhaps told women that they could not travel by locomotive for the sake of their own health, but there is perhaps another reason. There was a fear that if women were able to travel easily, they would do so alone, without a chaperone, without a man to keep an eye on them. It was assumed by some that given the chance, a woman without supervision would do unspeakable and unchristian things. Obviously, women wouldn't simply want to travel to holiday or see friends or family. The 'weaker sex' would automatically be drawn to extramarital affairs and debauchery. These women would then tempt men to be similarly wicked and immoral. The easily available travel network would open up the country and endless opportunities for women to be led astray, and therefore the railways were something to be feared. Perhaps the women would leave their families and have fun, without their men to supervise them. The rumour that a woman's uterus would fly from her body at speed seemed to circulate and serve to attempt to scare women into not travelling. If the women were too frightened to travel on these new-fangled machines, then they would perhaps stay home and repair that shirt and make stew for her husband's dinner instead of galivanting off and having fun.

In Jane Austen's masterpiece *Pride and Prejudice*, the haughty and deeply unpleasant Caroline Bingley says, 'A woman must have a thorough knowledge of music, singing, drawing, dancing, and the modern languages, to deserve the word; and besides all this, she must possess a certain something in her air and manner of walking, the tone of her voice, her address and expressions, or the word will be but half-deserved'.[1] Therefore, a worthy lady of the Georgian period, according to those in high society like Caroline, must have music, drawing, dancing, and languages, but also have an air of sophistication and carry herself well.

If they do not possess these attributes, they are but 'half

deserved' of any recognition. Perhaps it is telling that it is Caroline that says these words. For Austen, and women like her, it was possibly becoming an outdated notion that women were to be accomplished in these ways. Caroline's ideas reflected those of the upper and upper-middle classes. The achievements of what makes a woman deserving was becoming increasingly absurd and archaic to those who saw the world as Austen did.

The heroine of *Pride and Prejudice*, Elizabeth Bennett, is often mocked for belonging to a poorer family who made their money through trade. When Elizabeth's older sister Jane becomes ill, Elizabeth walks through muddy fields to be with Jane. Caroline comments on Elizabeth's clothing after she had walked alone across the fields: 'I hope you saw her petticoat, six inches deep in mud, I am absolutely certain; and the gown which had been let down to hide it not doing its office'.[2] Caroline is suggesting that Elizabeth had 'let down' her dress, both physically to hide the mud and also let down her sex by showing 'an abominable sort of conceited independence'.[3] Elizabeth is painted as wonderfully liberated and intelligent. She loves her sister Jane deeply and thinks nothing of walking three to four miles to see her, forgetting the norm of the period of being 'ladylike' and having a chaperone when out in public. Whereas Caroline sees Elizabeth's actions as 'scampering about the country because her sister has a cold',[4] to Elizabeth this walk was a natural reaction to her sister being ill. The word 'scampering' suggests an animalistic movement, as if Elizabeth is some sort of small rodent. Elizabeth needed to get to her sick sister, and without a carriage or time to wait for a chaperone, she set off alone, quite against the usual expected etiquette of the time. This shows her determination and independence, walking this distance alone across the muddy fields, especially in a time when women were rarely unaccompanied.

For the most part, the role of a woman remained much as it had done for centuries. Girls were brought up with the sole purpose of finding a husband, ideally one of good standing and with money. If she could secure a husband from a respectable family, who could provide her with wealth and links to a 'good family', it would of course help her rise in social class. However, this was not always possible, so many matches were made within their own social levels, always with the hope of one day climbing.

It was of course 'universally acknowledged' that a 'single man in possession of a good fortune must be in want of a wife'.[5] It was true that many men desired to be married as society and their families demanded it. It was expected that, regardless of someone's sexuality, they had to be married to someone of the opposite sex and have children, bringing about, no doubt, many deeply unhappy people. Upon marriage, the woman was absorbed into the husband's legal identity. She had never really had her own identity, as the 'daughter of' and now 'the wife of'. Her position was always one in relation to the man in her life and never her own.

Marriage was for life, as divorce was still a taboo subject. Often the only way out of an unhappy marriage was the death of either spouse. Girls could be betrothed to marry as early as twelve, and boys fourteen. Despite this young age, many did not say 'I do' until they were in their late teens or early twenties, when they were more secure financially and the boys had finished their apprenticeships. It was a long-term commitment to be attached to the same person for so long without any way out of what was essentially an arranged marriage.

Although some engagements were arranged quite early in a child's life, sex did not occur until after the couple were married, sometimes many months after the marriage ceremony. Girls and boys were usually at least sixteen when they entered into the physical side of their marriage, but there were exceptions to this general trend. Perhaps lessons had been learnt from the past, when child brides became mothers and their health was compromised.

Once the girl or woman was married, the authority over her passed from her father to her new husband. In the marriage ceremony today it is common for the father of the bride to 'give away' his daughter, placing her hand into her new husband's hand. This is the symbolic transference of 'power' from her father to her husband, passing on the supremacy from one man to another. Her life was never her own, and upon marriage, instead of autonomy, she merely had a shift in her overseer. There is less emphasis on this element in modern marriages, but the action of the father of the bride passing his daughter's hand into her husband's is still done, with the symbolism of this unspoken.

Women who did not get married, for whatever reason, were seen as outsiders and strange. A single woman without a fortune must be in want of some financial help. Women without husbands would struggle economically, unless by some good fortune they had some means of financial support themselves. Many women got married purely for money, their husbands providing for them, especially if their families were poorer or had fallen upon hard times. It was a bonus if they happened to like their spouse, a real boon if they loved each other and were happy together. Some were very lucky and enjoyed being with each other; others, as you will read in this book, were not so fortunate.

Single women were marginalised by society. It was seen as bizarre that someone would choose to stay single in a world full of married people. As with today, many simply did not wish to be married, however, this was not an option for the majority of people.

During this period, women could inherit property. This sounds wonderful, until you look more closely at the law. Women's names would appear on the will, but she would not be allowed to run the property. A man had to do this. A male relative or younger brother perhaps, had to do the day-to-day running of the property. It was his decisions, not hers, that would be considered when decisions, big or small, were taking place regarding renovations, changes to the architecture and décor. Despite the property being in her name, she could not change anything. If she was married, she could still own the property in name only, and it was her husband who would make the decisions regarding the upkeep and running of the property and lands. It would be well into the Victorian era before a law was passed to allow a married woman to own property and run it as she saw fit.

If her husband died and he happened to leave her the house and land in his will, she would not officially inherit. The moneys would be put into a trust to be overseen by a male relative. She could continue to live in the house, but her financial dealings were supervised. There was an assumption that she could not possibly manage her money successfully by herself and would need some male advice and supervision to help her protect her finances.

If she was left a widow or did not marry, she had few options to support herself. If she was educated, she could perhaps find a position as a governess or nanny in a grand house, or if she was poor, she could work in a factory, or mill or on a farm. There was, of course, always the option of 'the oldest profession', whether as the courtesan of a duke or a prostitute in a backstreet brothel. However, many would only do this as a last resort to avoid starvation of herself and her family, as it brought with it terrible risks of losing their good reputation on the marriage market and the very real danger of bodily harm or death at the hands of a violent man. Many became part-time prostitutes while working elsewhere, possibly a factory. She perhaps struggled to pay the bills with only one wage and was forced to put herself in danger to feed her family. The only other option was to rely on charity of family members to keep her from starvation. Charities took each case individually and only the most deserving cases were taken on. Not everyone had families that they could rely on for financial help or practical help with childcare, so many women who found themselves alone with a child, did as much as they could to pay their way in life.

Girls would be taught from an early age to sew, embroider, manage her household, and other practical skills that would show her to be accomplished. She would also learn to read and write, paint, dance, and play musical instruments and sing. Obviously these skills differed amongst the classes. A young lady belonging to the middle and upper classes would be taught languages such as French, Latin, and Italian. They would be taught embroidery and needlepoint.

A young woman from a poorer background would sew to make, repair and patch clothing, and darn socks for herself and those of her family, much more useful skills than the embellishment of clothing. This highlights the difference between the rich and poor that rather than the sewing just being a diversion from boredom, the poor women were sewing for practical reasons to clothe their families and save money. The rich women sewed for something to do.

A poorer woman would also be taught to cook by her mother, aunts, or older sisters, as she would need to cook for her family. She would perhaps be expected to cook for her family while her mother was tending to younger siblings. Only the middling sorts and the upper classes would have afforded staff to clean and cook for them. Girls from poorer families would also have had a hand in raising younger siblings or their brother's or sister's children who would sometimes live with them.

The boys of middle to upper classes would be given more in-depth education, even going so far as to live with the tutor in some cases, so he could be entirely submerged in his learning. Poorer boys would be given basic instruction in reading and writing and learn the trade of their father or if they were lucky, would be apprenticed to a local tradesman to learn a trade that would keep them gainfully employed well into adulthood.

Many working-class parents could not afford to send their children to school, but poorer girls and boys would perhaps go to a dame school if their parents were lucky enough to be able to afford the fees. Dame schools were small, privately-run schools. The name is almost a misnomer, as usually the lessons were taught in the teacher's own home rather than there being a purpose-built classroom. They were a cheap form of childcare for parents who were working and served as an early precursor of a nursery or infant school.

For a small fee, a woman from the village or town would teach the local young children to read and add, and sometimes how to write, although this was often only taught to the male students. Girls would be shown how to sew and knit in addition to their more academic subjects. This would potentially be a valuable source of income in the future for the girls. It would have been a very different experience from school-to-school as the volunteers had varying degrees of knowledge and skills to pass on to their students. Also, resources were limited for some, whereas other students had access to hornbooks, a thin piece of wood with the alphabet or *The Lord's Prayer* written on it. It is unsurprising that there would be a religious element to the teaching. The children would also learn the catechism and reading from the Bible was encouraged. Dame schools were in existence from the sixteenth century until compulsory education was introduced.

Another option for poorer parents was a blue coat school. The first blue coat school was set up in 1552 by Edward VI. It originated as a foundling hospital that educated children as they grew. The idea soon spread and the schools were dotted around the country. There are still blue coat schools today, but these are now typical government-run schools that still carry the name of their forebear. These schools would provide a basic education in an environment that more closely reflects that of a school we would recognize today. The children were separated into older and younger students and rudimentary reading, writing, and numbers taught, with a focus on religious education and prayer. They were very different to the dame schools due to their purpose-built classrooms and resources.

Some girls from wealthier families attended boarding school. There is an information pamphlet for a ladies' school in High Wickham in Buckinghamshire in the 1730s that advertises an education in 'English and French languages, dancing, writing, music, and all other female accomplishments'. The school lists its price per quarter, which was £3 and 11 shillings for full board and access to all subjects. Given inflation, this roughly translates to around £700 per quarter in today's terms. This would mean that a young lady's education would be around £2,800 per year, well out of the price range of many parents.

Women were seen as inferior to men and had been so for centuries. Girls grew up being told that they were substandard and lacking in moral courage, intelligence, and physical ability. They were not just the 'weaker sex', but deficient in all the faculties that mattered. Boys and young men, however, were taught that they were the strong leaders of the future and had to keep their women's changeable and potentially subversive behaviour in tight check for their own good. It was thought that women could not possibly be allowed too much freedom, or it would have terrible consequences for themselves, their husbands, their families, and society would suffer.

With such a stranglehold on women's movements still controlling their daily lives, women needed a way to escape. As the saying goes, 'necessity is the mother of invention', and women's need for autonomy drove them to invent a whole language using fans. This language had evolved from the signalling that took place in the French court of Louis XIV and Louis XV. Fans had become fashionable in Britain and were a staple accessory during the balls and most of the wealthier women had them. They used the fans to directly communicate with a gentleman. If a man caught a young lady's eye whilst she sat there waiting to be asked to dance, she could 'tell' him via movements of her fan. Equally if a man made advances towards a lady and she did not want his attention, she could tell him so via a different wave of the fan.

According to Laura Camerlengo, associate curator of costume and textile arts at the de Young Museum in San Francisco, 'records suggest that as early as the eighteenth century there was a discussion of these fan languages'.[6] Madeleine Luckel, who writes for *Vogue* magazine, states that 'not only are fans beautiful and practical objects to carry on a warm day, they are the means to a secret language that has been largely forgotten with time'.[7] It is amazing to think that a whole series of secret conversations were going on in the ballrooms, parks, and public spaces, and anyone not in the know was oblivious to these exchanges.

The earliest signals from fans were individual letters given in a basic semaphore communication. They were unsophisticated and took some time to transfer a sentence or thought. This signalling would later evolve into a more intricate interaction where whole sentiments were indicated with a single gesture. Whole sentences and commonly used phrases were shown to others with a specific wave or flutter of their fan.

The 'language' was a series of elaborate movements, such as carrying an open fan in front of her face meant that she wanted to meet him. Fanning slowly and deliberately meant that she was married and fanning quickly meant that she was engaged. Placing the closed fan on the left ear meant that she was no longer interested and twirling the fan in the left hand was a warning that they were being watched. Opening and shutting the fan meant that the man was being cruel, perhaps dancing with others and not her, and placing the handle of the fan to the lips meant she wanted to be kissed. This intricate series of movements was presumably understood by many women and their potential suitors.

These signals would become more widespread and by the mid-Victorian period had been written down in pamphlets and circulated throughout upper- and middle-class society. It was no longer an underground subversive language, but more of a generational form of communication, not unlike the way the use of emojis and social glyphs amongst younger generations is often misinterpreted and misused by older generations today.

Richer Georgian women would attend balls. These were the parties in which the young ladies would be presented to society so they might find their all-important husband. The eligible young ladies would dance with eligible bachelors in attendance and see if there could be a suitable match between any of the couples. The dances were intricate and teachers were employed to provide training. The less 'desirable' women were left without a dance partner. Their card, a paper they carried with a list of names the woman had agreed to dance with, would be empty and they were forced to sit it out on this strange mating ritual. The men, even the shy ones, would ask women to dance, as it was expected. Most men there would be eligible, so long as they had money and their reputation was good. A man without money would struggle to find a decent match. An honest social standing was paramount, otherwise if the man had a reputation of mistreating those around him or had rumours about squandering money or drinking to excess or gambling, then they would be avoided by all but the very desperate. Marriage was for convenience, not for romance or love, but it was important for both partners to know the other would socially conform to the expectations that the Georgians accepted to be the norm.

Pregnancy and childbirth were still huge killers for mother and baby, with numbers barely improving since the Tudor and Stuart period. Some sources suggest that up to twenty per cent of mothers died during childbirth or immediately after, around one woman for every five births. It is likely and shocking that the infant mortality rate was similar. This is possible because of the frequency of infection contracted due to unwashed hands or instruments used during the birth. Also, it was common for these infections to enter open wounds and tears during the birth of the child. This risk increased dramatically after the fifth child. Complications such as breech births and obstructed deliveries would often prove fatal to both mother and baby. Little could be done if the baby was the wrong way around or if the umbilical cord became wrapped around the baby. There was obviously no blood pressure monitoring for the mother or baby and no scans to check their health throughout the pregnancy. No monitoring was performed at any point so if anything had gone wrong, there was nothing that could be done.

By today's standards, the medical practices across the board were barbaric, particularly in women's health. Common prenatal care often consisted of purges, bleedings, induced vomiting, and starvation diets. The twisted logic behind this treatment was to keep the baby small, thus leading to an easier birth. If the mother was underfed, bled regularly, and made to be sick often, this would lead to the baby remaining small and therefore easier to birth. This horrific treatment of the mother no doubt led to the high mortality rate of both mother and child. The modern medical advice is to eat plenty of good nutritious meals with a little treat or two to cheer the mother up. Starving the mother will only result in the baby being underweight and possibly underdeveloped due to the missing nutrients in the mother's diet. Many expectant mothers during this time were also made to endure 'lying-in'. This entailed the mother to be lying in bed for many weeks or perhaps months in the run-up to childbirth, even if there had been no signs of early labour or health problems with the mother.

The 'lying-in' room would usually be a bedroom in the house not hospital. The windows were sealed shut with blankets lining the seals of the glass and often covered with blankets and heavy curtains. The theory behind this was to prevent the expectant mother from catching cold. With this in mind, the fire was kept stoked and burning hot, even in summer, and every breath of fresh air expunged and blocked from the searing and suffocating room. Blankets were piled on the bed and the unfortunate woman would be kept uncomfortably hot for weeks at a time. It must have been torturous for the poor women enduring the discomfort of being heavily pregnant along with the stifling heat of the 'lying-in' room. Not only would this room have been oppressive in the extreme, and dangerously depleting the oxygen needed for the woman and her unborn baby, but it would create a perfect breeding ground for bacteria, the very thing that they were trying to avoid. The mother-to-be would undoubtedly be sweating and it would be difficult to keep herself from dehydration in the baking-hot oven of a room.

It is believed that such practices led to the death of the much-loved Princess Charlotte, hours after she delivered a stillborn son in 1817. Although Princess Charlotte had been encouraged to walk a little for her health, she had still endured many weeks 'lying-in'. Charlotte was the only legitimate child of the Prince Regent, George, who would later become George IV, and his estranged wife Caroline of Brunswick.

The death of the little baby prince and his mother shook the country, leading to a public outcry of what could have been done differently to save them. They had loved the princess and were heartbroken for her and the loss of her baby boy.

Oddly enough, richer women were usually more likely to die during childbirth than their poorer counterparts. This was possibly because the poorer families could not afford to shut off an entire room of their house to allow the pregnant person their 'lying-in' period. The poorer women had more opportunity to have fresh air and the vital oxygen denied the richer women. It was also common for the richer women to be placed in a 'birthing chair' as soon as their contractions begun. This was an adjustable chair, sometimes with part of the seat cut away, and sometimes with stirrups for the woman's legs to be placed into. The idea of the birthing chair dates from at least the time of the Bible. In the book of Exodus in the Old Testament, it states that 'when ye do the office of a midwife to the Hebrew women and see them upon the birthstool'.[8] However, it was not the birthing chair's ancient usage or its connection to the Bible that encouraged the wealthy Georgians to adopt its popularity. The birthing chair offered an element of modesty to the proceedings of childbirth. It allowed the mother-to-be to be sat in an upright position, covered up, with her skirts about her knees or perhaps ankles. They saw no need for a lady of good breeding to lie flat in bed with the bedclothes up around her waist. That would have been most improper, most impolite, and most shocking!

Although the sitting up position has been argued to make for an easier and quicker birth, with gravity playing a role in the delivery, it has been argued that the birthing chairs had the opposite effect for the Georgian women. Perhaps it was the fact that even the midwives themselves were trying to keep the mother-to-be covered up at these pivotal times? The midwife would perhaps put her head beneath the woman's skirts and peer into the semi-darkness to see the progress of the baby, rather than lift the skirts out of the way entirely? It seems strange to us that modesty would be the primary concern given the high mortality rates of both mothers and their babies.

If the baby was stuck in the birth canal, then it was becoming popular to use tools to help the baby out. Forceps had been invented during the Jacobean period, but were not used more widely until the early Georgian period. Even then, many doctors did not like them and refused to use them. It has been thought that if forceps had been used for Princess Charlotte then her baby and the princess may have survived.

In 1830, in Germany, a physician, Bernard Heine, invented a new instrument to 'aid' childbirth. He called it the 'osteotome', a flexible hand-cranked saw that would become known as a chainsaw. If the baby was stuck in the birth canal, the saw would be used to cut through flesh, cartilage, and the pubis, the bone at the base of the pelvis. The theory was to cut through anything that was in the way of the baby getting out of the woman's body. The chances of the woman surviving this brutal vivisection was obviously slim to nil. She would almost always die once this 'procedure' was carried out and her consent was never sought. It was usually done when the woman had little chance of survival, but the baby had not yet been born. They took little care to ensure the mother's survival in the hope that the baby would be cut out safely.

There could be parallels made with modern women's health in certain parts of the world today. The decisions about a woman's own body are made without her consent, and she could likely die because the life of her unborn child is seen to take precedence over hers. Many women have died both in the past and present because their health is not considered or understood properly.

Caesarean sections did take place, but this was usually only after the mother had already died or was breathing her last. There was no careful surgery involved and the lower stomach as well as the womb were sliced open to retrieve the baby. It was not done carefully or with respect, and usually hacked at by whoever was in attendance, often without medical training other than learning by trial and error. It has been claimed by some that a caesarean could not take place when the mother was living, as there was no anaesthesia available. However, this is untrue. Laudanum, a mixture of opium and alcohol, and opium alone were used for many years for sufferers of chronic pain and for other surgical practices. They were used for menstrual cramps, sleep aids, toothaches, headaches, and a wide range of other ailments in adults and children, so why not for caesarean sections? The pain would have been managed to a degree and operations could have taken place to perhaps save both their lives. The chance of infection would have been great, even if the woman did manage to survive.

Introduction

There are no records kept determining how many babies lived after a caesarean section. It may be that the doctors thought they had nothing to lose, given that the mother had already passed away. However, when a decision was to be made whether the mother or child lived, it was often thought that the mother's life was worth little compared to the baby.

If the mother had lived through her surgery, chances were with such a large wound, she would succumb to infection after a few days anyway, given the lack of cleanliness of doctors' hands, beneath their nails, and the level of sterility of the blade used to make the incision in her lower stomach and womb. Even if by some wonderful miracle all these items were spotlessly clean, the bacteria would breed at the site of the wound after the blood was wiped away with a dirty apron, used cloth or even bedsheet already covered with various bodily fluids.

Even if she survived the trauma of childbirth or surgery, she still had a long way to go before she would be safe. If she avoided infection by some miracle, she could still die as her body was at its weakest and most prone to illness. A new mother was usually put on a liquid diet of tea and/or wine for the first week after birth. No solid food was allowed to pass her lips. This fasting so soon after giving birth would cause massive dysfunction in her intestines and stomach, all of this aggravated by having been forced to 'lying-in' in a hot room for weeks, perhaps months, beforehand. Also, if a new mother is drinking nothing but tea and wine, they are not getting the right nutrients and vitamins their body needs to survive, and if they were breastfeeding, their baby was also not getting any of the goodness he or she needed. These terrible misunderstandings and misguided medical advice of what a woman needed in pregnancy, childbirth, and the weeks and months that followed the birth of a baby, led to so much illness and unnecessary discomfort, pain, and in many cases death. It is a wonder any woman survived this horrific torturous time in her life. Even today, up to twenty-five per cent of pregnancies end in miscarriage and pregnancy can lead to many health problems. Despite knowing this terrible price she may have to pay, many women actively tried to get pregnant, knowing it was what society expected of them. She began her pregnancy with perhaps excitement, but no doubt a great deal of trepidation. In the Georgian period, those worries were very well-founded and the personal need for children and the pressure from society meant that many women got pregnant and risked their lives many times over. It was common to have a child every year to eighteen months during a woman's fertile married years. The risk to their life increased with every child, as they got older and played the odds of infection.

Those responsible for medical practices were tragically unaware of the importance of handwashing and clean linens during childbirth and it would lead to so many avoidable deaths. It wasn't until the 1840s, in the Victorian era, that clean hands and linens became the norm, although germ theory was not accepted until the 1870s. The washing of hands and bed linens during childbirth reduced the mortality rate from around twenty per cent to around six per cent overnight, proving its importance, although there were still those who refused to wash their hands.

Women were always seen as 'the weaker sex' and treated as second-class citizens. But why was this? The Bible story of Genesis was told to support the myth that women were inferior to men. It was after all Eve who listened to the serpentine devil in the Garden of Eden and ate from the Tree of Knowledge. It was because of her disobedience that all womenkind were cursed with the pangs of childbirth. It was because of her that every baby born was burdened with 'original sin', her sin of defying God's only rule. She was the reason that the pair were cast out of Paradise itself, and out of their God's love. She was to blame for everything, and therefore, every woman was to blame for Man's shame.

The story tells of how Eve talks Adam into tasting the Forbidden Fruit. Adam took the fruit from Eve and ate it, too, but it is her, the only woman in the story, who is blamed. God was not blamed for showing them the tree and refusing them the Forbidden Fruit. The Devil, disguised as a talking snake, is not blamed for encouraging Eve to eat from the tree. Adam is exempt from this blame to a great extent, so it is women who were inflicted with the pain of childbirth. This was possibly seen as a way to justify the brutality of the treatment of women during pregnancy and childbirth.

Eve was created to keep Adam company. She was to be his plaything in the Garden of Eden. She was not created in 'God's image' as Adam was, but was created as an afterthought. In the Bible, she is made from Adam's rib. God reaches into Adam's chest and creates her from that bone. Eve is therefore seen as an incomplete man. Adam was created from 'dust from the ground' and God 'breathed into his nostrils and man became a living soul'.[9] Eve was never created from that same earth or God's breath, but came from man. She is therefore 'less than' Adam, made from him, but imperfect.

Faith, as it had been for centuries, was deeply important to many people. The early eighteenth century seemed to mark a shift into an age of reason, moving away from the physical church. There were plenty of people who still attended church on Sundays and some still felt a strong urge to attend, although some simply found themselves there out of habit and social custom. There were of course those who attended church at Easter, Christmas, and other religious holidays. The upper classes would usually attend to make a good example for the less fortunate.

The vicars and priests would speak of damnation and hell's fire for those who did not attend, and perhaps this was enough to keep some repeat congregation members coming back each week. There was no fine for not attending church as there had been in the centuries earlier. However, God remained a big part of people's lives and belief in Him continued despite church attendance fluctuating throughout the century.

As the century moved on, a change seemed to sweep the country. A group of men in Oxford began to meet under John Wesley. The group distilled Christianity down into the key elements, such as the holy communion, observe the fasts and feasts, and to visit the sick and prisoners of the parish. At the centre of this Wesleyan movement was a focus of true faith in God and for God to be at the centre of their lives. This religious undertaking became known as 'The Great Awakening', and soon swept across Europe and the American colonies.

This 'Great Awakening' had a huge impact on the general population. It produced powerful preachers who, instead of speaking from pulpits to the pews, spoke to crowds outside. They still had their fine churches, but could preach from a pulpit, a town square or a field, they found God anywhere. They encouraged people to have a personal relationship with

God. This pulled people away from the ritual and ceremony that had brought people come rain or shine to the countless country churches throughout the nation. Instead, the 'Awakening' made Christianity a deeply personal experience, fostering a deep sense of spiritual conviction and redemption. It encouraged people to look inside of themselves and explore what they considered morality, setting their own standards for right and wrong and encouraging introspection.

John Wesley and his brother, Charles, had been in America as missionaries, and when they returned to England in 1738, found their beloved home country losing its faith and God. This deeply upset the men and they began attending prayer meetings searching for answers. The Wesley brothers started preaching and considered England their parish. The brothers toured the whole of England, Southern Scotland, Ireland, and the Isle of Man. Although not his initial intention, Wesley's message would ultimately separate his followers from the rest of the Church of England, and this group were called the Methodists.

The Methodists would continue to grow in popularity and their preaching and focus on personal faith continued to gain supporters. Both the Wesleyans and the Methodist Church allowed women to be ordained. This was done as early as the mid-1860s and really was revolutionary, considering that the Anglican branch of the Church of England did not allow women to be ordained until 12 March 1994, which is shockingly late in our history. For women to be accepted to be in the clergy was very forward thinking in an institution that had been dominated by men for millennia.

Fashion was at the forefront of a lady's persona that she

presented to the world. At the beginning of the eighteenth century, the dresses worn were quite modest and loose fitting. A lot of ladies' fashion consisted of layers. She would wear a chemise, which was a loose knee-length shift, made of linen. This was worn to prevent the rich expensive clothing of the outer layers coming into contact with the skin of the wearer. This undergarment would be easily and regularly washed, and the outermost layers were not, to preserve their delicate embroideries, lace, and fabric that were shown to the world. Lace and ruffles were often pinned onto the neckline and cuffs of the chemise so that these could be seen sticking out of the outer layers.

Stays, a forerunner of the corset, were worn on top of the chemise. Unlike many historical dramas on television and film, the stays were never worn directly on the skin. The stays would dig into the bare skin and be uncomfortable to wear. The chemise would always go underneath, making the wearing of the garment more comfortable. The bodice of the stays was stiffened with strips of whale cartilage, known as baleen, or lengths of cane. They were not yet tight-laced corsets, however, as television shows would let us believe. To tight-lace a corset, metal eyelets are needed, and these would not be invented until 1828. Without the metal eyelets, the fabric would tear and would not last long. The stays would be laced up through stitched eyelets, and tongues of fabric at the bottom of the bodice would allow for hip movement.

As the century rolled on, fashion dictated that the gowns became more close-fitting. In an odd way, some elements of the Tudor court became fashionable again, such as the stomacher. This strange invention was a V-shaped piece of fabric, often heavily patterned with lace, embroidery, or even gold and jewels, and pinned into place on the bodice, as the dresses fastened with a deep neckline. The more elaborate the pattern on the stomacher or petticoat, the more wealth that women represented. A woman from a poorer household could not afford to spend precious hours and money making a statement piece of clothing. Her wardrobe would be made up of simply-made utilitarian clothes: practical, unpretentious, humble, and without unnecessary adornments.

Hooped skirts became fashionable to achieve a bell-shaped silhouette. By the mid-1730s, the fashion took a turn for the ridiculous. The dresses of high society became comedic, with flat back and front and hips so wide that the wearer could not even reach the edges of her dress. To achieve this look, the women wore baskets on their hips beneath the skirts. These baskets were made from whalebone or cane and were known as panniers.

These panniers became so wide that the ladies could not sit side-by-side on spacious chairs or even pass through doorways without side-stepping awkwardly. It would have been a comical sight to witness the ridiculous lengths that these women had to go through to achieve simple everyday tasks, and even more humorous in a formal setting with the cream of society in attendance. In anticipation of the debut performance of Handel's *Messiah* in Dublin in 1742, female guests were politely requested to not wear their hooped skirts.[10] It would perhaps be for many practical reasons, from finding space for everyone in the auditorium given the huge space each of these skirts would take up, and for safety reasons. Given that the ladies' skirts were so big, they would be difficult to manoeuvre through doorways and if there was an emergency, perhaps a fire, there would be many potential casualties because doorways, corridors, and stairwells would be blocked by enormous skirts.

These panniers and this huge silhouette became popular amongst the wealthy ladies throughout a great deal of Europe because it showed their wealth. It showed that they could afford the many yards of fabric required for such a dress. Most people could not afford reams of fabric for just one dress, and certainly would not be able to afford the time and effort required to embroider or bead patterns onto a stomacher or collar or cuff of their chemise. Of course, wearing a dress with huge panniers, would have been incredibly impractical. Only ladies who could afford to sit and do nothing could wear such a dress. Most women had work to do, whether it was looking after their children or cooking or cleaning. Trying to do any physical activity wearing panniers would have been difficult. Even sitting down would be challenging and would have taken practice to position the whalebone panniers in a way to allow sitting to be feasible. It is a credit to these ladies that they could get in and out of their carriages and go up and down stairs wearing such outfits. It would take practice to do almost every daily task, sitting, standing, walking, moving through doorways, and perhaps the biggest challenge of all, going to relieve herself.

There was no disposable fast fashion during the Georgian period and fabric was prized. When a dress was unfashionable, it was recut, restyled, and sometimes unstitched completely to make a piece of clothing for a younger child or sibling or to gift to someone else, perhaps a poorer relative or servant. The rich did this too, as fabric was a precious commodity. Sometimes a richly decorated piece of fabric, particularly silk, could be donated to the church, to be used as an altar front or vestments for the clergy.

The textile industry was growing fast and producing a huge range of silks, wool, and cotton, all for home dressmaking. Some of these cottons were mass-produced block printed and became very popular during the latter part of the century and were readily available throughout much of Europe.

In April of 1782 a fashion article, from *The Ladies Magazine* reported that fashions had changed again: 'The Queen of France has appeared at Versailles in a morning dress ... said to be the universal rage ... it is drawn up in the front on one side and fastened with tassels ... .' [11] This style became known as 'the polonaise' and the skirts were a few inches shorter than had been the fashion, showing a shocking amount of ankle.

This fashion never really caught on in England, but the more fashionable English ladies did watch the French court with fascination. In England, the fashion opted for a much simpler version of French fashion, going for a style based on that of Ancient Greece and Roman fashion. The dresses were loose, made of muslin, with long straight skirts, high waistlines, gathered necklines, and narrow sleeves, supported with a bustle rather than a hoop or pannier. They moved increasingly towards what we recognize as a typical English Regency dress, as seen in many Jane Austen screen adaptations.

The French Revolution of 1789 had a profound impact on fashion. After the peasants had attacked the aristocracy and taken their lives, there was a severe distaste for all things frivolous and ostentatious. Wearing clothing that reflected this decadence was risky to say the least. It was thought that it was better to leave behind the theatrical frills and ribbons of the fashion icon Madame de Pompadour, King Louis XV's official mistress. Her clothing had been the envy of Europe and she even had a particular shade of pink created by Sevres porcelain factory named after her – 'Rose Pompadour'.[12]

Female followers of fashion looked to the French socialite Madame Jeanne Francoise Julie Adelaide Recamier as their new icon. Her great beauty and style exuded that new effortless neoclassicism that rejected the previous frippery. Her fashion was elegant and at the same time unassuming and it was exactly the right public statement to make. The clothing chosen was not just fabric chosen for its beauty and form, but a political statement, aligned to a social ideal and ideology. Every decision was important, given the political tensions across the English Channel.

The women in this book chose very carefully how they presented themselves to the world. The public face that they chose to show was important as it could make or break them in the eyes of society.

SARAH PENNINGTON

Unfortunate Mother

≈

Lady Sarah Pennington is such an interesting woman. The little that is known about her earlier life shows real strength and determination. She married and had children, but when that marriage began to sour, she took control and left her cruel husband to start her own life elsewhere. She wrote a well-received book, which is seen by many readers today as ground breaking in its feminist ideas of womanhood. In the book she outlines her motherly advice to her daughters and to all young women, telling them how they should behave and how they should follow their hearts regarding what is the best course of action for themselves, regardless of faith or expectations in love. A mother giving this kind of advice to her daughters was shocking as most people, regardless of gender, were beholden to the church for spiritual and moral guidance. To suggest that a young woman should follow her own moral compass and not the church's was unusual.

Lady Sarah was born in Bath in Somerset in 1720, although her actual birth date is unknown. She was not poor, but did not belong to the aristocracy at birth. The record keeping at innumerable churches varied. Some administrators were careful and obsessive, recording every christening in their parish, with the names and dates. However, some were less meticulous and did not record any details, other than higher born parishioners.

Her father, John Moore, was probably also born in and around the Somerset area in about 1695. She had no in-depth formal education. She would have been given instruction in reading, writing, and mathematics, with a religious element, too. With this relatively basic education, she must have been naturally gifted with a curious mind and a drive to learn. All her education would likely have been done at home, rather than in a traditional classroom environment. Many young ladies did not attend school as we would recognize it today, instead having a tutor visit the house to teach for a few hours a day. She was lucky to have even this, as many girls from poorer backgrounds were home-schooled by their mothers, who lacked the relevant knowledge and skills. She absorbed her learning well and became an avid reader into her teenage years. It is likely that she kept a diary, as was the fashion, however, if she did, the pages sadly do not survive. What a wonderful and insightful read those pages would have been. They were perhaps destroyed later by her abusive husband.

The first time she really comes into records properly is when she married Sir Joseph Pennington of Warter Hall in the East Riding, of Yorkshire. He was a commissioner of customs, who was responsible for the collection and management of revenue and enforcement of restrictions on items in and out of the country. He was two years her senior and became Fourth Baronet Muncaster upon the death of his elder brother John Pennington on 26 March 1768. He was highborn and his family owned property throughout the North of England.

Sir Joseph was born in January of 1718 and was christened on 20 January in Warter in Yorkshire. His parents were well connected. His father, also Sir Joseph Pennington, was the Second Baronet Muncaster. His mother was the Honourable Lady Margaret Lowther. She was the daughter of John Lowther, First Viscount Lonsdale, and Katherine Thynne, who was the daughter of Sir Henry Fredrick Thynne, who was created First Baronet Thynne of Kempsford in the county of Gloucester on 15 July 1641.

Newlyweds Sir Joseph and Lady Sarah came to live at Muncaster Castle in West Cumbria on the edge of the Lake District. Muncaster is a beautiful castle with so much history. Its pele tower dates from the fourteenth century, built on top of Roman foundations dating to around the second century AD. The rest of the house was added to over the coming centuries. Muncaster has been home to the Pennington family for at least 800 years, perhaps even longer.

Their marriage was not a love match, but a marriage of convenience and logic. Women from middling to richer families were expected to marry into equally wealthy families or those who were even more well-off. This elevated the woman's family, made connections for business and secured their children's status.

The Penningtons are an ancient family with royal connections. In 1464, Sir John Pennington is said to have given shelter to the then King Henry VI whilst he was wandering in a daze after the Battle of Hexham, one of the many skirmishes of the Wars of the Roses. The king was found aimlessly walking on the surrounding hills by some shepherds, who directed him to Muncaster Castle. Sir John welcomed the king out of the cold and he stayed at Muncaster Castle for some days, allowing him to recuperate back to full health due to their hospitality. As the Pennington family had shown such loyalty to the king, he rewarded the family with a glass bowl which came to be known as 'The Luck of Muncaster'. It was said that if the bowl ever broke or was taken from Muncaster Castle, the house and the family would fall. The bowl survives to this day and the family and the house continue to go from strength to strength. The Penningtons remained in royal favour for many years to come and were therefore a good choice for Sarah to marry in to, knowing their royal connections, wealth, and their ancient family name. It made sense for her to marry Sir Joseph, but sadly she knew nothing of his personality until it was too late.

Lady Sarah and Sir Joseph would soon grow to despise each other. Perhaps Lady Sarah imagined a domestic idyll, a doting husband, happy children running around the expansive grounds of their beautiful home. However, life for her would be very different from this ideal and she would realize her husband's penchant for cruelty only after they were married. Many young brides entered their marriages feeling hopeful and positive. Some were lucky and found good matches where their husbands were good men and they loved each other or at the very least were content. However, this was not the case for many, who discovered their new husbands to be cruel, distant, or oppressive, tormenting their wives with various forms of abuse.

Sir Joseph was a notorious scoundrel, well-known wastrel, heavy drinker, gambler, and womanizer. His family knew of his repute, but his new wife would only discover it after they were married. He certainly found himself with a reputation for self-destructive and narcissistic behaviour, so much so, stories about him are still told to this day about his character. He squandered much of the family fortune and almost lost the family home of Muncaster as a result. Lady Sarah soon despaired of her new husband and often reproached him for his wild conduct. She would chastise him, but he did not like his wife telling him to stop wasting money and drinking so much, and it often made his temper even worse. There is no record of physical violence by Sir Joseph aimed at his wife, but according to the stories passed down in the family, he certainly abused her in many other ways, such as intimidation, verbal, and emotional abuse. He would often leave the house for days at a time and when he finally came home, he was very drunk, massively in debt, and even more argumentative than normal. This obviously left Lady Sarah exhausted, frustrated, and deeply disappointed with the way her life had turned out.

Despite this, the couple did have six children, although this may have been to appease the social expectation to have children rather than Lady Sarah wanting to sleep with the man who was a bully. It would be expected that a married couple would have children, even if the couple did not feel like their marriage had a future. It is entirely possible that the couple had children for the sake of society and for the Pennington family name. Although he had a bullying nature, there is no evidence that he ever sexually assaulted his wife.

Their children were Joseph, the eldest, named after his father, Jane, Margaret, Catherine, John, who would become 1st Baron Muncaster, and Lowther Pennington, who became 2nd Baron Muncaster and then succeeded as the Sixth Baronet Pennington of Muncaster in the county of Cumberland. All their children would go on to make good marriages themselves and live relatively long lives. John would serve as a Member of Parliament in the constituencies of Milbourne Port, Colchester, and later Westmorland.[1]

We do not know if the bullying extended to his children. There are no records of physical abuse of his children, but there are oral stories passed down to the current family of the way he treated the children. According to these verbal stories, he seemed to be apathetic about his children, not caring about them at all, which is of course a form of abuse.

Sir Joseph's bullying got worse over the years. Twelve years into the marriage, the fighting came to a head. During a particularly heated argument between the pair, Lady Sarah had reached her limit with his temper, packed her bags and left him. Unsurprisingly, there is no record of what the argument was about. Perhaps it followed yet another one of Sir Joseph's binges, where he had lost a lot of money again. It is known that Lady Sarah did not want her husband to do this, as his overindulgences were becoming more and more frequent. He locked the door after her and kept the children before she had a chance to take them with her. He did not do this because he loved them and wanted them close to him, but because he knew it would hurt their mother to be separated from them. It really did hurt her deeply, she missed them so much. Sir Joseph's cruelty made Lady Sarah despise her estranged husband even more, rendering their relationship irreconcilable.

It must have taken so much courage to leave her husband. It would not have been unheard of to separate from a spouse in this way, but it would be very rare and certainly gossip-worthy to voluntarily leave a marriage. The fact it was a wife leaving a husband was not typical at all and incredibly brave of her. Women had no tangible rights at this time in history. She would get no legal advice in regards to getting her children back, no financial support to put food in her belly, or intervention for her housing situation. She would have been completely alone. Divorce was still frowned upon and was only rarely allowed through very specific circumstances and a costly private Act of Parliament.[2] Even if a separation had been agreed by both parties, there was still a terrible stigma attached to the estrangement. Marriage was seen as being for life, no matter how bitter, violent, or abusive it was. 'Until death do us part' was the marriage vow and only death severed the vow between the couple. Sadly, in some cases, extreme action had to the taken to leave their marriage or perhaps death would have come prematurely for an unfortunate number of women. As divorce was a rare outcome, few women escaped violent and abusive marriages.

Their private arguments and growing resentment behind closed doors could no longer be contained and kept quiet once Lady Sarah left and it turned into a very public scandal.[3] Muncaster Castle is many miles away from neighbours, but this did not stop rumours being spread around the local area about the couple. They were the Lord and Lady of Muncaster, the biggest, grandest house for many miles, so their names and likenesses were known by the locals as celebrities of sorts. Perhaps the servants overheard their arguments as it would have been difficult for them to be ignorant of them. It is easy to imagine the shouting behind closed doors, the smashing of glasses, and the slamming of doors as those arguments became heated. The servants would be aware of the icy looks and atmosphere at mealtimes as they brought the food into the dining room and laid it in front of their master and mistress. It would be the servants who cleaned up the smashed glass and crockery and repaired or replaced other damaged items. The lady's personal maid could perhaps be a shoulder to cry on. Lady Sarah was alone at Muncaster and had no one else to talk to, so it is entirely possible that she was sometimes caught with her guard down in the quieter moments and poured her heart out to a friendly servant who listened in horror and interest.

Sir Joseph's portrait hangs at Muncaster Castle in the Main Hall to this day, and for some reason, the light above his portrait keeps going out. Despite repeatedly being fixed, and the wiring of the house checked many times, the light over his portrait will not work long term. The staff at the house jokingly suggest that it is perhaps poetic justice that the man is left in the dark after his terrible treatment of his wife and children. Across Muncaster's Main Hall from Sir Joseph's painting, is a portrait of Lady Sarah and her mother, Mrs Moore. Lady Sarah sits next to her mother in the portrait. It is telling that they are sitting side by side; they are allies united against Sir Joseph. Mrs Moore is wearing a blue dress with a plunging neckline. She is sitting at a writing desk, perhaps about to begin writing letters to friends or family. She is not looking at her work though, but sits facing away from the desk and staring across to the portrait of him across the hall. She does not look happy, but deeply scornful as she stares across the Grand Hall at her vile son-in-law. Lady Sarah's mother looks very youthful and as if she had given birth to Sarah when she was little more than a child herself. They could be sisters. She sits at a right angle, facing fully to the right of the portrait. Even her chair is turned to fully face the front of the portrait. She has nothing to hide and nothing to be ashamed of. Lady Sarah, on the other hand, has her back entirely to her shameless husband. She wears silver and her dress seems to shine in the light over their portrait. It is as if she cannot even look at the man she married. The way the portraits are placed across the Grand Hall from one another, it looks as if Lady Sarah has turned her back on her husband, as she did in real life due to his behaviour. In contrast, Mrs Moore stares at her despicable son-in-law, as if she is forever bewildered and disgusted by the man.

When Lady Sarah left Muncaster and her hostile husband, she found herself making her way back to her home town of Bath. There she began to write what would be her defining book, *An Unfortunate Mother's Advice to Her Absent Daughters; In a Letter to Miss Pennington*.

The book has been written about extensively throughout the years. There is a whole chapter devoted to it in *Flirtation and Courtship in Nineteenth-Century British Culture*. Editor Ghislaine McDayter describes Lady Sarah's book 'as much a confession as it is a text of etiquette' [4] in that Lady Sarah outlines her own 'scandalous'[5] past and 'social misdemeanours'.[6] She writes openly about her failed relationship with Sir Joseph and his behaviour towards her. She writes about her decision to leave him and her regrets and heartbreak about leaving her children. McDayter refers to their marriage as 'uncongenial',[7] but this word does not fully encapsulate how turbulent and toxic their relationship truly was. It suggests an impoliteness, or perhaps rudeness, however, the feelings between them were far more serious leading to their irrevocable separation.

First published in 1761, Lady Sarah's book directly addresses her daughters, Jane, Margaret and Catherine, although it appears to specifically address Jane, her eldest daughter, known to her as 'Jenny'. She must have only been around eleven years old at this point, perhaps only ten. Margaret was a year younger and Catherine a year younger still. They were all still so young, but certainly old enough to realize their mother was not living with them anymore and definitely old enough to miss her and be affected by the increasing frequency of arguments between their parents.

Although the book is particularly addressed to her daughter(s) it is thought that many young women read her work and took her advice to heart. She advises young women to be strong and not to tolerate cruelty from their husbands. Many young women were entering marriage blindly, saying 'I do' without knowing their husbands or the families they were becoming a part of. A great number of these women found themselves, like Lady Sarah, in desperate situations, loveless, alone, and miserable. Perhaps the readers of Lady Sarah's books had been instilled with the confidence and strength to leave the men they discovered to be damaging to them.

The first lines of the book are heartbreaking. They read 'My Dear Jenny, Was there any probability that a letter from me would be permitted to reach your hand alone, I should not have chosen this least eligible method of writing to you'.[8] This opening line suggests that writing a book was the only way that she was able to reach her daughters. Sir Joseph had cut her out of his life entirely and banned her from seeing her daughters in any way. This presumably included writing to them. Perhaps he had given strict instructions to the servants at Warter to deliver all the mail to him personally. Sir Joseph was a powerful man and could have easily strong-armed the servants to pass on any letters or parcels from Lady Sarah. He was an intimidating figure and as their boss, had their jobs and accommodation in his hands. One word from him would have made them homeless and jobless with no reference to find other work. The terrified servants would do as he told them, so letters from their former mistress would not reach the children. It is easy to imagine Sir Joseph sifting through the correspondence on his desk, his dark unforgiving eyes scanning the handwriting on the addresses to see if his wife's writing was there amongst the mundane letters. Perhaps he had an occasional moment of intrigue when he thought he recognised a hand. It is entirely possible that Lady Sarah had attempted to contact her children this way. It was the only method of communication bar visiting someone face-to-face. It is not difficult to imagine Sir Joseph, upon seeing a letter from his estranged wife and mother of his children, angrily tearing the letter up into tiny pieces and watching the remains of it burn in the fireplace. It is possible that she wrote many times, and her letters were destroyed. This is perhaps what happened to any personal papers she had had in her rooms after she left. It is easy to imagine her angry husband bursting into her room and pulling papers and books off the shelves and desk, and carrying them through to the Great Hall, where the fire burned furiously. Him perhaps giving excuses to the children as they ran around, helplessly unable to prevent their mother's memory being destroyed in front of them.

It is difficult to imagine the pain that Lady Sarah felt not seeing her children, particularly her daughters, with whom she seems to have had a very close relationship. It seems such a desperate move to write and publish a book, just to be able to send a message to loved ones. It shows the hopelessness in her attempts to contact her children. It also indicates a potential worry on her part about her children's welfare, particularly that of her daughters. It is possible that Lady Sarah was uneasy about her children being under the guardianship of her unkind husband. Perhaps she worried that they were being mistreated, too. It is possible that she felt guilty about leaving the way she did, replaying those last moments in her head, wondering what she could have done differently to change the sad outcome.

In her book she goes on to state: 'The public is no way concerned in family affairs and ought not to be made party in them; but my circumstances are such as lay me under necessity of either communicating my sentiments to the world, or of concealing them from you.'[9] She acknowledges that the public should not hear of their family disputes and would probably not care to hear about their troubles, disputes, and subsequent separation. It is so distressing that she had to decide between revealing to the world their family situation or her daughters growing up entirely without their mother's love or guidance. It was an impossible situation for Lady Sarah as by telling the world of their arguments and estrangement, she risked her own reputation in a time when a woman's standing was paramount. She was the one who left the marriage and therefore she was seen as the one to blame for the breakdown of their holy vows. She perhaps wanted to get her side of the story out in public to gain sympathy. She certainly had been wronged.

The publication of her book, however, was not met with the derision she would have expected. Lady Sarah was 'never condemned and ostracised'[10] as many women would have been in the same situation. Many women who left their husbands were shunned by the local community and never really accepted into polite society again. To her surprise, her work was met with positive acclaim. Perhaps it was her 'eloquent defence'[11] of her actions and her explanation of her unpleasant and impossible position she had been in in her marriage. To some, her situation highlighted the uncomfortable and painful situation of women entering marriage. It was also used to highlight the unfortunate place that women have in society.

Lady Sarah attempts to explain her situation to her daughters in the book. She explains the 'most extraordinary nature' of the events that led to the children being left without their mother. She wrote that the children were left without the 'tender care of an affectionate mother'. It is sad to think of the young children left without their mother at so tender an age. From what is understood, Lady Sarah was a good mother, warm, and affectionate. She was quite the opposite of their father, who seemed to be very cold, aloof, and irritable.

She wrote, 'you were then too young to be able to form any right judgement of her [their mother's] conduct, and since that time it was very probable that it has been represented to you in the most unfavourable light'.[12] She writes this as if she is talking to her daughters in person, which is quite heartbreaking. It is almost an apology that the girls were so young when she left. She states that as all the children were young when she left the family home, they were unaware of what really happened. The eldest would have only been eleven or twelve years old and the youngest would only be a toddler the night that door slammed shut behind her. As all the children were pre-teen, they would have known little of what was happening. The youngest of her children would have barely remembered her and by the time they were old enough to verbalize their thoughts, Lady Sarah would have been nothing more than a vague blurry memory. Perhaps the oldest children, although they would of course remember their mother, would not have been fully aware of the intricate details of their parents' increasingly public arguments. They would grow up without her there, without her calming influence, but with their father's anger and bitterness.

Without her there to give her account of what went on, their father would have told the children his version of events. He told them the 'unfavourable' account of the arguments. Sir Joseph was easily able to poison the children's minds against their mother, exaggerating and telling outright lies about Lady Sarah and why she left them. He was in the perfect position to slur her name. If he had barred the servants from allowing her entrance to the house and he burned her letters to the children, they had no way of knowing how their mother truly felt about them. Sir Joseph could 'prove' their mother wanted nothing to do with them. As far as they were concerned, she had never visited them and they had never even received a letter from her. Sir Joseph could point to this absence as evidence that their mother wanted nothing to do with any of them anymore.

She continues to write that in future 'suspend your belief of all that may have reached your ears with regard to me and wait the knowledge of those facts'.[13] Here, she asks her daughters to try not to make judgement of her, but wait until they know facts of her relationship with their father. There is a suggestion that she hopes that when the girls are old enough, they will understand their mother's actions better.

She also gives life advice for her daughters. She mentions presenting dinner, and other mealtimes, cleaning, and general house related management. She writes: 'Aim for perfection, or you will never attain an amiable degree of virtue. Be religious without hypocrisy, pious without enthusiasm. Endeavour to merit the favour of God, by a sincere and uniform, obedience, to whatever you know or believe to be his will.'[14] Religion was important to Lady Sarah, as it was to the majority of people during this time. She advises her children to be good, god-fearing Christians.

She writes 'and should afflictive evils be permitted to cloud the sun-shine of your brightest days, receive them with the submission, satisfied that a Being equally wise, omniscient, and beneficent, at once sees and intends the good of his whole creation'.[15] Perhaps that is how she felt? Sir Joseph was her 'afflictive evil' that darkened what would have been her brightest days as a young mother. She believed that all this hardship, the cruelty she faced from her husband, the end of her marriage, losing any contact with her children, and becoming homeless was all part of God's plan. That perhaps He was testing her devotion to her faith. Did she feel then that she had succeeded in proving her worth to Him? Perhaps it could be read that she wished her daughters to be strong enough to rise above their 'afflictive evil' and do as she did, removing herself from the 'darkness' that had enveloped her life.

The last page of the book reads: 'Thus have I endeavoured, my dear girl, in some measure, to compensate both to you and to your sisters the depravation of a constant maternal care, by advising you, according to my best ability, in the most material parts of your conduct through life, as particularly as the compass of a letter would allow me.'[16] It is heartbreaking and beautiful that she refers to her eldest daughter Jane, or 'Jenny', as 'my dear girl'. These last pages are almost an apology to her. The fact that she is absent and not able to be there with them, instructing the girls as a mother should.

She continues: 'May these few instructions be as serviceable to you as my wishes would make them! And may that Almighty Being, to whom my daily prayers ascend for your preservation, grant you his heavenly benediction; may he keep you from all moral evil, lead you into paths of righteousness and peace, and may he give us all a happy meeting in that future state of unalterable felicity, which is prepared for those, who, by patient continuance in well-doing, seek after glory and immortality.'[17] Here, Lady Sarah states her hopes and wishes for the girls. She hopes that God will guide them to do right and lead a good life. More than anything, she seems to want to see her children again. A 'happy meeting' is longed for by Lady Sarah more than anything. She signs the book off, 'I am your truly affectionate mother, S. Penningon'.[18] This once again shows how she wishes to be viewed by her children. Perhaps she uses the word 'truly' as even years later she worried about her children believing lies told about her. She probably rightly assumed that little in the way of 'truth' was told about her in her absence. She wanted to be seen as 'affectionate' by her children. It is doubtful that the children experienced affection once their mother left. Sir Joseph was not an affectionate, warm man at all. Perhaps she wanted to offer herself as this role to remind her children of the warmth that she had provided as a mother, albeit for a relatively brief time.

Although she quite rightly blamed her husband for the initial breakdown of their marriage, she took full responsibility for her part in its failure. In her book she states that in circumstances such as hers, a woman must look to her own conscience as to what to do, rather than blindly cling to her marriage vows. She managed to avoid the censure that many women would have faced in those circumstances. In fact, her book remained in print for years to come and stretched to numerous editions and has been included in many anthologies throughout the nineteenth century. She would also go on to write another two books, *Letters on Different Subjects*, published in 1766, and *The Child's Conductor*, published in 1777, but neither came close to the popularity of her first book.

She died in August of 1783. The exact date or the cause of her death is sadly not recorded. She was mentioned in *The Gentleman's Magazine* in a glowing and clearly sympathetic obituary.[19] She was obviously well-known and liked enough to warrant them marking her death. It is a shame that no more information is known about her passing. Her cause of death, according to Lorna Sage, was 'severe and uncommon afflictions'[20] which could be any number of terrible ends.

Lady Sarah Pennington was never reunited with her beloved children. When she died aged only sixty-three she had not seen them for many years. The stress and agony of not seeing her children grow up cannot have helped her mental or physical health. She was a three-times published author, penning the books in her own name, in a time when female writers were still unusual. Despite the very small, intended readership of her first book, it became a bestseller. She saw no reason why words spoken in front of a member of the clergy should force her to stay in a loveless and toxic marriage, and this alone made her philosophy so fresh and unique. She saw her own safety paramount and did not stay with a violent abusive man as so many no doubt did. Her strength to leave that marriage and her determination to contact her children made her stand out from the many married mothers in the country. She went to such lengths to make her children feel loved.

MARY WOLLSTONECRAFT

The First of a New Genus

Mary Wollstonecraft was one of the founding feminists of her age. Many feminists since have cited her life and works as influences for their philosophies and views, a wonderful accolade for her. She was a writer and long-time advocate for women's rights[1] during a time when women had so few rights. She led an unconventional life guided by her own sense of morality and not only spoke but took action against injustice wherever she saw it. Mary was also the mother of the famous Gothic writer Mary Wollstonecraft Shelley, the author of *Frankenstein: The Modern Prometheus,* and a magnificently headstrong woman in her own right.

Mary was born on 27 April 1759 in her grandfather's house on Primrose Street in Spitalfields in London.[2] Her mother was Elizabeth Dixon, or Dickinson in some documents, perhaps due to a mishearing of her spoken name. She was an Irish woman from a wine merchant family. Mary's father was Edward John Wollstonecraft, an English weaver who specialised in silk. Mary was the second born of their seven children. She had four brothers, Edward, Henry, James, and Charles, and two younger sisters, Eliza and Everina. She would stay closer to her sisters than her brothers, but they were a close family.

Her childhood was a deeply unhappy one. Her father was a bully of a man. He regularly assaulted her mother, herself, and her siblings. He was very aggressive with them all and was feared, not loved, by his family. Years later, Mary would recount the terrifying stories of her sad childhood. A tragic start to her life and that of her siblings, living in fear of their bullying father.

The area of Spitalfields was busy and overcrowded. It was a manufacturing centre where items were made and taken to and from the market. Houses were overflowing with hungry and overworked desperate people and were in some cases barely fit for human habitation. Factories and front rooms where weaving often took place were equally cramped and badly lit. Wages paid for a fraction of the sorrow and pain their hard work brought them. Edward Wollstonecraft's offices were close to where they lived.

When Mary was around six years old, the family moved to Barking, a small market town in the county of Essex, which has now been swallowed up by East London in the borough of Barking and Dagenham. Edward must have struggled to find work as a silk weaver in their new town and strangely made the decision to become a farmer. It was an odd choice for a man who had never had any training or knowledge of farming. He was possibly forced to leave the weaving profession because of his increasing anger towards his customers or fellow traders in the area. He had perhaps gained a reputation as an unreliable worker, and it is not difficult to imagine him being rather cantankerous, rude, and argumentative with his customers.

Edward was unsurprisingly not a good provider for his

family. He squandered what little money he made on gambling or drinking. Their mother Elizabeth struggled to feed and clothe her family as a result. Edward continued to fritter money away and the family were forced to move to possibly downsize their house or rent. They perhaps had to move to avoid debtors finding where they lived. Or maybe it was another harebrained scheme that her father had been tangled up into that forced them to move. He was prone to squandering money on the next 'big earner, get rich quick' business scheme, or gambling away what little they had on a 'dead cert'.

The family would be forced to move for the third time before she was ten, this to Beverley in Yorkshire, a much more rural setting compared to the noise of London. Mary loved her time in Yorkshire. She loved the house and garden they lived in and the natural world they were surrounded by. It was a world away from the loud city life she had grown up in. The family had space to breathe the clean air and enjoy a quieter life. The beauty of nature was a great comfort to Mary and her siblings as their father's alcoholism and violence spiralled out of control. Home life must have been a harrowing reality for the Wollstonecraft children. Mary found herself with her siblings out in the fields that surrounded them. The rural childhood idyll of climbing trees and swimming in the river was in stark contrast to their home. How desperate must they have been to stay outdoors away from the place that was anything but homely. She and her eldest sibling, Edward, two years her senior, would protect the younger brothers and sisters, but it was usually Mary, Edward, and their mother who bore the brunt of the violence and cruelty.

As Mary grew older, she became increasingly concerned for her mother's well-being. It is entirely possible that she witnessed violence or perhaps even sexual assaults enacted on her mother by her father. There is an anecdotal story of the young Mary curled up at nighttime on the landing outside her mother's bedroom so as to prevent her father hurting her mother further.[3] Presumably she knew that she was using herself as a human shield, stepping into her mother's place to be attacked and hurt. Whether or not she targeted her father's anger away from her mother that night is unknown. It is quite tragic that a young child felt the need to protect an adult, when it is the adult's job to protect their family. A father should protect his family, not be the source of their pain. He was a bully and a deeply unpleasant individual who made his family despise and fear him. This horrible situation shows that even from a young age Mary had a strong sense of justice and felt the urge to fight unfairness. She did not want to be hurt herself, but put herself in danger to protect her mother, a woman she perceived as weaker than herself.

She would also play a maternal role to her younger sisters, Eliza and Everina, perhaps because she felt a responsibility as the eldest girl to take on this role. She could also have seen herself as their protector and mother substitute as their actual mother was increasingly feeble and silent.

Later on in life her little sister Eliza was suffering greatly with what has in more recent years been diagnosed as postnatal depression. Mary also realised that Eliza's husband, Meredith Bishop, was adding to her pain being an overly controlling individual. There is no mention of Bishop being physically violent with Eliza, but he certainly seems to have been a domineering person. Eliza was clearly not happy with her lot in life and wanted her marriage to be over, perhaps regretting starting a family with a man she had grown to despise. Mary was so worried about her younger sister that she made arrangements for Eliza to pack up and leave her home, away from the baby and her husband. Mary left with Eliza and they hid themselves away at Hackney, where Eliza, away from the sources of her sadness and stress, began to recover emotionally and physically. Being a first-time mother can be overwhelming. It would have been highly unusual for a mother to leave home away from her child and husband. It was seen as a woman's place to be at home caring for her child, looking after the home, and doting on her husband. It was expected that she should want to do this for them and give up her own needs and wants to provide the care they needed. The fact that Mary was willing to dismiss the current norms shows how ahead of her time she was. However, this advice horribly backfired for Eliza, who faced public condemnation for her actions. Although she had left her husband, she was still technically married and therefore could not remarry and was made a social outcast. She was doomed to a life of hardship and poverty.[4] Mary no doubt felt terrible for her younger sister's situation, especially as she was instrumental in making it happen. She did, however, believe at the beginning that she was taking the best course of action for Eliza's mental health and long-term happiness. Eliza would make a full mental and physical recovery although tragically Eliza's little daughter did not survive long after their separation.

Later in life, when Mary wrote her book *A Vindication of the Rights of Woman* she attacked the social system that forced women to run away from their marriages as there were no other options available to them. She was no doubt writing of Eliza when she penned this chapter. Had there been other options available for Eliza when she felt trapped, she could have perhaps stayed with her daughter which could have saved her life. Sadly no advice or financial support was there to be offered to the likes of Eliza and her story is a tragically common one.

Mary's education was not a good one. Whilst they lived in Yorkshire, she started to attend a day-school. It was an inexpensive school, but was enough to provide her with the basics in reading and writing, although little else.[5] Mary later praised the school for its inclusiveness, as public schools were usually exclusively attended by boys and only offered education for an extortionate fee.

Mary had two close friends in her childhood that she maintained throughout her life. The first was Jane Arden, later Jane Arden Gardiner. Arden's father, John, was a scholar and one of Mary's teachers. He perhaps sparked her love of literature and natural philosophy, a philosophical approach to physics and nature together, a strange mixture of science and philosophy. The two friends would attend lectures by John Arden and discuss various books they had read. After Mary moved away from Yorkshire, the two girls wrote letters to each other regularly, well into their adulthood.

The atmosphere of learning is something that Mary very much appreciated at the Arden household. It had a relaxed and cerebral atmosphere, in complete contrast to the heavy, tension-filled environment in her home. In some of her letters to Arden, she expresses her feelings of deep depression and low mood that seemed to plague her life.[6] The feelings of anxiety and depression are perhaps something that she would have been prone to naturally, but certainly would not have been helped by her volatile and violent childhood. It is entirely possible that

that level of trauma stays with someone for the rest of their lives, affecting them in their relationships, friendships, and even the way they view themselves and their own self-worth.

The second friend important to her was Frances 'Fanny' Blood. Lifelong friends, they wrote to each other regularly throughout their teenage years and well into adulthood. They were introduced by mutual friends, the Reverend Clare and his wife. Mary adored the couple and would spend a lot of time with them in Hoxton, part of the Hackney area of London. She talked with them about different subjects and read books he suggested, such as Jonathan Swift and John Locke. Mary perhaps viewed the Clares as parental figures. The Reverend certainly presented a much more positive paternal role model than her biological father, being calm, well-read, intelligent, and supportive. Between her time with the Clares and Fanny Blood, Mary found her kin and would later credit Fanny and the Clares for her love of reading and for opening her mind[7] to the wider world of academia and learning. Blood would go on to become an illustrator and educator.

In 1778, aged around twenty-one, Mary left home. She was deeply unhappy there. Her father was as cruel as ever and her long-suffering mother still being bullied by him. The atmosphere there was one of heaviness and past distress. The ghosts of previous arguments and violence played out in her head and she was desperate to leave. The children were almost all still at home at this time, the youngest, Charles, only eight. The eldest son, Edward, named after his father, preferred the name Ned, to perhaps distance himself from his violent father. It is understandable that he wanted to be known by a different name to his father, given the terrible violence they had all suffered. He also perhaps wanted to have a different given name as he worried about being like his father. Ned had recently left home to be closer to his place of work and despite Mary begging to go with him, he left without her. She was desperate to get away from the pain and torment and must have been deflated to discover that her brother was leaving without her. Their mother did not want another child to leave the nest, and refused to let Mary go with Ned.

The family lived in rooms belonging to a bank clerk called Thomas Taylor. Taylor was an intelligent young man who often entertained Mary by chatting to her about Plato, Aristotle, and other Ancient Greek philosophers, a subject she found interesting and had spent time reading up on. Perhaps Taylor was attempting to flirt with the now twenty-year-old Mary, but she did not respond, either as she was not interested him or perhaps did not realize Taylor was trying to make advances. She had little to no experience of men having spent a large chunk of her life looking after her siblings or with Jane Arden's family, talking about literature, history, religion, science, and philosophy.

In 1778 she finally got the opportunity to leave the house, finding a position as a lady's companion to Sarah Dawson, an elderly widow living in Bath. A lady's companion was a throwback to the days of ladies-in-waiting where a woman who had a certain level of sophistication would be paid to accompany a wealthy woman around and do minor personal duties, such as pack her bag for overnight travels and accompany her on those trips. The closest male equivalent of this role would be a valet in a grand house, but probably the best description of this role in modern terms would be a personal assistant. It was a job that could potentially be a very useful way to acquire style, refinement, and contacts to help in better marriage prospects or to perhaps be left with a small fortune when or if their mistress died. Mary hated her role and perhaps did not see the possible benefits worth her time spent miserable. She intensely disliked Dawson as a person and as an employer. She was too demanding of her time and condescending to her, believing Mary's intelligence to be very limited. Perhaps she spoke down to Mary because she was from a less wealthy family and assumed she was less intelligent as a result. She remained in Dawson's employ for two years, which no doubt felt much longer, doing a job she hated. She so despised the role that when she wrote *Thoughts on the Education of Daughters* in 1787 she listed the many terrible drawbacks of working as a lady's companion. Seven years after leaving the employ of Mrs Dawson, her experiences there still grated on her so deeply that she wanted to discourage young women from taking on such roles. She had little to say about the perks of the job, but was scathing and brutally honest about the drawbacks of her former occupation.

She eagerly left Mrs Dawson's employ in 1780 in response to a sad letter she had received telling her of her mother's illness and impending death. Her mother had always been a frail woman, but now was dying[8] and Mary became her main carer until her eventual passing. Poor unfortune Elizabeth did not live long after her daughter returned to look after her. Perhaps Elizabeth had desperately held on to life until her daughter had arrived, only dying after her arrival, feeling the relief that she got to see her one last time. After her death, Mary moved in with the Blood family, happy to be away from the family home again.

Very soon after Elizabeth's death, Edward remarried and

none of the family approved of this. It is easy to see why they did not like this idea. Their mother had only just died, and it was unseemly for a widow or widower to remarry too soon after the death of their spouse. Edward had always treated Elizabeth with cruelty and hostility in life and this was another example of how little he cared for her, finding her 'replacement' so soon after her death. It is understandable why his children did not want to see him remarry. They perhaps did not want their father's toxicity to spread into another family group, distributing his own brand of misery and fear to his new family. They had all been so unhappy growing up, and the thought of their father and his new wife possibly having more children to bully, filled them with horror. They married anyway, but there are no records of children from this second marriage.

After the death of Elizabeth, Mary understandably did not want to return to the employ of Mrs Dawson. Who could blame her? It is at this point, whilst living with her friend that she realised that she had romanticised Fanny Blood. Perhaps due to her unpleasant time with Mrs Dawson, she had glamourized her friend somewhat, believing her to be a kindred spirit. She had perhaps thought of Fanny as her redemption, the person to help her emotionally deal with the stress and despondency she felt working for her employer. They do say that absence makes the heart grow fonder, as it is easy to romanticize people at moments when they are distant in miles or memories. Upon seeing her again and living with her, Mary realized that her friend was very old-fashioned in her world view, not like Mary at all. Fanny liked the idea of being a wife and mother, which was not a problem to Mary, but Fanny also thought that all women should aspire to have that life and wish for nothing. She had very differing views to those of Mary who had seen first-hand what the dream of domesticity had done to her mother and sister. Nevertheless, Mary stayed with her friend, despite their very different views. She even helped Fanny's brother financially occasionally and helped him with his paperwork while they lived together. She liked to make herself useful, perhaps as a thank you to the Blood family for allowing her to stay with them.

Mary had imagined a beautiful world with Blood. A female paradise where the two could rent a room together and be each other's support, both financial and emotional. Sadly, the harsh financial reality of life hit them hard and they quickly realized that they could not afford it. How wonderful it would have been to have a female Utopia where they were each other's sustenance. They would be independent of men and enjoy their lives free of social constraints.

Mary decided that she, Blood, and her sisters would set up a school in North London. They started Newington Green School, a school for girls only, but although Mary and her fellow founders were hardworking, the school fell short of the ideals they dreamt of. Reading, writing, simple mathematics, and sewing were the flavour of learning. If parents wished their daughters to have a more comprehensive education, then they had to keep their girls at home and teach them their preferred curriculum. It seems to jar against what Mary stands for in feminist ideals. Those girls under her care were given the same education as they would have had elsewhere: basic, ordinary, and sparse. It is disappointing that the girls were not given a more inclusive and wide-ranging education, one with sciences, mathematics, engineering, and languages. An education which would encompass a more complete learning to parallel and even surpass the boys' schools.

Mary would thankfully later change the way she felt about women's education, perhaps because she saw the level of intelligence, debate, and questioning amongst her pupils at Newington. Mary possibly assumed that society was right to only educate women up to a basic level due to their future roles like so many others had done. I like to think that she maybe saw in her young female pupils a spark of cleverness that she had not expected to see, a spark that could change the future. Perhaps her pupils inspired her to reflect on her own views and make a change for the better.

The status quo would not last for long though. Fanny met and fell in love with a young man, Hugh Skeys, and left for Lisbon, Portugal soon after they were wed. Skeys thought that a warmer climate would help Fanny's failing health.[9] She had never been a particularly healthy person and often had bouts of sickness that incapacitated her. Poor Fanny's mental and physical health continued to fail, despite the change of scenery and warmer climate. Her health got suddenly worse when she became pregnant, and Mary left the school to nurse her.[10] She appears to have been a naturally caring person who seemed destined to be a nurse and protector of the weak. It is possible that as Fanny's body was trying to provide for the growing life inside her, it was no longer able to sustain the woman herself. All her goodness was going to the baby and Fanny was getting none of the nourishment, leaving her weak and ever closer to death. Sadly, Blood died on 29 November 1785 upon the birth of her child. It seemed that all of Fanny's life force was taken to sustain her child and when the baby was born, her mother had no more life left. In Mary's absence, the school failed to prosper and had to close within a year. She was so devastated by Fanny's death that Mary based part of her first novel on her friendship with Fanny, *Mary: A Fiction*, written in 1788.[11] She would never forget the friendship she had found with Fanny Blood, as although they did not share ideals about life, she was a fixed point for Mary in her ever-changing world.

After Fanny's death and the closure of her school, Mary managed to get a position as a governess. She was to teach the daughters of an Anglo-Irish family, the Kingsboroughs, in Ireland. She struggled once again to get on with the lady of the house, Lady Kingsborough.[12] Perhaps both had strong personalities, or perhaps opposing views of what femininity and womanhood meant. It is possible given Mary's experience with her previous employer that she entered this job already feeling aggressive towards Lady Kingsborough. This initial internalized anger towards the rich woman, not unlike the infamous Mrs Dawson, may have in turn made Lady Kingsborough dislike her instantly, which could have become a self-fulfilling prophecy, leading to an unpleasant working environment. The children, on the other hand, loved Mary as a person and as a teacher. She was natural with no pretences, so unlike other governesses that had come before her. She spoke to them honestly and passionately. One of the daughters, Margaret, would go on to write female-emancipatory fiction and health advice. She stated that it was Mary that 'had freed her mind from all superstitions'.[13] The superstitions could have referred to Margaret's religious faith or her political affiliations. Given her aristocratic background, it was expected that she favour the more conservative political stance. However, she was rather liberal and supportive of women's rights and had very modern views of education, possibly due to Mary's influence. Margaret would later teach Mary's second daughter Mary Shelley. She is a lovely link between mother and daughter and one wonders if King ever told stories about her mother to her young student.

Her time spent as a governess would lead Mary to write her only children's novel in 1788, a collection of short stories, with the snappy title *Original Stories from Real Life; With Conversations Calculated to Regulate the Affections and Form the Mind to Truth and Goodness*.[14] The stories were morally instructive tales for children, a genre that was quite popular. There are stories such as *The Treatment of Animals, Anger-History of Jane Fretful, Lying, Honour, Truth, Small Duties, A History of Lady Sly and Mrs Trueman*, and *Anger, Folly produces Self-Contempt and the Neglect of Others*. There are twenty-five short stories in total, all of them moral tales and warnings for children to be good people. These sorts of tales were popular, although it would be many years before the Grimm brothers wrote their famous fairy tales. It was around this time that she decided to embark on a career as a writer instead of a governess. She was angry and frustrated with the career options open to women. So few women made a living from writing and it seemed an unusual, perhaps even radical choice. Women had written novels and had works published, but few before her had really set out to achieve this and fewer still had made a full-time career from it.

She wrote to her sister Everina in 1787 and explained that she hoped to be 'the first of a new genus'.[15] Mary could see that the life that she wanted was not available to her as a woman, so she wanted to create her own, carve out her own niche for herself. Plenty of male writers managed to make their living, some a great living, from their words, but as a woman, she had no same gendered role-models to follow. She bravely decided to quit her job as a governess, move to London, and find a place to live. She was helped by her friend and liberal publisher Joseph Johnson, a real supporter of radical thinkers.[16] She showed a natural talent with languages and learned German and French quickly,[17] translating German and French texts into English and vice-versa. Notable books she translated were *Of the Importance of Religious Opinions* by Jacques Necker, a Genevan banker, statesman, and reformer, and the German education reformer Christian Gotthif Salzmann's book *Elements of Morality, for the Use of Children*. She wrote a great deal of reviews, mostly of novels for Joseph Johnson's *Analytical Review*, a notable periodical that despite its relatively small readership was feared by the conservative factions within William Pitt the Younger's government.

During this time, Mary's world was expanding. Her work and her name were beginning to open her up to prominent thinkers and writers in society. She met some prevalent thinkers of the day, such as the radical pamphleteer Thomas Paine, one of the English-born American Founding Fathers, political activist and theorist, philosopher, and revolutionary. She also met the English journalist and philosopher William Godwin, a man who would change the course of her life.

Godwin was born on 3 March 1767 and is considered one of the first champions of utilitarianism, the ethical philosophy which supports 'the greater good'. He was also the first advocate of anarchism, a political philosophy that is suspicious of all justifications of authority that demand unnecessary obedience, such as capitalism, social hierarchy, and nation-states. This was typically a left-wing movement and is often referred to as the libertarian branch of the socialist movement or libertarian socialism. His radical liberal stance was adored by many on the left, but he was treated with suspicion by those on the right, the more conservative thinkers and politicians who were nervous of his open-minded viewpoint.

When Mary first met Godwin, they were at Joseph Johnson's house. Johnson was hosting a dinner party for another author of their mutual acquaintance, and guest speaker, Thomas Paine. Godwin had attended to hear his hero Paine talk, but apparently all he heard was Mary, who talked incessantly to him all evening, much to his disappointment. She talked so much that Godwin missed several opportunities to speak to Paine about his own philosophies and opinions. Godwin also could not hear Paine as he spoke to other guests and was left barred from joining their conversation. It is rather amusing to imagine the scene. Godwin longingly watching the charismatic Paine across the room, surrounded by enchanted guests hanging on his every word and laughing along with his jokes; whilst Mary, mesmerised by Godwin, was hanging off his arm as she talked. They were not impressed by each other. Mary was upset with Godwin for ignoring her at the dinner party, as she had given him her full attention all night. Godwin was annoyed that Mary prevented him speaking to his hero Paine. It was not a positive first impression. They would later meet again and this time fall in love and marry.

She did not let this unpleasant night put her off pursuing her interests. She made connections with the Blue Stocking Club,[18] a secret underground movement consisting entirely of women who supported educational reform and cooperation. She became tangled in a love affair with the already married artist Henry Fuseli. He was married to Sophia Rawlins, one of his former models. It does seem that Mary was the one who was chasing the relationship rather than it being a fully mutual connection. She seems to have loved his gothic artwork and his mastery of light and shadow, and perhaps struggled to separate the art from the artist, referring to 'the grandeur of his soul, that quickness of comprehension, and lovely sympathy'.[19] She does sound like a 'fan-girl' and quickly became infatuated with the artist after meeting him. Mary rather strangely proposed a platonic living arrangement with Fuseli and his wife. Unsurprisingly, Mrs Fuseli was not happy with this indecent proposal and Fuseli cut off all communication with her.[20] Mary assumed that Mrs Fuseli would agree to the idea of a young woman who was infatuated with her husband moving into their family home. Perhaps because her own views of marriage and relationships were so unconventional, she assumed that other people would accept this. She was wrong. Mrs Fuseli did not agree in any way and Mary was mortified.

To avoid further humiliation, Mary fled the country. She ended up in France, far away from the embarrassment of the situation. To take her mind off recent events, and to perhaps refocus her mind, she wrote a popular pamphlet *A Vindication of the Rights of Men, in a Letter to the Right Honourable Edmund Burke; Occasioned by His Reflections on the Revolution in France* in 1790. This pamphlet was initially published anonymously,[21] but with some confidence and some say boldness, she would later that same year put her name to the pamphlet. The conservative politician Edmund Burke responded by writing a pamphlet criticising Mary's *The Rights of Men*. Burke's criticism so angered her that she spent weeks writing a cutting response. She was not going to take criticism without fighting back.

Whilst in France, she got to see the first rumblings of the French Revolution. She referred to the Revolution as 'a glorious chance to obtain more virtue and happiness than hitherto blessed our globe'.[22] Perhaps she romanticized the Revolution and hoped for a change of fortunes for the poorer French people. The idea of 'Liberte, Egalite, Fraternite' was a beautiful one that aimed to reduce the chasm between the rich and poor. The unimaginable wealth that the aristocracy enjoyed was shocking. The lavish lifestyle of the rich was in sharp painful contrast to the poorer classes who were forced to eat whatever scraps they could find. They would certainly have eaten cake if they could have got their hands on it, but all dietary staples were scarce due to the poor harvests that sparked the beginnings of the Revolution. The ideals behind the Revolution were primarily that everyone should have basic needs met, bellies filled, housing for all, and a more equal distribution of wealth. As we know, sadly, what began as a cry for freedom and equality, turned into a bloodbath, that would end the lives of between 600,000 and 1,300,000 lives. A lot of very rich aristocrats and royalty were killed, however, the revolutionary crowds bayed for more blood and soon began killing the servants of the rich and those with even more distant connections to the big houses. It began as such a lovely idea of no hunger, no homelessness, no poverty, but turned into something ugly and vicious, killing anyone who wore silk or lace, served at a rich house, or was related to anyone connected to the aristocracy.

Burke wrote about the events of 5-6 October 1789, praising Queen Marie Antoinette as a symbol of elegance and beauty of the Ancien Regime. He wrote how she was surrounded by 'the furies from Hell, in the abused shape of the vilest of women'.[23] Mary argued with Burke about his interpretation of the events, writing in direct answer to him: 'Probably you [Burke] mean women who gained a livelihood by selling vegetables or fish, who never had any advantages of education.'[24] Burke's comments cruelly dismissed the poorer women around Paris at this time as amongst the 'vilest' people and 'furies from Hell'. The 'furies' were figures from Roman mythology and were not even human. Dwelling in the Underworld, they were the torturers of evil sinners. Perhaps he referred to the women as 'furies' as they were attempting to make money in the busy marketplace as the rich people were being taken away, and this itself was like a form a torture to Burke. Mary corrects Burke, explaining that they were just women who were making a living selling their wares. They were desperate to make some money to feed their families. To add to the difficult time they now faced with bad harvests and few jobs being available, the women had never had the benefit of education and that was not their fault. The women did what they had to do to make money. Perhaps Burke had led a very sheltered and privileged life and had a shock when he saw the poor women on those violent days. Perhaps that shock was made even more stark and deplorable as they stood side by side the ill-fated Queen Marie Antoinette. The women had had none of the privilege and pampering that the queen had enjoyed. Their skin would have been weather-beaten, a far cry from the milky white complexion of the queen. The women's simple clothing would have hung in rags, nothing like the laces and silks of the queen.

After the French Revolution, the women of France, followed

by others in the most fashionable places in Europe, adopted various fashions which commemorated the deaths of many of the aristocracy. While incarcerated and awaiting execution, rich women were often forced to have a haircut so as not to interfere with the guillotine's blade. The hair was cut roughly with a dull knife which often nicked the skin and left bald patches. To avoid this indignity, many wealthy women whilst in prison would get a servant to cut their hair in a less severe way, leaving some length on top, but still short around the neck, not unlike a modern 'pixie cut'. This allowed the women to have some self-respect as they climbed the steps to their death. It is amazing to think that the fashionable haircut that is still popular today has its roots in something so political and heartbreaking.

Women also started wearing chokers around this time. This was meant to symbolize the beheaded people who lost their lives during the Revolution. These chokers were usually made from ribbon, or perhaps a strip of fabric from a dress that had been altered. Red scarves, red ribbons tied around the arms and criss-crossed across a person's back, or red shawls also became a way to commemorate the Revolution across Europe. The colour not only symbolized the blood spilled on the guillotine platform, but also was a direct reference to Charlotte Corday, executed on 17 July 1793, for assassinating the Jacobin leader Jean-Paul Marat. As the story goes, as she climbed the steps of the platform to her death, she wore a red shawl and the crowd was transfixed by her. Red had always been seen in the Catholic faith as the colour worn by martyrs. Perhaps the colour also struck the crowd because of its association with death. Corday possibly appeared as if she was already covered in blood with her red shawl wrapped around her body. It could have been quite shocking to the crowd to see a soon-to-be-executed woman draped in the colour of blood. It is perhaps easy to see why this fashion became popular. It became a nod to the blood shed during the Revolution and a way to remember the victims or the perpetrators of their bloody ends.

Mary arrived in Paris just around a month before Queen Marie Antoinette and King Louis XVI were guillotined. Her arrival in Paris could not have been worse. She had joined a few British people in the city and their safety was far from guaranteed. Many at home had advised Mary not to leave for France. Britain and France were on the brink of war and travelling there was not advised[25] in fear of hostilities beginning at any moment. The city was a ticking timebomb, with a highly-charged electricity in the air, ready to spark in an instant. Whilst in Revolutionary France, Mary was careful to stick with the moderate Girondins rather than the more radical Jacobins.[26] She had to tread cautiously, lest she say the wrong thing or upset the wrong people. Mary was either lucky or unlucky to see King Louis XVI being taken away and tried before the National Assembly. She was strangely moved by this, writing 'the tears flowing insensibly from my eyes, when I saw Louis sitting with more dignity than I expected from his character, in a hackney coach going to meet death'.[27] It seems as if Mary was genuinely moved to see the king brought down so low. Perhaps seeing him in person she realised that he was only human, an ordinary living breathing person, rather than a fantastical creature of a royal. It would have been a gruesome and terrible event to witness. The knowledge that the king was being taken away to face his death would have upset her so much.

When France declared war on Britain in February of 1793,

Mary and her fellow British expats tried to leave for Switzerland, but they were denied permission to travel across the border. They had left it too late, despite being told to move on much earlier. Life was very difficult for them in France during the war as you may expect. They were under police surveillance and had to get six Frenchmen to write statements to vouch their allegiance to the Republic. Their own assurances of their allegiances were not enough for the increasingly paranoid and desperate French people. On 12 April 1793 a law was passed that all foreigners were forbidden to leave France, making life very difficult for anyone not French-born, particularly any British people left behind. They had become prisoners there, with every stranger staring at them, suspecting them of terrible treachery. During the next few months, Mary would witness many of her friends murdered by the guillotine.[28] To see the Revolution happening around her and to witness strangers being carted off to be killed must have been horrendous enough, but to lose friends this way would have been horrific. The pain from this experience must have left a mark of sadness on her for the rest of her life.

To perhaps make human connection again after witnessing such horror, Mary found herself in love. It could be that given the heightened tensions around her, she felt her emotions more keenly. She had not long completed her work on *The Rights of Woman* and given the revolutionary atmosphere of Paris, she decided to throw caution to the wind and sleep with a handsome American adventurer called Gilbert Imlay, even though they were not married. Social norms had long died away in the ruins of revolutionary France. It now seemed insignificant to expect anyone to adhere to society's rules when society itself was in the grip of change and upheaval. Sex before marriage was such a small indiscretion when compared to murder, revolt, and complete social disorder.

Imlay had served with the New Jersey Line in the American army during the American Revolutionary War. He would later style himself as 'captain', although there is no evidence that he was ever officially given this title. Perhaps he wanted to project himself as a leader when he left the army, hoping that no one would ever find out. If he called himself a captain, then maybe people would treat him with more respect. He perhaps felt he had had no respect from people around him, so styled himself a captain to try to regain some level of reverence and regard. To those who knew him, he was shrewd, but ruthless in business. If he saw a weakness in a rival businessman, he would think nothing of exploiting this limitation to his own advantage. He seems to have been callous and hard-nosed in his business dealings and although successful at making money, did not do so ethically. Needless to say, he was not well liked professionally or even personally. He did not have friends who stayed long after discovering what kind of a man he was. He could be amiable, even charming, when he needed to be, but people seemed to be able to see through the façade of his pleasantries. He would serve in the US Embassy and became known for penning the highly successful non-fiction book *A Topographical Description of the Western Territory of North America* and a novel, *The Emigrants*. Both these works promoted the country and encouraged people to go and settle in America. His literary success would only serve to boost his ego further and arguably make him even more unpleasant.

Despite his obvious flaws, Mary quickly became enamoured

with him. This time the attraction was mutual. She soon became pregnant and gave birth to her first child on 14 May 1794. She decided to name her daughter Fanny, after her best friend Fanny Blood, and the baby was given her father's last name.[29] Despite not being married and thus being looked down on by society, Mary was overjoyed to become a mother. The two appeared to have cohabited with their baby and presented themselves as a married couple. Had their neighbours known they were not married, scandal would no doubt have followed them. She wrote to her friend and told her that 'my little girl begins to suck so manfully that her father reckons saucily on her writing the second part of *The Rights of Woman*'.[30] It is a humorous idea that Imlay was suggesting that the baby was so 'manfully' feeding and strong, that she would take after her mother, writing scathing attacks on a man-led society. It is telling that the strength her daughter had was perceived as masculine from the beginning. It did not occur to anyone that women and girls could also show strength and stamina. Perhaps Fanny Imlay would have gone on to write like her mother had she lived. Tragically, Fanny would take her own life, aged only twenty-two. She sadly seems to have inherited her mother's tendency for melancholia. Fanny would not likely have remembered her mother's struggles with mental health when she was a baby, but perhaps there was a genetic element to her proclivity to self-harm.

Mary continued to write obsessively throughout her pregnancy and the difficulties of being a new mother and all that motherhood brings. It is challenging enough to be a mother for the first time without adding the extra pressure of writing. Paris was still in the depth of the Revolution all around them and this must have been a frightening experience, especially being alone with a baby amongst the bloodshed and horror. It is hard to imagine just how alarming this would have been for her. She is responsible for keeping her baby safe and healthy in a country gripped with rebellion and insurrection.

She somehow managed to write *An Historical and Moral View of the French Revolution* as a sort of exposé of The Reign of Terror. She managed to get a copy of her book out of France to London, where it was published in December 1794.[31] This publication shed light on the violence and original wishes of the Revolution for the people back in Britain. She had become for all intents and purposes an undercover reporter, secretly getting her book out of the country and reporting it to an unsuspecting world. Rumours about the Revolution had been whispered abroad, but few had realised the extent of the horror before reading Mary's book.

There may have been growing acclaim for her book abroad, but at home behind closed doors, things were less than perfect. Mary's husband soon became bored with the domesticity at home and left one day, deserting his daughter and her mother. He had promised to return to their home in Le Havre in Northern France at some point, but as time went by, Mary began to realize that Imlay had lied and had abandoned them. She perhaps thought he had fallen out of love with her or perhaps found someone else. Whatever the reason, he never returned home. For many years she clung on to the hope that he would return to her and Fanny one day. She wrote letters to him regularly and tried to appeal to his sense of duty to his daughter and her love for him. The letters are tinged with sadness and desperation, a lonely, abandoned woman. She was a woman alone with a young child in a foreign country at war with itself. She had witnessed cruelty and horror and many of her friends had been imprisoned, tortured, and executed.

The isolation and the overwhelming dejection she felt led her to attempt to take her own life in May 1795. It is thought that she took an overdose of laudanum. Imlay saved her somehow, although there is much conjecture as to how he was responsible for saving her life.[32] She had just returned to London the previous month and perhaps hearing of this, Imlay visited her just in time. It continues to be debated how he came to visit her just in time to save her from her overdose. He perhaps visited and then she attempted to take her own life in a different room while he was at the house. This does not seem to be the case, however, as this was not a cry for help, but a genuine feeling of desperation, sadness, and hopelessness. Despite his continued rejection, she still had strong feelings for the father of her child. She came up with a rather odd plan to win him back. She decided to begin a money-making venture on his behalf which involved locating a Norwegian captain who had stolen a large amount of silver that Imlay was attempting to get past the British blockade of France. It sounds harebrained, but Mary was determined. She set sail for Norway with her young daughter and her maid Marguerite, although she would make the final leg of the journey alone, leaving Marguerite to look after her daughter on the Swiss border. Whilst travelling, she wrote a series of letters to Imlay explaining her plan and her progress finding the captain and his stolen silver. A lot of these letters were eventually published in 1796 as *Letters Written During a Short Residence in Sweden, Norway, and Denmark*.[33] Whether these letters were originally intended to be published, we do not know, but they somehow found their way to the publishers. The letters outlined her escapades during her time abroad. It is interesting to imagine what Imlay would have thought about this venture. Each letter he received gave him the next chapter of her Scandinavian adventure. Did he read her letters with delight, bemusement, or confusion? It is unclear whether she was successful or not in her attempt to track down the Norwegian captain and the stolen silver. It seems the outcome was sadly lost to history. She returned to England even more heartbroken. Perhaps she did not retrieve the silver and Imlay continued his coldness towards her, or perhaps she found the silver and this did nothing to win him back. Whatever happened with the silver and the Norwegian captain, Mary was broken upon her return and attempted a second time to take her own life. She left a note for Imlay in which she wrote, 'let my wrongs sleep with me! ... May you never know by experience what you have made me endure.' She goes on to write that she was 'the victim of your [Imlay's] deviation from rectitude'.[34] She blamed Imlay's cruel treatment of and apathy towards her for her feelings of helplessness. Although his actions did not help her mental state, his abandonment was perhaps the final straw for her mental stability. Considering her mental and emotional suffering after witnessing close friends being executed during the French Revolution and being left with a small child to raise alone, he deserted her when she needed him most. She did not see her suicide attempt as anything but a rational response to extreme circumstances.

She attempted to take her life the second time by jumping into the River Thames. She apparently walked out one wet night for about half an hour to make her clothes heavy with the rainwater. She was witnessed jumping in and pulled from the water by a stranger passing by.[35] Her soaking wet and still conscious body was dragged from the Thames, but she felt heartbroken that she had not succeeded in taking her life. It is tragic that someone with so much talent and intelligence should suffer so much with their mental health.

Mary seems to have managed to step out from under the black cloud of depression and suicide ideation long enough to take up her literary career again. Perhaps she found that by throwing herself into work, it took her mind off the overwhelming sadness and redirected her negative thoughts into something productive and all-consuming. She began to become involved with Joseph Johnson and his circle of friends again. Amongst their number were three notable women: Mary Hays, a self-taught author of poetry and novels all focusing on women and their lives and history; Elizabeth Simpson, later Inchbald, an English novelist, dramatist, actress, and translator whose two novels, *A Simple Story* and *Nature and Art*, received high acclaim and recognition; and Sarah Siddons, a well-known French actress and one of the first 'IT girls' of the eighteenth century. Also present at these intellectual meetings was William Godwin. Although their first meeting had not gone well some years previously, the two struck up a mutual friendship and admiration. It would be a unique courtship that would eventually lead to a passionate affair.[36]

Despite their rather wobbly beginning, Godwin had found himself warming to Mary. He had stumbled across her *Letters Written in Sweden, Norway, and Denmark*. Upon reading this, he became smitten with her. He had later written that 'if ever there was a book calculated to make a man in love with its author, this appears to me to be the book. She speaks of her sorrows in a way that fills us with melancholy, and dissolves us in tenderness, at the same time that she displays a genius which commands all our admiration.'[37] It seems as if he had fallen in love with her through her written words, forgetting that night when they first met and he was unimpressed by her chattiness. Her words now had the opposite effect on him, drawing him towards her, rather than repelling him.

They quickly started a physical relationship as she soon became pregnant for the second time in her life. Godwin despised marriage and pushed for the abolition of the institution in his book called *The Enquiry Concerning Political Justice and Its Influence on Morals and Happiness*, published in 1793. Despite these strong feelings, Godwin and Mary married when she realised that she was pregnant. It was important for them both that their child would be legitimate, unlike Fanny born only three years earlier. Upon the completion of the marriage paperwork, Godwin realised that his future wife and her former beau Imlay had never been married. This information became public knowledge somehow and Godwin and his now wife lost many friends over this revelation. Sex before marriage was still a taboo subject and many shunned the couple because of it. Mary had not only had a child out of wedlock, but she and Imlay had posed as if they were married, cohabiting in a time when it was frowned upon by society. They both drew negative attention: Mary because of her past perceived indiscretions; and Godwin because of his very unusual and vocal stance on marriage, which now made him seem like he was hypocritical becoming part of the institution he condemned so wholeheartedly.

They were married 29 March 1797 much to the surprise of

many who had read Godwin's work. Perhaps some thought that they had already been married. It is fair to remark that the two had a rather unusual marriage. The couple lived in Somers Town, a popular part of North-West London. However, Godwin also rented rooms only twenty doors away at Evesham Buildings in Charlton Street to sleep in if he so wished. These rooms were used as office space for Godwin's writing, and the two cohabited when it suited them, and slept apart when they wished. They perhaps planned their sexual liaisons around their own schedules and slept in Somers Town when it was convenient for them both. There is no account of the two taking other lovers during this time, although they do seem to have lived very separate lives for much of their married life. They loved their independence and despite living so close to each other and being married, they often communicated via letter. Although their relationship was unconventional even for today, it worked for them. It was a stable marriage, although a sadly brief one.[38]

Mary gave birth to her daughter on 30 August 1797. The little girl would grow up to be none other than the Gothic Goddess herself, Mary Wollstonecraft Shelley, the writer of one of the most well-loved horror novels of all time, *Frankenstein: A Modern Prometheus*. Sadly, little Mary would grow up without knowing her mother. It is believed that a part of baby Mary's placenta broke apart during the birth, became lodged in her mother's body, and soon became infected, killing her when her baby was only a few weeks old. Mary lived for several days in excruciating pain. This was an all too common story for post-partum women. It killed so many women and was no respecter of age, wealth, or social status.. A post-partum infection had killed her friend Fanny Blood, along with countless other women who were from every echelon of society from countesses to cooks, from baronesses to basket weavers. Of course, only the richest and 'most important' women's deaths were recorded. The uncountable poor women who died in similar circumstances were mourned and missed no doubt, but their names went unwritten. Mary's death was recorded as 'childbed fever', a strange umbrella term that was often used to describe any death of the mother shortly after the birth of their child. It would likely have been septicaemia that killed her.[39] Blood poisoning after an infection would not have been necessarily recognised as such at the time. Pregnancy and post-partum infections were the most common cause of death of adult women and must have been a terrifying and inevitable part of their lives. 'Childbed fever' was listed on countless death certificates during this time and described many deaths from various unspecified infections.

Godwin was devastated by her death. He was a new father, left to look after his baby daughter, and the now three-year-old Fanny Imlay. Without his wife, he was lost. He was rather cruel towards his stepdaughter and continually reminded her that she was not his own child. Perhaps this was out of a strange coping mechanism or he genuinely resented her presence. He wrote to his friend Thomas Holcroft about his grief: 'I firmly believe there does not exist her equal in the world. I know from experience we were formed to make each other happy. I have not the least expectation that I can now ever know happiness again.'[40] Godwin here sounds as if he is experiencing deep depression and hopelessness following the death of his wife. He is convinced that because she has gone, he will never again feel happiness because they were made to make each other happy.

She was buried in the churchyard of St Pancras Old Church in Somers Town close to where the couple had lived together. Her gravestone reads 'Mary Wollstonecraft Godwin, Author of Vindication of the Rights of Woman: Born 27 April 1759: Died 10 September 1797.[41] Her body would be later moved by her grandson Sir Percy Shelley, third Baronet to his family tomb at St Peter's Church in Bournemouth.[42]

Godwin must have started writing about his wife straight away. Once again, this could have been a way to cope with his grief and keep himself busy during the days and weeks that followed her death. He poured his grief into his book *Memoirs of the Author of a Vindication of the Rights of Woman*, published in 1798. He no doubt believed that he wrote from the heart about his late wife's life and loves. However, he strangely included details about her illegitimate child and various love affairs and even suicide attempts,[43] leading the readers to be horrified and scandalised. It was an odd decision to include these very personal details about his late wife. Robert Southey, the Romantic poet and poet laureate, was outraged, accusing him of 'the want of all feeling in stripping his dead wife naked'.[44] and it lead to many satires being written such as the *Unsex'd Females*, a poem by Richard Polwewhele (1798). Southey's use of the word 'stripping' is interesting, suggesting that Godwin has taken away from her the layers of concealment that are needed to survive. It also sounds monstrous to strip the dead body, and that too is parallel to the shock and scandal that followed the publication of Godwin's book. He portrays his late wife as a person full of feelings and passion, but someone who was balanced and perhaps slightly subdued by his reason.

He also suggests that she was not as religious as her writings perhaps suggested. Godwin's opinions of her seemed to form into fact as time went on. It seemed as though Godwin's writings became true in the minds of those who read his book and as the nineteenth century continued, Godwin's image of Mary inspired works of art, such as poet Robert Browning's *Wollstonecraft and Fuseli*. William Roscoe, a lawyer, banker, and Member of Parliament, took up his pen to write: 'Hard was thy fate in all scenes of life/As daughter, sister, mother, friend, and wife/But harder still, thy fate in death we own/Thus mourn'd by Godwin with a heart of stone.' It would seem that Roscoe felt little sympathy for Godwin, believing him to be merely capitalizing on her death by exposing all her secrets after her death. It does seem very strange with hindsight that he would reveal his dead wife's secrets to the world in this way. What his motives for doing this, we may perhaps never know.

There are at least three plaques commemorating Mary's life and legacy. There is a green plaque on the wall of Newington Green Primary School, near to the site of the school that she set up with her friend Fanny Blood and her sisters Everina and Eliza. Sadly, the original site has been demolished and built upon. There is also a controversial sculpture of her in Newington Green. It is a symbolic depiction of her rather than a realistic one. Some have criticised the sculpture as showing traditional depictions of beauty, rather than showing Mary as she really was. There are actual portraits of her painted during her lifetime so a realistic image would not have been difficult to find as source material. There is a blue plaque at 45 Dolben Street in Southwark, London, where she lived from 1788 and finally, a plaque on Oakshott Court, close to the site of her final home, The Polygon in Somers Town, also in London. It is wonderful that her legacy is being remembered. Her determination is remembered well through her work, her values, and her feminist tendencies.

Although Mary's life was unusual in the way she conducted herself, she would become an icon to the modern feminist movement in the twentieth century. Virginia Woolf, herself a feminist icon of the twentieth century, would later describe Mary's life and works and 'experiments in living' as 'immortal'. Woolf would see Mary as trailblazing and a symbol of what womanhood should be. Someone who lived their life the way they wanted to, someone who did not adhere to anyone's rules but her own. Mary Wollstonecraft's life and works became iconic. She became the poster girl for the modern feminist movement in Europe. A woman who refused to be defined in typical terms and followed her heart in love and work.

DIDO ELIZABETH BELLE

A Spark of the Abolitionist Movement

❧

The amazing thing about Dido Belle isn't that she was mixed-race. A lot of children were born to black slave women in the eighteenth century. It is not that her father was wealthy; plenty of titled British captains and entitled admirals tore around the Caribbean capturing French and Dutch ships and stealing their contents, whether it was sugar, tea, tobacco, or people. The amazing thing about her was that despite this inauspicious start in life, she would be taken to England by her mother's attacker, Sir John Lindsay, and settled into a relatively comfortable life at the grand Kenwood House. She was not a servant, but treated as a member of the family.

Dido Elizabeth Belle was born into slavery in 1761 in the British West Indies. Her mother was an enslaved African known as Maria Belle, although her surname is spelled without an 'e' on her daughter's baptismal record.[1] Little is known about her mother, apart from her name, although that is unusual, given that she was an enslaved person and their humanity was often taken from them. Countless thousands of names were lost in an attempt to remove the identity of slaves. Some enslaved people were renamed by their captors and taken far from home, separating the person from their own sense of self. This has had very long-term consequences for the families of those who were enslaved, as it is almost impossible to find the names or birthplaces of their ancestors. It is just one of the tragic and far-reaching effects of the deplorable systematic abuse of enslaved humans.

There are mentions of Dido's mother while she lived at the property with Lindsay's relatives, but not documented fully. We do know that Maria was finally 'bought' her freedom. The documentation for this is dated 22 August 1774.[2] She was gifted a parcel of land in Pensacola in Florida by Lindsay, with the proviso that she builds a house on the land within ten years. She left England to claim her land. It does raise questions as to why Lindsay gifted her this land. Did he feel a pang of guilt about the way he treated her? He did rape her when she was just a child and then essentially kidnapped her. Was the land really to silence her? He perhaps 'gifted' her this land to make sure she was far away from Lindsay. This 'gift' does seem strangely out of character for a man who would happily sexually assault an underage girl, getting her pregnant.

Plenty is known about her father, unsurprisingly. He was Sir John Lindsay, a member of the Lindsay family of the Evelix branch of the Clan Lindsay, originating from the lowlands of Scotland. His family tree can be traced back centuries, a long line of prosperous titled landed gentry. They were a prominent family who had been wealthy and powerful since the time immediately following the Norman invasion. Lindsay had a distinguished naval career and served as the captain of the British warship HMS *Trent*, based in and around the West Indies.[3] Lindsay was the son of Sir Alexander Lindsay, third

Baronet and his wife Amelia, daughter of David Murray, fifth Viscount Stormont.

It is possible that Lindsay found Maria on board a Spanish slave ship that his forces had captured in the Caribbean. Between the years 1757 and 1767, Lindsay was sailing round Jamaica, Haiti, West Africa, America, and Cuba. It was during this period that the British were engaged with the Seven Years War, fighting with France and her allies over the ownership of the colonies of America and the islands of the Caribbean. The Royal Navy's ships were used to protect the trade routes used by British ships in this area. They were there to police the waters, making sure that no one could stop the British trading ships delivering their goods. The abolition of the British slave trade did not come into effect until 1807, but up until then, the Royal Navy's ships were there to protect the British slavers. They were also encouraged to capture enemy ships and cargo as prizes for the Navy and bonuses for themselves. The cargo included anything on board the enemy ships, from sugar, tea, silks, weapons, or tragically people. This is possibly when Lindsay encountered Maria. She was only fourteen when Lindsay's forces captured the ship, and only fourteen when Lindsay raped her and got her pregnant. Maria gave birth to her daughter Dido when she was fifteen years old.[4] The Pensacola property record, when she 'bought' her freedom, confirmed her age stating that 'the sum of two hundred milled dollars … paid by Maria Belle, a Negro Woman Slave about twenty-eight years of age', dated 22 August 1774. As terrible as the description of her is, it does confirm being a fourteen-year-old child at the time of her sexual assault and subsequent pregnancy.[5]

Lindsay had five illegitimate children from five different

women. Dido was the first in 1761, then came John Edward Lindsay the following year, Ann Lindsay and Elizabeth Lindsay (later Palmer) both in 1766, and another John Lindsay in 1767. The latter two were named in his will bequeathing them £1,000 to be shared by his 'reputed children'.[6] Elizabeth Lindsay and her half-brother John Lindsay would keep in touch with each other as adults, although there is no evidence that the other half-siblings had any contact. It is telling that Lindsay acknowledged all those children, giving them his surname, but not Dido. At least four of the five women were of African heritage and with the exceptions of Maria and Dido, had their baptism records at the same place, Port Royal, near Kingston, Jamaica, where the Royal Navy had a base to repair ships. It is very likely that these other unfortunate women suffered a similar encounter with Lindsay before their babies came along.

After the war, Lindsay returned home to England with his new baby daughter Dido and her unfortunate abused mother Maria. Lindsay took the two to stay at Kenwood House, the home of his uncle William Murray, 1st Earl of Mansfield, and his wife Elizabeth Murray, Countess of Mansfield. Sir William had many prestigious jobs during his lifetime, such as Lord Chief Justice of the King's Bench, Lord Speaker, Attorney General for England and Wales, and the Chancellor of the Exchequer. They were a very wealthy family and Kenwood House remained a fine house. Sir William and Elizabeth were childless, possibly not by choice, so perhaps Lindsay thought they would appreciate having a child in their home. Maria was allowed to stay at the home, too, although we do not know in what capacity she was kept there. She could have been a guest with her own room, attending meals, but it is more likely that she was expected to work there, cleaning, cooking, and washing as she had not yet 'bought' her freedom from Lindsay. Maria had her daughter baptized Dido Elizabeth Belle in 1766 at St George's Church in Bloomsbury.[7]

The name Dido is taken from Ancient Greek mythology. She was the founder and first queen of the city of Carthage in 814 BC. The details of this came from Virgil's epic poem *Aeneid* written in around 20 BC. Dido was described as clever, enterprising, and resourceful. She uses her intelligence to run away from her callous and unfeeling brother Pygmalion after she discovers that he was responsible for her husband's death. Perhaps Maria wanted her daughter to inherit the intelligence, strength, and resourcefulness of her namesake.

Dido was by this time five years old. This is very old for a child to be baptized as it usually takes place within days of a baby's birth due to the old Catholic idea that unbaptised babies remain in limbo if they die. It might have taken this long to get Lindsay to agree to the baptism at all. It would also perhaps take time to save up enough money to pay the church the sum to have the child baptized. Perhaps it was down to Lady Elizabeth as it was five months after the Countess' arrival that Dido was baptised. It certainly suggests that Dido was thought of as more of a daughter than a servant. Even though she was older by the time she was baptized, the fact that she had this ceremony at all shows that at least some in the household loved her and worried about her spiritual wellbeing.

In the church records, Maria is recorded as her mother, however Lindsay is not recorded as her father. There are a lot of reasons why he possibly never wanted to have his paternity of Dido recorded in the official records. Perhaps he did not want to be linked to the enslaved African woman he abused, perhaps he did not think of Dido as his daughter, or perhaps he wished to distance himself entirely from the two because he feared the reaction of others in his family and the wider community. However, his other children from enslaved Africans were acknowledged and carried his name. Lindsay did not attend the baptism, perhaps for the same reasons his name is missing from the records. He seems to have wanted to distance himself from her. Perhaps Lady Elizabeth and others within the household began becoming more vocal about getting the child baptized. Maybe Lindsay was tiring of the conversation, and he eventually just conceded to the baptism.

William and Elizabeth Murray at Kenwood House seemed to have raised little Dido well. She was educated alongside the Murrays' niece, and Dido's cousin, Lady Elizabeth Mary Murray. Lady Elizabeth's German mother had passed away and the Murrays had taken the girl in to live with them as their daughter. When Dido was brought into the home alongside her cousin, the two were treated as sisters.

It was not unheard of that an aristocratic family would become the legal guardian of an illegitimate relation on behalf of a relative. However, it was very unusual for a wealthy family to become legal guardians of a child with mixed heritage. Dido was taken in as a member of the family, an equal to her fair-skinned cousin Elizabeth. Dido, born into slavery as the daughter of an enslaved woman, was not taken to the house to work as a servant. Many sadly thought that the colour of someone's skin determined their 'worth' in life and it was often expected that they undertook the dirty and menial jobs. Dido did not work a great deal during her life. She was raised as a lady along with her cousin in an aristocratic British family. She was one of the lucky few who grew up wearing silks and slippers and never faced the hardships endured by her mother.

Dido learnt how to read, write, and play music, as well as being taught manners and deportment as would any young lady growing up in that world. She was even granted an annual allowance to spend on what she wished. However, she was not always treated equally as although she lived in the fine house, she was not allowed to attend balls and parties with her cousin Lady Elizabeth. This was primarily because she was illegitimate, but possibly also due to the inherent racism of the time. She was not invited to the ball thrown by Lady Elizabeth's stepmother in 1782. Dido was also not allowed to go riding with Lord Mansfield and her cousin to visit neighbours. Was this done in an attempt to protect Dido from the characteristic racism of the time or was it the Murrays themselves who were being racist, stopping her from attending the parties and having fun?

As Dido grew older, she began to tend to the dairy and poultry yard at Kenwood House. This was a common pastime for gentlewomen of the time, reminiscent of Marie Antoinette's obsession with being a shepherdess and milkmaid. Marie Antoinette had her own hamlet built in the grounds of the Palace of Versailles known as the Hameau de la Reine. The hamlet was built so she could live out her rural fantasies of being a peasant farmworker, even going so far as to having milk yolks made for her so she could parade around feeling like she was working. Dido was not pretending like the former queen, but tended to the animals every day. She fed and cleaned out their pens, collected eggs from the chickens and milked the cows.

She occupied a strange and unusual position in the house.

Georgian Feminists

According to colonial law, she had been born into slavery so it was unheard of that she would be treated as a lady to a great extent. She was still expected to work within the house, although not as a domestic servant and not all the time. It was a unique position.

Dido often assisted Sir William Murray in his paper and letter writing, taking dictation. Sir William, by this time in his sixties and possibly beginning to suffer from arthritis or bad eyesight, would have welcomed the help. This showed her high level of education, being able to read and write at speed.[8] She had a neat hand and never complained about writing his letters for him. The job of secretary was usually done by a man in their employ. It wasn't until much later in history that women fulfilled the job. It perhaps shows that Dido was trusted and seen as an equal in many ways. She would hear of important business transactions and be party to sensitive information about visitors to the house. She must have been trusted a great deal by Sir William and those who attended meetings at the house.

Thomas Hutchinson, an American and former governor of Massachusetts, visited Kenwood House and wrote about his encounter with Dido in his diary in 1779. He wrote that she was 'neither handsome nor genteel-pert enough'.[9] It is a cruel assessment, considering that the only portrait we have of her shows her to be very beautiful. The word 'pert' has two meanings and it would be interesting to know which Hutchinson meant. It can describe someone who is cheeky and fun, or refer to the pleasing shape of her body. He also commented that Dido 'was called upon by my Lord every minute for this thing and that and showed the greatest attention to everything he said'.[10]

That he calls for her 'every minute' perhaps suggests that she is overworked and put upon by her legal guardian; or it could imply that she had become vital to him. He perhaps loved her and wanted to be in her company. Dido listening carefully to his every word, could perhaps suggest that she feared him and the consequences of not listening to him when he spoke. It could also of course be that she genuinely wanted to hear what he said. Perhaps they had a father-daughter relationship, or perhaps it was more of a patient-carer relationship. They spent a lot of time together during this time, and while there is evidence of both forms of relationship, we cannot be sure which they shared.

Whatever the early relationship was between Dido and her legal guardian, things would change after the death of Lady Mansfield in 1784. Her cousin Lady Elizabeth left Kenwood House the following year after her marriage to George Finch-Hatton, a politician in the House of Commons and a Fellow of the Royal Society. The couple seemed to love each other, which was not of course always the norm in Georgian marriages amongst the aristocracy. Elizabeth was twenty-five when she married Finch-Hatton, which was quite common for the time. She spent her married life relatively happy between her new husband's two vast estates of Kirby Hall in Northamptonshire and Eastwell Park in Kent. Without her cousin and best friend at Kenwood House, Dido was left with Sir William. It was suddenly very quiet at the house.

Lady Mansfield's death had come as a great shock to everyone. After her passing, Dido began to spend even more time with Sir William. He was not old by today's standards, but he had retired from work in the government and his health was beginning to fail. His wife had previously cared for him and helped him get around the home. It is possible that he had mobility problems due to arthritis, other joint pain, or perhaps an old injury flaring up and getting around their big house was beginning to be a problem. Dido had always been there to help Sir William with his administrative tasks, however, now she found herself taking over from Lady Mansfield, helping the increasingly frail man with everyday tasks, such as helping him wash and dress, and putting an arm around him to help him up the stairs. She became his full-time carer. Sir William seemed to show her affection and even love, perhaps treating her more like a daughter now that his niece had left and his wife had passed away. He perhaps missed his niece and mourned his wife, and Dido brought him the warmth and care he had lacked since his beloved wife had passed away. The two were closer than ever. In turn for her kindness, he ensured her health and happiness. He gifted her five guineas each birthday. This does not sound much for a very rich man to gift a woman who has grown to be like a daughter to him, but according to the Bank of England's inflation calculator website, the sum is worth around £736 in today's money.

She also received an annual allowance of £20, which would be well over £2,400 today. Dido was given a portion of the allowance every three months, so she was never given a lump sum. In contrast, her cousin, Elizabeth received £100, which is well over £12,300 in today's money, excluding money she received as gifts. Elizabeth was an heiress in her own right, but still received more money than her cousin. This would have further limited Dido's power, being the poorer relation. To put these figures into context, an average annual wage for a woman working as a housekeeper in a rich household ranged between £20 and £70, whilst a Royal Navy lieutenant would make £100 a year.[11] It seems that women, despite how hard they work, have always been underpaid compared to their male counterparts. An average three-bedroom house with a garden outside of London would set someone back around £200[12] and it would have been far beyond the reach of most ordinary people.

The only known portrait of Dido is by David Martin completed in around 1778. It is oil on canvas and shows Dido and her cousin Elizabeth both staring out at the view. Dido is moving behind her cousin in the picture, but Elizabeth has her hand reaching back to grab her arm. It looks as if Dido is walking quickly behind her cousin, perhaps even running through the portrait, shown by the flick of her scarf flowing behind her. Dido is wearing the most stunning silver gown that seems to shine and a beautiful green and gold sash that is full of movement. She wears a turban, a common fashion accessory at the time, as people of colour were expected to cover up their natural hair during the week when out in public. On Sundays they were 'allowed' to venture out with their hair uncovered. Therefore, what seems like a fashion choice, is perhaps more of a forced expectation of society and seems a lot less pleasant. It certainly changes the way we view this portrait and one wonders whether Dido resented wearing her turban as a fashion accessory and whether she saw it as a sign of repression. Did she look in the mirror and see her true self, or did she see a different version of herself, moulded to suit the sensibilities of the white English middle to upper class eighteenth century society she lived in?

Her clothing is analysed carefully in the 2018 television miniseries *A Stitch in Time*, presented by the fashion historian Amber Butchart. Dido's life is discussed in detail and her beautiful dress and turban are scrutinised, as is the fashion of the period. Amazingly talented historical costumiers and seamstresses Ninya Mikhaila and Harriet Waterhouse recreated the dress and turban, using Martin's painting as inspiration. However, as the portrait only shows one side of the clothing, and the construction of the dress, such as seams could not be seen by the dressmakers, it was necessary for them to delve into historical dress patterns and other portraiture of the period to fill in the gaps. By the end of the show, they had reconstructed this iconic dress and brought a little piece of Dido Belle back to life. Her dress in particular was a stunning creation and it is thought that the fabric was an iridescent silver-blue, which would have shimmered in the candlelight.

In the portrait she carries a bowl of fruit and has a large feather in her turban. These two items are to perhaps set her apart as being more exotic than her book-reading cousin. She wears a string of pearls around her neck and dangly pearl earrings. The pearls were also seen as exotic and expensive items and were often associated with pureness and virginity. She has one hand up to her face and the expression on her face looks playful and cheeky. Perhaps the two best friends and cousins had been gossiping or discussing a secret. Elizabeth wears a more conventional pale pink satin dress with lace at the neck and sleeves. She has English flowers in her hair and holds a book in her hand, perhaps showing her intelligence. The difference between their dresses is telling. Elizabeth's dress follows the up-to-date fashion of the period with flounces and flowers, ruffles, and even layers of a fine fabric overlaying the pink silk, which is perhaps voile or something similar. She has lace around the elbow length sleeves and a frill of lace around the square neck of her gown. Her stomacher looks to be richly embroidered or covered with lace, both of which would have taken a lot of time and money to create. Dido's dress is a far simpler one, free flowing in its silver-blue silk, without any of the embellishments that her cousin's dress has. The deeply scooped neck of the dress and her long sleeves are free from lace and frills. Both cousins wear pearls around their necks, Dido with one string of larger pearls, her cousin with two strings of smaller pearls.

Overall, the portrait looks as if Dido has been taken unaware, as if the paintbrush captured her as the artist painted her cousin. Her expression is one of cheekiness and embarrassment as she holds her hand up to her face. Dido's posture is one of movement, as if she is walking or running, and her cousin's hand reaches out as if to stop her leaving the portrait.

It was not unusual for paintings to feature black people, but they were usually cast as servants or a novelty to parade in front of guests. They are shown standing nervously in the background of the painting, waiting on their 'master' to give orders. They were also often included to show the wealth of the sitters, being able to afford an enslaved person.

It was nothing new to exploit those considered unusual or different. During the Renaissance, Cardinal Hippolytus Medici, who would become the Lord of Florence, had a menagerie of animals and people from different countries. He brought them out to 'perform' their native languages,[13] parading them around in front of his guests and getting them to speak in their own languages to show their differences. They were nothing but curiosities to him, just something he could exploit and use for his own gain.

There were people from all over the world being held captive against their will. Although Dido was shielded from a lot of bigotry living at Kenwood House, being surrounded by people who loved her, she would still no doubt have faced terrible comments and stares around the neighbourhood for just being herself. Society was very monocultured and very judgemental, anyone with a different skin tone was often the target of unwanted attention, harassment, and discrimination.

Dido lived in a time when the transatlantic slave trade was at its height. Britain had grown fat profiting off the backs of the unfortunate people that they had enslaved. Britain relied on this despicable slave labour in the Caribbean and American colonies continuing to thrive and they ensured it did by any means necessary. It was in Britain's best interest to not only turn a blind eye to the human suffering, but to actively participate in it and allow those who traded in human life to be given easy passage. As is often the case in history, the rich got richer, and the people at the bottom of the pile, continued to be hurt, abused, and mistreated, trampled on by those above. However, public opinion on the slave trade was beginning to shift as people became more aware of the horrific human suffering involved.

Before he retired, Sir William was Lord Chief Justice of the Court of King's Bench, the most powerful and influential judge in England. He presided over many court cases, most of which were high profile, carefully watched by the public. The press would report these prominent court cases, all of which were major crimes, such as murder, major thefts, and heists, and cases of embezzlement. He would later be involved in examining the legality of the transatlantic slave trade. This captured the public imagination like never before.

The most prominent of Sir William's many cases was that of James Somerset on 22 June 1772. After much deliberation, Sir William ruled against Charles Steuart who wanted to forcibly make James Somerset return to his life of servitude. Somerset was an enslaved West African, who had been 'sold' in Norfolk, Virginia to Steuart. Somerset was sent far and wide in England where he was taken. He was sent to deliver messages and letters between various businessmen on behalf of Steuart. Perhaps Somerset came across other enslaved peoples or perhaps other abolitionists. Whatever happened on his travels for his 'master', whoever he met, led Somerset to refuse to return to the servitude of Steuart. This led to Steuart starting legal proceedings against Somerset and being brought in front of Sir William in his courtroom.

To everyone's shock and some satisfaction, Sir William found in favour of Somerset, meaning that Steuart could not legally force Somerset back to his side. When the verdict was announced, it sent legal and political shockwaves across Britain and its American colonies. Although this was only one case, it was seen by many as the beginning of the end of the transatlantic slave trade. Although it was thirty-five years before this dreadful chapter of our history was ended, this case was seen by some as showing that slavery was from that point illegal in England and was held up to be a landmark contribution to the abolitionist movement.

It was possibly the influence of raising Dido that made Sir William such a staunch supporter of the abolitionists. Seeing her as a beautiful, lively, pleasant, helpful, intelligent, and caring person, may have helped Sir William question the general acceptance of the transatlantic slave trade. Thomas Hutchinson, Sir William's American friend, would recall a conversation he had with a slave owner he met during the trial. When discussing the case, the slave owner had been less than happy about the outcome of the proceedings at court. He knew that if slavery was going to be made illegal in England, then it would impact his own financial security and selfishly did not want it to end. As the public perception of slavery became more sympathetic following the trial, the slave owner cannot have liked where it seemed to be headed. He seemed to resent Sir William as it was his court ruling that was seen as the beginning of the end of the slave-trade. Hutchinson reports the slave owner's response to this conversation: 'no doubt ... he will be set free, for Lord Mansfield keeps a Black in his house which governs him and the whole family'.[14]

The slave owner seems to be under the impression that Dido, thoughtlessly referred to as 'a Black' in his comment, is the one who 'governs' the family. Perhaps he is suggesting that she has usurped the power of not only Sir William, but the whole family and is bossy and has taken over the decision-making in the house. Even though it was Sir William's ruling that it was Steuart who was in the wrong, it seems as if the slave owner puts the entirety of the blame on to Dido. It is strange and yet very telling that the slave owner blames the mixed-race woman and not the rich white man, although it was Sir William's actions he disapproved of. It shows the vein of inherent racism that ran through society and the prejudice and discrimination Dido faced every day.

England's black communities lived predominantly in and around the cities of London, Bristol, and Liverpool, where sea trade was prevalent and there were large populations. The black communities there originated from all over the world and from many different backgrounds. They perhaps found the black communities in these cities provided a connection, a social link, and even a collective political network they struggled to find elsewhere. Being so far away from home, it was perhaps a link to their own culture, language, and maybe even family.

The case of James Somerset was an interesting one for many reasons. Through these black communities it was thought that Somerset came into contact with Elizabeth Cade, Thomas Walkin, and John Marlow. All three became his godparents when Somerset decided to be baptized in August of 1771 at St Andrew's Church in Holborn, London. It has been speculated that rather than a burning desire to be baptized because of his faith, he became Christian to become free. There was a widely held belief that a Christian became a free man or woman upon their conversion. There was an incredibly complicated system of legal, moral, and theological rules and arguments involving the status of enslaved people and Christianity. This led to a massive influx of black enslaved people and servants getting baptized, and the records show this increase in numbers. It is still unclear to this day whether Christianity was agreed to 'free' a person from enslavement or not, however, it is certainly understandable why so many did it.

Dido's biological father died 4 June 1788, aged around fifty-one. He had been promoted to rear admiral a year earlier, but due to his failing health, the role was more symbolic than active. He died at Marlborough while on his way to Bath for medicinal purposes. He was buried at Westminster Abbey. In his will, he finally acknowledged that he was the biological father of Dido. Perhaps with his impending death, he felt a pang of guilt about the way he had behaved towards his daughter.

Dido's legal status was never certain during Sir William's lifetime.[15] She was never sure whether she was free or a slave, or something in between. She could have easily still been classed as a slave, given her status at birth, despite her current living arrangements. Sir William passed away on 18 March 1793. It is unclear what exactly led to his death. There is no mention of a long-term illness, other than the previously mentioned joint pain and general slowing down of his body. He had complained for some time about feeling tired and was lethargic. He went to bed earlier each day, and on that fateful night, did not wake up.

Sir William left a will including land worth £26,000 and a not-so-small fortune. The land would be worth well over £3,000,000 in today's money and would be the equivalent of several lifetimes' worth of work for the average skilled labourer of the time. As her legal guardian, he left Dido an annuity of £100, and a lump sum of around £500,[16] which is around £40,000 in today's terms. It is rather telling that Dido was given a considerably smaller sum than her cousin Lady Elizabeth. It is unclear whether this difference was due to the colour of her skin or her illegitimate status. Within the complicated class system, it was not unusual for an illegitimate child to be given significantly less financial recompense than their legitimate counterparts, yet still be considered a member of the family.

In a complete contrast from Dido's earlier life at the magnificent Kenwood House, her later life after Sir William's death was spent in a middling class and yet comfortable lifestyle. Her own house was certainly not as big and grand as Kenwood, but was still luxurious. She had spent thirty-two happy years at Kenwood and it must have been a heartbreaking time for her leaving it for the last time. Perhaps she only left Kenwood House after Sir William's death as she knew he needed her. Perhaps she felt compelled out of duty to care for the increasingly frail old man or perhaps she stayed because of her love for him. Dido married a senior servant or valet called John Davinier. He was born Louis Jean Charles Daviniere in Ducey in the Normandy area of France.[17]

There is a 2013 film *Belle* about her life with Gugu Mbatha-Raw in the title role. The film, although visually beautiful, is not a fully faithful retelling of her life as the filmmakers and director have taken some artistic liberties with the truth. John Davinier, played by actor Sam Reid in the film, was the son of a reverend in Hampstead in the film, however, the real Davinier was not. Nor was he a lawyer, and as a result had nothing to do with the Zong massacre, where at least 130 enslaved African people were murdered on 29 November 1781. They were all thrown overboard to drown so the crew of the British slave ship Zong could claim insurance when the boat reached Jamaica. It was a dreadful loss of life because the doomed enslaved Africans onboard were considered 'cargo' and nothing more. As with a lot of historic films and television shows, a lot of artistic licence was taken with the film, despite Dido's own life being exciting enough. Sadly, the Zong massacre was not fiction, but an all too real chapter in our history.

The records show that Dido Belle and John Davinier were married on 5 December 1793 in the fashionable Church of St George's in Hanover Square. It should be noted that although the church was 'the' one that high society wanted to be married in, the church also saw its fair share of commoners and servants who worked for the rich people get married there. Records show that some who got wed there, could not read or write, as they signed the marriage register with an 'x',[18] the usual 'signature' for those who were illiterate. It is rather sad to think about that level of illiteracy being so prevalent in society. As some servants did get married at this fashionable church, it shows that they were making enough money to pay the church for their marriage licence and therefore, although illiterate, were making a wage large enough to pay for more than their everyday necessities. Many would be working in jobs that did not require them to read or write so learning these skills would not have been necessary. They would be servants, factory workers, farmers, or miners – menial, 'unskilled' jobs. None of these jobs would require them to learn to read or write so many poorer families found work in these professions. Few paid as well as the servant, though, so this was one of the most sought-after jobs a poor person could wish for, as they could from time to time get leftovers, a bonus at Christmas, and holy days off.

The newlyweds had a new house built for them at the exclusive Ranelagh Street North, at number fourteen.[19] This address was close to St George's Hanover Square, an elite address that few could afford, where they would rub shoulders with the great and good of Georgian society. The fact that they could afford to commission a house to be built for them proved that they were comfortably well-off, as building from the ground up is an expensive way to find accommodation.

The couple seemed to have had a happy life together. They

welcomed three children, all sons. John, named after his father, Charles, named after John's grandfather, and William Thomas. Charles, born 1795, and William Thomas, born 1800, survived until adulthood. Sadly, John must have passed away sometime around 1804, making him aged ten at the oldest. No doubt he succumbed to one of the many childhood diseases and infections that claimed innocent lives in their countless thousands. In a time before antibiotics, a simple ear infection or a nasty cut could kill a loved one, especially a child whose immune system was still not fully functional. Edward Jenner created the smallpox vaccine in 1796, but a lot of other childhood diseases were still rife, with their vaccines being decades away in some cases.

Dido passed away in 1804, leaving her remaining boys without a mother, and their grieving father without a wife and friend. She was only forty-three when she passed away. Her body was buried in July of that same year at St George's Field at Westminster. The area where she was buried was redeveloped sometime during the 1970s and her grave has been lost to history. No one can seem to find a record of where her grave was moved to, or even if a record was kept. We do not even know what was carved on her gravestone. It is very sad that her grave marker has been lost and is telling of a careless or thoughtless society that records were not kept of where graves were moved to.

Her sons William Thomas and Charles would go on to have an excellent education, learning English, Greek, Latin, French, accounting, drawing, mathematics, and land surveying.[20] They would work for the East India Company, with William based in England and Charles in India. Charles would join the army, connected to the East India Company, in 1811 and worked his way up through the ranks to captain by 1827.[21]

For a mixed-race woman, born illegitimately into slavery, to be elevated to the status of a lady is an incredible story. She married well and lived in a fashionable area of London, having her house built when this was the more expensive option. Her children were very well educated with one son becoming a captain in 'charge of infantry recruits'[22] at the headquarters of Fort St George, in Chennai, India, formerly known as Madras. The fact that her own flesh and blood rose through the ranks of the army, that in her time helped slave owners with their 'cargo' is so telling of the changes in attitude and persistence of Dido herself. She saw herself as an equal to the white men around her, unusual for that time for any woman. Perhaps her childhood growing up as an equal to her cousin Lady Elizabeth in Kenwood House helped her to see herself as more than a match for anyone she met. Had she been treated poorly during her time there, perhaps being bullied and abused, she would have been a very different person, lacking cleverness, confidence, and courage.

Dido, it could be argued, was responsible, in part for a spark of hope for the beginnings of the abolitionist movement. Without her and her influence on her legal guardian, perhaps history would look very different. It is all conjecture of course, but had Sir William not brought her into his home, perhaps he would have seen the world differently. He may have prescribed to the outdated ideas that so many of his brethren believed, the illusion of white superiority.

Without Dido's positive impact on Sir William's life, perhaps he would have found in favour of the slave owner Charles

Steuart and allowed him to forcibly return James Somerset back to Steuart's home. If this had happened, then perhaps the abolitionist movement would have lost momentum and public support, holding back the Slave Trade Act of 1807 and the final absolute Slavery Abolition Act in 1833. Of course, there were other factors and individuals leading to this eventual all-encompassing ban on the trading of human life, but Dido Belle certainly played her part in the story of abolition. She changed hearts and minds and brought about the beginning of the end to a terrible chapter in our history. She lived in a time of abysmal inequality and found herself rising from an illegitimate daughter of an enslaved women, to the unofficially adopted daughter of a knight of the realm. A meteoric climb through the ranks of society, that was unheard of. She is unique in so many ways, her position and status in society, her intelligence, her impact on others around her, and her place within the Earl of Mansfield's family.

JANE AUSTEN

A Hopeful Romantic

৯

Jane Austen is arguably the most well-known and beloved English female author of her age, or possibly any period. Many people who have not read Austen dismiss her work and assume it is filled with posh ladies in silk playing pianoforte and taking tea with other posh ladies, gossiping about their tediously closed off high-born world. There are moments of piano playing and indeed tea drinking, but her work is far from taking itself seriously. Some think of Austen as twee, quaint, and frivolous, but her writing is scathing and clever, poking fun at the very people she was acquainted with, dripping in cynicism, and a dry sense of humour. She is best known for her wonderfully sarcastic tone of writing in her six published novels and her exploration into values, etiquette, relationships, marriage, and money.

She was born in Hampshire in the harsh winter of 1775 on 16 December. Due to the particularly icy weather, Jane would not be baptized until April the following year. It was highly unusual for babies to be baptized so long after their birth, with the event usually taking place no more than a week after the baby was born due to the belief that unbaptized babies went to Hell if they died before the ceremony.

Her father George Austen was the rector of the Anglican parishes of Deane and Steventon.[1] He descended from an old and wealthy family of wool merchants. As was the tradition, the eldest sons inherited the wealth on each branch of the family. However, George's branch of the family fell into poverty and he and his sisters were orphaned as children and taken in by extended family. It was common for sons without access to the family fortune to enter the clergy or the army, both professions providing not only a wage, but often accommodation and life-long job security.

This background could be why Jane wrote so often about inheritance and how unfair the system was. Perhaps her father often mentioned his childhood and what an uncomfortable and impossible situation he was left in after his parents had died. Perhaps he talked about the financial hardships he and his remaining siblings had faced upon becoming orphans and how unfair it was that they had found themselves punished twice; first, by losing their parents, and the second time when they were left penniless.

Aged sixteen, George went to St John's College, Oxford. This is likely where he met his future wife, Cassandra, who came from the prominent and wealthy Leigh family. Her father was the rector of All Souls College, Oxford, and she grew up with great privilege and money amongst the landed gentry. The two had had very different lives up to this point.

George and Cassandra became engaged in around 1763 after they exchanged miniatures.[2] This was a common gift between lovers who were about to be married or newlyweds. The miniatures could be full face or sometimes just a closeup of the soon to be wife or husband's eye. It was a happy match and children would soon arrive. They would have a big family, with two girls and six boys. Little George, their second eldest child, born in 1766, soon showed signs of illness and intellectual delay. He was prone to seizures and may have been deaf and mute. His mother had him fostered, perhaps for George's own good, or perhaps because she couldn't cope with a child with such health issues. Little George's new living arrangements could be seen as either very kind or very selfish. The family focused on their other children and George's name was rarely mentioned.

According to Professor of Literature Park Honan, who wrote extensively about the lives of many great novelists and poets, the Austen home was an 'open, amused, [and] easy intellectual' one.[3] This environment would perhaps sow the seeds for a young Jane to grow academically, to hone her skills as a writer, and to sharpen her wit. If intelligence, discussion, and reading was part of her day-to-day life during childhood, then it is possible she absorbed this.

The Austens had to rely on the patronage of other family members and often hosted visits from relatives. According to writer and literary critic Deirdre Le Faye, the visits were like 'the bright comets flashing into an otherwise placid solar system of clerical life in rural Hampshire'.[4] A clerical life in rural Hampshire must have been a very quiet and sedate one. The 'bright comets flashing' were the visits and subsequent parties away from the dull parish she was used to. The visits must have been so exciting, seeing the rich lives of the fashionable, beautiful young things in the poshest parts of the city. Young Jane must have experienced so much of Georgian society, the good, the bad, the rich, and the poor. Le Faye writes, 'the news of their foreign travels and fashionable London life, together with their sudden descents upon the Steventon household in between times, all helped to widen Jane's youthful horizon and influence her later life and works'.[5] These excursions during her formative years could easily have inspired her to write. They would certainly have polarised the worlds Jane was used to. The well-dressed ladies and gentlemen of London, with their theatre, parties, high fashion, and clinking glasses, were a world apart from the life she was used to in the quiet country parish with her family. She increasingly saw home as slow, tired, and old-fashioned, whereas London was new, shiny, and provided an endless parade of fascinating individuals. News of foreign travels from these strangers would have transfixed most in attendance. Foreign travel for most people was just a dream. Only the richest could afford foreign holidays, and few poorer people had stepped outside the county where they were born.

The Austens were not poor by any means. They had a fine house, although not palatial, they were all clothed well, although not the latest fashion, and did have money to travel to extended families' houses, albeit not abroad.

In 1783, Jane and her sister Cassandra were sent to Oxford to be educated. Their governess, Mrs Ann Cawley, taught them the expected subjects. The same autumn they started with Mrs Cawley, both girls were sent home as they had contracted typhus fever, an endemic disease spread by body lice and rat fleas. It was usually contracted by malnourished poor people although was not unknown entirely from wealthier individuals. The disease is characterised by red spots, delirium, and an overwhelming feeling of lethargy. Jane almost died from the disease,[6] as did many hundreds of thousands of people during the first half of the nineteenth century.

Perhaps due to fear of losing Jane, her family decided to homeschool her for the next two years. It was common enough to homeschool children, sometimes with a governess, tutor, or a parent. In 1785, she and Cassandra began attending Reading Abbey Girls' School, run with a rod of iron by Mrs La Tournelle.[7] Perhaps young Jane seemed stronger at the end of those two years. Lessons with her probably included spelling, French, dancing, drama, music, and, of course, needlework. Sadly, both girls would not be allowed to continue at the prestigious school beyond another year, as the fees were too high for the family.[8] Education was mostly for the rich, and only the children of wealthy parents got to enjoy more than the very basics of learning.

Their education continued at home, with neither attending an official educational establishment again. Luckily, Jane's family were open to her curious hungry mind and her learning continued away from the classroom. According to Irene Collins, an Austen biographer, Jane 'used some of the same school-books as the boys'.[9] The boys being Jane's brothers, who would have attended the schools she could not. It appears that Jane was given access to her father's library and that of a family friend Warren Hastings, a British colonial administrator. The two libraries amounted to a large and varied collection, allowing her a glimpse at a unique anthology of interesting and unique books. Perhaps her father felt a pang of guilt for not being able to continue paying for Jane and her sister to go to school. He also supplied the girls with quality paper and materials for writing and drawing.[10] As the girls were given the same books the boys used in school, and plenty of paper and writing supplies, they were given the best chance they could have without attending school. Luckily, Jane and her sister were naturally intelligent and had the drive to read and research for themselves. Even with the tools, many would not have had the determination to learn alone.

The Austen household entertained themselves by staging plays in the rectory barn. According to Professor Penny Gay, the 'barn is fitting up quite like a theatre, and all the young folks are to take part'.[11] These plays were published works by recognised playwrights of the time, such as David Garrick, a very famous playwright, actor, and theatre owner, and Richard Sheridan, a playwright, and Whig politician. Jane's older brother James often wrote an additional prologue and epilogue to the plays and they were performed in front of the family. At first, Jane was simply an audience member, but later she would perform with her brothers and sisters.[12] Most of these plays were comedies and this is where perhaps she honed her skills, being exposed to these satirical pieces throughout her childhood and early teenage years.[13] She began to experiment with her own dramatic writing, perhaps inspired by the many plays she had been fortunate enough to see and by her brother James' writing. Jane would write three plays during her teenage years.[14]

She entertained her family with poems and stories she wrote.[15] Even at the early age of eleven she was skilfully exaggerating the monotony of everyday life and parodying common plot devices in 'stories full of anarchic fantasies of female power, licence, illicit behaviour, and general high spirits'.[16] Between 1787 and 1793, Jane wrote an impressive compilation of works, consisting of twenty-nine stories in three bound notebooks, referred to as the *Juvenilia*. Jane called the three notebooks *Volume the First*,

Volume the Second, and unsurprisingly, *Volume the Third*. They contain 900,000 words.[17] The *Juvenilia* are housed at the British Library and is a remarkable collection and well worth viewing.

The *Juvenilia* are often seen as 'anarchic' and 'boisterous', perhaps showing an early example of her humour and love for satire.[18] Richard Jenkyns, a former professor, lecturer, and public speaker in Classics and classic literature at various prestigious universities over his career, compared Jane's early work to that of eighteenth century novelist Laurence Sterne. An Anglican cleric, Sterne was known for his controversial writing. He wrote the much-debated religious satire *A Political Romance* in 1759. It was so shocking to its readers, that many copies were destroyed. By comparing the two writers perhaps Jenkyns was noticing their love of parody and sarcasm, however, he may have seen parallels in how their work was received by the public.

Amongst the collection of works in the *Juvenilia*, there is a satirical novel that has been translated as *Love and Friendship* (sic), believed to have been written by Jane when she was only fourteen in 1790.[19] In this pastiche novel, she mocks the well-known 'sentimental novel' or 'novel of sensibility' very popular during this period.[20] The novels of sensibility were those that featured an emotional journey, a character who expresses deep sentiments, and a plot interwoven with frequent moments of both distress and tenderness. These novels would expressly attempt to 'tug on the heartstrings' of the reader and some well-known and well-loved writers of this period built their careers on this genre. Oliver Goldsmith's *Vicar of Wakefield* in 1766, Henry Brooke's *The Fool of Quality* in around 1770, and Maria Edgeworth's *Castle Rackrent* written in 1800, all plunge unapologetically into sensibility and emotive writing. This is also why later Jane chose to title her masterpiece *Sense and Sensibility* as such, as a nod to this growing genre of novel.

In 1791 she began *The History of England*, a thirty-four-page manuscript, in which her sister Cassandra included thirteen beautifully detailed watercolour miniatures. As with all Jane's work, the writing was done with a very tongue-in-cheek view of history, parodying the style of writing usually used in history books of the time. She mocked the supposed superiority and attitude of the typical history writer, particularly Oliver Goldsmith, who in 1764 had published his very serious historical text of the same title.[21]

Honan in his 1987 book about Austen's life suggests that it was not long after writing *Love and Friendship* that she decided to 'write for profit, to make stories her central effort'.[22] This must have been a big decision indeed, as although many women were writing during her lifetime, such as Frances Burney, Charlotte Smith, and Jane West, it was still not seen as a viable profession for women to do for a living. It shows how forward thinking she was to consider such a career.

Jane wrote about marriage a great deal and all her heroines from her novels were married by the last chapter of her books. It was, however, a ceremony she was never involved with. Arguably, the love of her life was an Irish-Huguenot gentleman by the name of Thomas Langlois Lefroy. He was a few months younger than Jane and heavily involved in the legal system, rising to be the Lord Chief Justice of the Queen's Bench for Ireland.

Jane was clearly attracted to the handsome Irishman and the two had moments of flirtation. In a letter to her beloved sister Cassandra, dated Saturday 9 January 1796, Jane confides in her about how she would be shocked by the way 'my Irish friend and I behaved. Imagine to yourself everything most profligate and shocking in the way of dancing and sitting down together'.[23] Presumably the pair had flirted at the side of the dance floor, perhaps whispering plans for their possible future together, contrary to the traditional courtship rules. The dances at balls were very structured and were performed in regimented lines, but perhaps their fingers laced together rather than palm-to-palm or they smiled at each other as they passed one another. Their behaviour would not have led to them being dismissed from the ball, but it would have raised eyebrows that they spent so much time with each other. It was polite and expected for a woman to accept a dance from any gentleman who asked, if she liked him or not. Perhaps Jane only danced with Lefroy, and this too was scandalous enough for her to feel the need to confide in her sister. It is easy to picture Jane as a character in her own novels, sat at night in a shared room with her sister, discussing this man as they did each other's hair. Jane refers to Lefroy as a 'very gentlemanlike, good-looking, pleasant young man'.[24] She is perhaps being coy to her sister writing this. It sounds polite and not the words of someone in the first throes of a love affair.

Jane wrote to Cassandra that she expected an offer of marriage any time from Lefroy and that she would refuse him unless 'he promises to give away his white coat'.[25] This is in reference of Lefroy's 'one fault' of adoring the character Tom Jones, created by Henry Fielding in his masterpiece *The History of Tom Jones, a Foundling*, published in 1749. Lefroy reportedly loved the titular character so much that he began dressing as he would, choosing to wear a rather impractical white morning coat. The character of Tom Jones has a reputation for being a ladies' man and defending their honour. He is injured badly when a bottle of liquor is thrown at his head when trying to defend his beloved Sophia Western from rumours that she had had sexual relations with a soldier from the local regiment.[26] It does seem that Lefroy wished to emulate the main character from his favourite book, wanting to be seen perhaps as dashing, honourable, and attractive to the opposite sex. Whether he was really any of these things is left up to our imagination.

The affair would end only days later on 14 January 1796. Jane writes once more to Cassandra: 'At length the Day is come on which I am to flirt my last with Tom Lefroy and when you receive this it will be over – my tears flow as a write, at the melancholy idea.'[27] The reason for this sudden end to their relationship? 'There is a report that Tom is going to be married to a Litchfield Lass'.[28] She is clearly heartbroken by this revelation and feels the need to share this news with her sister. We will never know what Lefroy's true feelings for Jane were. He seemed infatuated with her, then married someone else. It is believed that Lefroy's family intervened in the couple's relationship and forcibly talked him out of pursuing the connection between the two. There could have been many reasons for this, but the most obvious for the family to want their relationship to end, was a practical one. Neither Jane nor Lefroy had any money to bring to the marriage. They were both reliant on other members of the family to support them. Lefroy was yet to make his name in the legal world and relying on a great uncle in Ireland to finance his education. Jane was living off her family's money, so neither of them were financially independent. This would have made marriage very difficult for them. The idea of marriage was to better one's own prospects, and as neither of them had money, their marriage could have been disastrous, taking away any chance either of them had to marry further up the social scale. When Lefroy visited Hampshire, he was carefully kept away from the Austen house and news about his visit kept quiet. Perhaps he knew it was the right decision, despite his affection for Jane. He maybe did not want to be within her presence because he might not be able to find the right words, or perhaps he worried he would lose his resolve and propose after all.

She continued to think of him as her lost love, however. There have been parallels drawn between the good-looking Lefroy and the gorgeous Mr Darcy from her seminal novel *Pride and Prejudice*. Some have taken this idea further, suggesting that both Tom Lefroy and Jane Austen are represented by the characters of Mr Fitzwilliam Darcy and Miss Elizabeth Bennet. It is an interesting thought that Jane based arguably her most iconic and most loved characters on the man she adored and herself. Mr Darcy is far more attentive to Elizabeth than his real-world counterpart and perhaps she made Mr Darcy into the man she wished Tom Lefroy had been. Someone she would settle down with, someone to stand by her, someone who was worthy of her, and someone she could live with happily forever after.

It is heartbreaking that Jane never got to marry her muse. Perhaps she gave Elizabeth Bennet and her other heroines the opportunity she never had, marrying the men of their dreams and fulfilling their 'purpose' as was seen at the time. Although Jane often satirized popular romantic novels, her comments made about Lefroy in her letters certainly suggest that she genuinely liked him, if not loved him. These feelings were so strong that no other suitors ever seemed to measure up, and she turned down all other advances from eligible bachelors.[29] She continued to think about Lefroy for many years. It was common for friends and neighbours to occasionally call upon each other, visiting each other's houses for tea to catch up on local gossip. Jane was at one of his relative's houses for tea and wrote to Cassandra about the visit, once again mentioning Lefroy. She wrote how she wanted desperately to ask his relatives how he was and could not bring herself to do it.[30] Perhaps she did not want to sound as if she was still infatuated with him as maybe she was frightened of the answer. No one had measured up to him in her mind, but maybe Lefroy had found happiness with someone else.

She was not merely moping about the loss of Lefroy. She continued to write new material and make changes and tweaks to her existing works. She started writing her first full-length novel *Elinor and Marianne*. This book was written initially as a series of letters. There are no surviving manuscripts of this draft, but she would rework it many times and this novel would be anonymously published in 1811 as *Sense and Sensibility*.[31]

Jane wasted no time and immediately started working on her second novel, known in its first incarnation as *First Impressions*. It would be renamed as *Pride and Prejudice* in 1796. She completed the first draft a year later aged only twenty-one. As with all her novels, she would test the popularity of her work by reading them aloud as the completed chapters to her family at night. *Pride and Prejudice* soon became an 'established favourite'[32] of her family, which must have been pleasing to her and give her confidence to continue. Possibly without her knowledge,[33] Jane's father approached Thomas Cadell, a London-based publisher, to ask him if he would consider publishing *First Impressions*. Cadell returned Mr Austen's letter and refused to publish her work. Looking at the later success of the book, it is almost unbelievable that Cadell refused to publish it, and one presumes he lived to regret his decision.

After completing *First Impressions*, she returned to her first novel, the yet to be published *Elinor and Marianne*, changing its epistolary format to third-person narration, which brought the novel together. This left the novel resembling, but not quite yet, *Sense and Sensibility*.[34] After finishing revisions on *Elinor and Marianne* in 1798, she started work straight away on her third novel *Susan*, which would eventually become *Northanger Abbey*, a wonderfully satiric take on the traditional Gothic novel.

George Austen shocked his family and the people in his parish when, in December 1800, he announced his retirement from his ministry. It seems as though he did not discuss his retirement with his family before announcing it from the pulpit one Sunday. The family were to leave the quiet familiarity of Steventon and relocate to number four Sydney Place in Bath, Somerset, a regular secular house. The move suited George and Cassandra Austen and their older children, but the younger daughters, Jane and Cassandra, were not informed until plans were already under way that they were to move fifty miles from the only home they had ever known.[35]

Once in Bath, Jane's productivity seems to have slumped. She did make some revisions to the novel that would become *Northanger Abbey*, but started and then abandoned a fourth novel *The Watsons*. Her writing between the years 1795 and 1799[36] had been incredible, writing and revising novel after novel, then the move seems to have stopped her creativity entirely.

According to journalist and biographer Claire Tomalin,[37] this lack of creativity after the move suggested that Jane was suffering from depression and perhaps anxiety after the move. She maybe missed her old life and the tranquillity and inspiration it brought. Her unhappiness in her new situation could have led her to withdraw into hopelessness and a downturn in her usual productivity.

However, there is a different way to look at this change in her writing habits. According to literary critic Robert Irvine,[38] it is just as likely that Jane's output was so vastly reduced because she was for the first time in many years enjoying a busy social life. Perhaps she spent more time writing when she was at the vicarage, because of the boredom and relative lack of social occasions to attend. Bath offered a great deal of opportunities for the young ladies to attend balls, parties, and other social events. Jane possibly then did not actually suffer from depression at all, but something resembling elation and excitement about her new life in Bath. Instead of spending her long days writing and revising her work, she instead had a busy social life, being invited into town to shop, parade, and had occasions to make dresses for, such as parties and balls.

Bath was a thriving, fashionable, and elegant city and rose to be a very popular place for the elite to visit. Ralph Allen, a local man, made his money organising a postal service much like the one we know today. He invested this money in limestone quarries, from which the beautiful honey-coloured stone was used to build the city. Allen joined forces with John Wood the Elder, an English architect, with the ambitious vision to build Palladian style architecture from Italy. Many of the buildings, such as those on Queen Square, look like one grand building from a distance, but are in fact many individual houses, sharing one impressive common frontage.

The fine houses popped up all around the city, contained within the city walls. Holding a fashionable address on The Circus, The Royal Crescent, or others built by Wood, showed that someone was wealthy and chic. The rich would walk the promenades and parks of Bath, wearing their finest by day, taking tea and gossiping. By night, the city was transformed. Beau Nash, an opportunist and card shark, ran nocturnal Bath like his own personal high-class dominion. He would meet new people as they entered the city and decide whether they would join his 500 to 600 strong 'Company'. Only the 'best' would be allowed to join the Company. Nash would match ladies with suitable dance partners, broker marriages, and escort unaccompanied ladies as if he was a patriarch, pimp, and poser all in one. He also regulated the gambling tables by removing compulsive gamblers and those who became violent and warning less experienced players against risky games or fellow card sharks. He was a one-man police force , an enforcer, and a bit of a cad, too. Nash was a great ally and could really help someone make it in the town, but equally, if Nash was an enemy, he could make someone's life very difficult.

It is unclear whether Jane was accepted into Nash's fashionable and elite company, but she certainly had many options whilst living there. She could easily have spent her free time making friends and dancing rather than spending many hours writing. Perhaps she honed her skills at the card tables and met the great and good as they passed through the thriving city.

Irvine points out that during this period in her life, Jane moved around a great deal. She travelled around from her new home in Bath to London and the southern counties, meeting with friends and attending balls. She had a busy and no doubt fun time, never staying anywhere for very long. This travelling would not have been particularly conducive to writing novels.[39]

Thanks to the letters Jane wrote to her sister Cassandra at least weekly, sometimes every other day depending on what was going on in their lives, there is plenty known about her life. There is, however, a gap in this writing for a significant time between 1801 and 1804.[40] It is believed that Cassandra destroyed all of Jane's letters written during these years. It is unlikely that they fell out, as they had always been so close, even as children. What is more likely is that the letters contained a subject matter which Jane or her sister, or perhaps both, wished to forget. They perhaps agreed to destroy the letters because of their content, thus deleting the subject written about. It is believed that letters to her brother were also destroyed. Perhaps she was such a prolific writer of letters, as well as novels, that it was impossible to keep them all. So many of her letters were destroyed, that only a small handful of examples of her signature remain today. As a result, anything bearing her handwriting is very valuable.

During the Christmas of 1802, Jane received her only proposal of marriage. She and Cassandra had been visiting Catherine and Alethea Bigg, old family friends. Their younger brother Harris Bigg-Wither had just successfully completed his education at Oxford and was at home. After reacquainting themselves, Bigg-Wither became so enamoured with Jane that he proposed straight away. She accepted. They had known each other since they were children and he brought with his proposal financial stability. On paper, he was a far superior catch to her former beau, the handsome Lefroy. Bigg-Wither was the sole heir to his family's vast estates and land in and around the Basingstoke area. By marrying him, she could secure her own financial future, she could buy her parents a house and pay off their debts, find a suitable match for her unmarried sisters and brothers, and find gainful employment for her brothers. She and her family would never have to worry about money again and her children, if they had them, would be comfortably off. It made perfect sense to marry Bigg-Wither.

The very next morning, she withdrew her acceptance of the marriage proposal.[41] Perhaps after a sleepless night of worry, or perhaps a vivid nightmare of marrying Bigg-Wither, she decided she could not go ahead with the wedding, and the cons far outweighed the positives of becoming Mrs Jane Bigg-Wither.

Despite the many perks the money and connections the marriage would have brought, perhaps Jane made the right decision. Irvine describes Bigg-Wither as somebody who 'seems to have been a man very hard to like, let alone love'.[42] He sounds a deeply unpleasant person. His own relative, a Mr Reginald Bigg-Wither wrote: 'Harris was not attractive - he was a large, plain-looking man who spoke little, stuttered when he did speak, was aggressive in conversation, and almost completely tactless.'[43] What a catch!

The description does remind me of Mr Collins from *Pride and Prejudice*. The obsequious little man who is entirely without warmth, grace or self-awareness is a wonderful love-to-hate character. Mr Collins also proposes to the heroine Elizabeth Bennet, who promptly refuses him, despite the perk of his having the incredibly posh and snobbish Lady Catherine de

Sir Joseph Pennington. The light above his painting frequently malfunctions; perhaps a faulty fitting or do the Muncaster spirits dislike him due to his behaviour towards his wife and children?

A portrait of Lady Sarah Pennington.

Muncaster Castle in West Cumbria, where the Pennington family still live to this day. (Paul Hudson)

A founding feminist, Mary Wollstonecraft.

Left: A portrait of Mary Shelley, daughter to Mary Wollstonecraft.

Below: A plaque marking the home of Mary Wollstonecraft

Portrait of Dido Elizabeth Belle Lindsay (1761-1804) and her cousin Lady Elizabeth Murray (1760-1825). The original is in Scone Palace, Perthshire, Scotland.

Jane Austen, a wonderful writer and keen commenter of society.

Jane Austen's beautiful Hampshire home, of Chawton Cottage

Above: A plaque marking the spot the original Elizabeth Fry Refuge was located.

Left: Elizabeth Fry, A woman who advocated for prisoners, when so many had dismissed them.

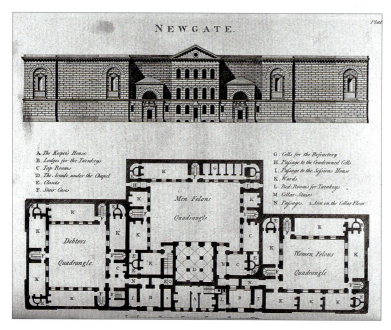

A plan of Newgate Prison as it would have been during Elizabeth Fry's lifetime.

Hester Stanhope, a true adventurer, shown here wearing her turban.

Above: The updated plaque that briefly describes the horror of the Peterloo Massacre

Right: This painting shows Peterloo, where Mary Fildes showed such passion.

Anne Lister, the first modern lesbian, an entrepreneur and diarist.

The beautiful Shibden Hall, once owned by Anne Lister. The tower to the left of the photograph was built by Lister herself, as a library. (Calderdale Museums Services with Bankfield Museum & Smith Art Gallery)

The first ichthyosaur found by Mary Anning. The fossil is now housed in London's Natural History Museum.

Mary Anning, who was a palaeontological pioneer.

The statue of Mary Anning at Lyme Regis, UK, unveiled in 2022.

A portrait of Ada Lovelace, who was the mother of modern computing.

Burgh as his patron, as well as the parsonage as her home. Mrs Bennet chides Elizabeth for not marrying Mr Collins, but her father congratulates her and tells her: 'An unhappy alternative is before you Elizabeth. From this day you must be a stranger to one of your parents. Your mother will never see you again if you do not marry Mr Collins, and I will never see you again if you do.'[44] Jane has Elizabeth Bennet delighted at her father's reaction, although it is unsure what her family really thought of her refusal of the real-life Mr Collins. Elizabeth's refusal makes sense to us as readers as we see how obnoxious Collins is, but financially, she has made a great mistake. Overall, Elizabeth is right to refuse, as her future happiness and sanity is more important to her, than her financial security. In the novel, it is Charlotte Lucas who agrees to marry Mr Collins after Elizabeth's refusal and it is perhaps a glimpse into the life that Jane dodged. Charlotte barely sees her new husband, she is left alone at the parsonage most days, and despite the fact Charlotte refers to herself as 'content', it is not the kind of happiness that Jane wished for. She has Elizabeth refuse the advances of Mr Collins, but allows her to find long-term happiness with Mr Darcy, someone Jane sadly never found for herself.

When writing to her niece Fanny Knight, she asked her what she thought about her situation regarding the recent marriage proposal. Her niece answered her with her honest thoughts, telling her 'not to commit yourself farther, and not think of accepting him unless you really do like him'. She followed this with sage council: 'Anything is to be preferred or endured rather than marrying without Affection.'[45] I think it is safe to assume that Jane shared this notion. She was not going to marry someone for whom she had no affection or even respect.

She always had her heroines married by the end of their stories, but only to men who deserved their love and admiration. In possibly an autobiographical moment in *Sense and Sensibility*, Elinor Dashwood states: 'the worse and most irremediable of all evils, [is] a connection for life'.[46] What she is saying here is that one of the worst things that can occur to a woman is a marriage with someone wholly unsuited to them. Perhaps this real-life event and the words of her niece gave her the inspiration to make Elinor Dashwood so wise and modern.

Her writing continued and she found herself picking up her unfinished novel *The Watsons*, making changes. Perhaps she was inspired to write again after some time away from the novel. The plot centres around an impoverished and disabled vicar and his struggles to bring up his four daughters. Biographer Kathryn Sutherland describes the novel as 'a study in the harsh economic realities of dependent women's lives'.[47] It is suggested by Honan that Jane abandoned this book shortly after her father passed away on 21 January 1805. It could have been grief that led to her to stop writing, or it could be that her and her family's circumstances were now too close to resembling the characters in the book. It must have been uncomfortable to write such a book given her own late father's profession and the now difficult financial situation the family found themselves in.

The sudden death of the Reverend George Austen left Jane, Cassandra, and their mother in desperate circumstances. Four of the older brothers, Edward, James, Henry and Francis (Frank), all offered to pay annual contributions to help their mother and sisters. The youngest brother, Charles, did not make a financial contribution to the family, but this could have been due to him serving abroad. It is possible it was some weeks before he even heard of his father's death, given that the Admiralty of the Royal Navy had promoted him to commander of the sloop HMS *Indian*, based at St George's Town, the first permanent English settlement on the islands of Bermuda.

The second eldest boy, George, named after his father, did not contribute either, but for good reason. He was born with severe epilepsy along with many other conditions and had not grown up in the family home. Little is known about the boy once he left the Austen home and it is not known if any contact was sustained between the family who cared for him and the Austens. It is unclear whether the boy lived beyond childhood.

In the four years that followed, the family had to move around a great deal. It was a challenging, uncertain, and turbulent time. They managed to remain for some time at their rented apartment in Bath, but eventually had to leave the city in the early summer of 1805. They lived for a short time with family members back at Steventon and then moved to a cottage in Worthing. They also spent time living with Frank, Jane's older brother, and his new wife in Southampton. It was four years of upheaval for the family and must have been very difficult for them all, never being sure how they would manage financially. The family were finally settled in Chawton Cottage near Alton, Hampshire, by 7 July 1809.

Once settled, the calm that overcame her life seems to have been what Jane needed to complete her novels. A woman's primary functions were to be a wife and mother and while writing was actively encouraged as a hobby, it certainly was not to be the main source of her income. Books were of course not only written but published in her lifetime, however they were often published anonymously or under a pseudonym, such as in the case of George Eliot.

Jane published four novels whilst staying at Chawton, and they were all relatively well-received. Through her brother Henry's London contact, Thomas Egerton, she published *Sense and Sensibility*, which like all of her novels, with the exception of *Pride and Prejudice*, was published 'on commission', where the author takes the financial risk. For *Pride and Prejudice*, Jane sold the copyright for a one-time-payment.[48] She had become soured by her dealings with publishers as she had previously sold the copyright of *Susan*, the novel which would become to be known as *Northanger Abbey*, to the publishers Crosby & Co for a sum of £10, who then did not publish it. This left Jane angry and she did write to Richard Crosby demanding to have her copyright back. She bought it back from him and looked for a more reputable publisher

Despite her fight to get her work published, when her work was in the public domain, it was received well. *Sense and Sensibility* was published on excellent quality paper and was on sale for 15 shillings, the equivalent to a huge £58 per copy in today's money. The elite, fashionable, and beautiful young things loved her work. It was said that even the Prince Regent, the soon to be King George IV, was a big fan of hers, having a set of her completed works at all of his many royal residences. Jane, however, was not particularly enamoured by the prince's attentions. The Prince Regent's librarian, James Stanier Clarke, a former naval clerk, quietly suggested that she should dedicate her newest novel, *Emma*, to the future king. Jane disapproved of the prince's womanizing, gambling, and lavish lifestyle, spending money so carelessly. Having been brought up with a modest and frugal attitude to money, she must have been appalled by the prince's spendthrift and decadent over-the-top existence. She begrudgingly did dedicate the book to the prince. If she had not, the prince's ego would perhaps have been hurt, and his people would have made it difficult for Jane to be published elsewhere.

Her work was published in much larger volumes than normal, into many thousands of copies. It is unclear whether the decision to publish the books in such great volume was down to the publisher or author. It is thought that Jane made £140 from *Sense and Sensibility*, which today stands at around a decent £9,000.[49] This would have allowed her some comfort and independence. After the success of *Sense and Sensibility*, her subsequent works were said to be 'from the author of *Sense and Sensibility*' rather than the previous authorship of 'By a Lady'.[50] It is a rather tragic fact, that Jane's name never appeared as the author of any of her books in her lifetime. A female writer was still something taboo and treated with suspicion.

Jane started feeling unwell early in 1816. By the summer of that year, friends and family had started to notice her deterioration.[51] A vast majority of biographers fall back on Zachary Cope's 1964 posthumous diagnosis of Addison's disease, also known as primary adrenal insufficiency, a rare and long-term condition characterized by the body's inadequate production of steroid hormones cortisol and aldosterone within the adrenal glands. It leads to abdominal and gastrointestinal pain, weakness, and weight loss. It may also lead to low blood pressure, vomiting, mood swings, darkening of the skin, lower back pain, and loss of consciousness. However, a lot of her symptoms could also be explained by Hodgkin lymphoma, a cancer that starts in white blood cells called lymphocytes, of which side effects include non-painful, but very itchy swellings on the neck, under arms, and groin.

Whatever her illness, she slowly seemed to fade from her former self. She was fully aware that something was wrong and chose to pass it off as 'bile' or 'rheumatism'. Despite feeling ill, she continued to work on the ending of her novel *The Elliots*, then moved on to write *The Brothers*, a novel that would be published in 1925 as *Sanditon*. The plot circled around her heroine Diana Parker, described in the novel as an 'energetic invalid'. It does not take much detective work to assume that Diana Parker is in fact based on Jane herself, who by this point is almost entirely sofa-ridden. Although in the novel, Jane mocks hypochondriacs, perhaps she felt that she was imagining her illness. She abandoned the novel only twelve chapters in as her illness began to overcome her and sap her energy. She wrote of herself that she was turning 'every wrong colour' and that she was living 'chiefly on the sofa'.[52] Jane put her pen down on 18 March 1817, never to pick it up again.[53] By the end of the following month, she was bed-ridden.

Her sister Cassandra and her older brother Henry were worried about their sister and took the frail Jane to see a doctor in Winchester. According to historian Janet Todd, she was suffering from agonizing pain by this time, she had given up on life and wished for the end to come quickly. She must have felt so ill to have wished for her own death.

She got her wish only weeks later on 18 July 1817. She was only forty-one years old.

Through his connections, Henry managed to get his sister a burial plot in the north aisle of the nave of Winchester Cathedral.

In her epitaph, Henry praised her personal qualities, prayed for her eternal salvation and mentioned the 'extraordinary endowments of her mind',[54] but did not explicitly mention her achievements as a writer, as pointed out by Le Faye.[55] It seems strange to us that her writing skills and immortal works are not mentioned in the great writer's epitaph.

In the weeks and months that followed Jane's death, Cassandra and Henry worked with publisher John Murray to discuss getting *Persuasion* and *Northanger Abbey* published as a set. Henry once again wrote about his sister, in a biographical note dated December 1817. Sales were good, but sadly all her novels were out of print by the end of the 1820s. Despite this, her books were still popular and were borrowed regularly from libraries throughout the country.

Jane had many admirers and there was even an early example of fan fiction based on one of her characters appearing in *The Lady's Magazine* in 1823.[56] The writing refers to Jane's genius and suggests that aspiring authors look to her for inspiration and that even established authors are jealous of her talent.

A publisher and fan of Jane's, Richard Bentley, purchased all remaining copies of her novels before they went out of print. He then published the collective works as illustrated volumes as part of his Standard Novels series. In 1833, Bentley published a full collected edition of her works. Since then, her novels have never been out of print, which is quite an achievement.

It is tragic that Jane did not live long enough to see how popular, beloved, and enduring her works would become. Her name is synonymous with fantastically scathing writing hiding behind good manners and afternoon tea. She created such wonderfully vivid characters, ones who were very likely based on people she knew, albeit exaggerated to comedic or dramatic effect. Her heroines all defy gender norms in one way or another, pushing for more agency in their own lives. The overarching theme that runs throughout Jane's novels is the inequality faced by women in the Georgian society she lived in. She wrote of the world she inhabited and of the problems she knew many women in her position faced.

HESTER STANHOPE

Non-conformist Adventurer

❧

Lady Hester is very likely one of the most exciting and unique women you have never heard of. A British adventurer, she travelled around the Middle East, exploring places few Westerners had ever stepped foot. Considered the first to use modern archaeological principles, she was a trailblazer and never conformed to society's norms if she could help it.

She did for the most part lead a charmed life, living in the lap of luxury for much of her life, and meeting the great and good of Georgian society both at home and abroad. She was born on 12 March 1776, the eldest daughter of Charles Stanhope, 3rd Earl Stanhope, and his first wife Lady Hester Pitt, the sister of William Pitt the Younger. Lady Hester spent much of her childhood at her father's impressive estate at Chevening, until around 1800 when she moved in with her grandmother, Hester Pitt, Countess of Chatham at her home in Burton Pynsent.[1]

Her father, also known as Lord Charles Mahon, was a British statesman, inventor, and scientist. He dabbled in politics, supporting William Pitt the Younger, before severing his political links with Pitt after he strayed from his liberal beginnings. Stanhope was also the chairman of the Revolution

Society initially founded in honour of the Glorious Revolution of 1688. The society expressed sympathy for the French Revolution and supported Thomas Muir, one of the Edinburgh politicians transported to Botany Bay. Stanhope was not shy to publicly support or condemn various political and social events during his time with the society.

An accomplished scientist, Stanhope was elected a fellow of the Royal Society as early as November 1772. He devoted a huge amount of his fortune to his experimentations and philosophical work. He is responsible for creating an impressive range of items, such as a rather unsuccessful method of fireproofing buildings, an improvement to canal locks, an iron printing press, which was a method of producing plaster moulds of pages to be printed known as stereotype matrix and stereotype plates, a method of tuning music instruments, and a one lens microscope which still bears his name.

His daughter seems to have inherited his scientific and mathematical mind. She would later go on to move into a branch of science untouched by her father.

Hester seemed to bore easily in life and was not one to stay anywhere for long. In 1803, she moved in with her uncle, William Pitt the Younger. Here, she would live quite happily, and manage his household for him. He had appointed himself Prime Minister by this point, but he was still unmarried, and needed the help of his niece to run the house and add a feminine touch. She would also act as hostess to the many dignitaries and leaders he met with daily. This social political life came easy to Hester, as guests commented on her beauty and her conversation. She seems to have been a natural at speaking to dignitaries, leaving them dazzled by her charisma. Even when her uncle ended his term as Prime Minister, she continued her role at his side as a private secretary and his personal assistant. She had made herself indispensable to him.

Pitt the Younger died in January 1806, aged only forty-six, due to a peptic ulcer and many other underlying health problems. On his death, Hester was awarded an annual pension of £1,200, which is the modern equivalent to just short of a whopping £89,000 in today's money. A princely sum of money to set her up in a good life for many years to come. This sum showed how much her hard work was appreciated by Pitt having made herself invaluable to him during her time working as his personal assistant.

She stayed in London for some time, but soon found herself tiring of life there and decided to move to Wales. She was content for a while, but when her brother Major the Right Honourable Charles Banks Stanhope died in the Battle of Corunna in 1809, she felt she needed to leave. She had been very close to her brother and his death abroad led her to pack up and leave Great Britain for good.

Her love life may have prompted this departure as well. Her former lover, Granville Leveson-Gower, 1st Earl Granville, married another woman, despite potentially long-lasting feelings between them. Hester had never admitted to any remaining feelings between the two, but the couple had been together on and off for some time according to society gossip. Also hotly rumoured was Hester's relationship with Lieutenant-General Sir John Moore. Her beloved brother Charles had been Moore's aide-de-camp, and the two were reported friends. Hester and Moore had written to each other throughout his fighting in the Peninsular War.[2] Hester's niece, Catherine Lucy Wilhelmina

Powlett, Duchess of Cleveland, believed that they flirted and were even perhaps considering marriage. There is nothing more than hearsay about the nature of their relationship, but once again, society gossip was rife about their spicy love affair. Sadly, their relationship was doomed. Despite the flirtation and possible marriage plans, it would all come to nothing as Moore, like her brother, was killed in the Battle of Corunna.[3] This could have been the point at which Hester decided that she would never marry, with her hopes dashed when Moore was killed.

When she stepped off the dock at Portsmouth harbour, it was the last time she would ever be on English soil. It was perhaps a conscious decision to never return to England, or perhaps it was circumstance that kept her away. She left with her brother and chaperone, James Hamilton Stanhope, who accompanied her as far as Rhodes. She was joined by her maids, Elizabeth Williams and Anne Fry, and her physician and later biographer, Charles Lewis Meryon. During her time on the Greek islands, she met Michael Bruce, who was primarily known for smuggling Antoine Marie Chamans, the Comte de Lavalette, out of France during the Bourbon Restoration in 1814. He was also a short-lived Member of Parliament, but found himself now accompanying the unlikely group around Europe. He and Hester would become lovers, although this could have purely been a physical relationship, rather than it being one based on deeper feelings.

It is suggested that when the party arrived in Athens, they were met by none other than the infamous Lord Byron. George Gordon Byron, or 6th Baron Byron, was a university friend of Bruce and the latter introduced Hester to him. Bryon described her as having 'a great disregard of received notion in her conversation as well as conduct'.[4] These are rather insulting words from Byron's mouth, given his own outlandish and unorthodox lifestyle. Byron would later claim not to have wanted to get into a debate about women's rights with Hester because 'I despise the sex too much to squabble with them'.[5] This quote shows how he dismissed women as being inferior to men, and only thought of them as amusements and diversions when it suited him. Perhaps he did not wish to engage in an argument as he knew he could not win such a debate against Hester. She was noted for her quick wit, intelligence, and sharp tongue at times, too, so Byron could have been intimidated by her. Her intelligence was maybe seen as a threat to Byron, who seems to have sidestepped any attempt to speak to her about anything more than simple pleasantries about the weather. Any serious debate or in-depth discussion was dodged by Byron. It is fun to imagine Hestr smiling to herself as she watched Byron storm off into the distance after each of her endeavours to begin a conversation.

The group went on from Athens to Constantinople, present-day Istanbul, capital of the Ottoman Empire. From here, they intended to travel to Cairo, which was still recovering from the recent chaos following Napoleon's invasion of Egypt and the bloodshed and upheaval that followed. It is incredible that she chose to go there at all, given the country's recent troubles.

Their journey to Cairo was fraught with danger and bad luck as the ship encountered a massive storm off the coast of Rhodes. It capsized and soon fell beneath the waves, sending their possessions to the bottom of the Aegean Sea. With the loss of all their clothing, the party borrowed outfits from some kind passing Turkish sailors. Despite it being a traditionally Muslim country, Hester refused to wear a veil, as females usually were expected to wear, choosing instead to wear the clothing of a Turkish male. She wore slippers, a turban, and a robe. Even when a British frigate picked up the stranded travellers to take them to Cairo, Hester continued to wear clothing traditionally worn by a man. She bought new clothes when they reached their destination, but chose a long purple velvet robe, embroidered trousers, waistcoat, jacket, saddle, and sabre, not the clothing usually associated with an English gentlewoman. It was in this clothing that she went to meet with the Pasha, a high-ranking Ottoman man, similar to the British peerage or knighthood.

Her choice of clothing can be seen in many ways. It could be seen as a terrible slight on the religious norms of the country, not wearing a veil as expected. It is entirely possible that it was seen as such by some who met her. Maybe it shows a conscious or subconscious decision to break with tradition and usual gender norms. Perhaps away from English shores and the strict social rules, she felt liberated to wear the clothing she wished to wear, dispensing with stays, paniers, and layers of heavy fabric, opting for free-flowing material. There are even suggestions that she shaved her head and wore a turban in public. Again, this shows her complete departure from the social norms of the day, and as it would take many months for her hair to grow back, shows how her decision was a long term one. She clearly had no intentions to return to English society any time soon. At home, the hair fashion was as severe as any of the other rules there. Even men grew their own hair long and powdered their hair or wore wigs if their own hair was not long enough. The rule for women's hair was 'the bigger, the better', with women often adding fake hair to their own to increase the volume, with some styles at the end of the eighteenth century reaching into the skies like giant white powdered mountains atop their heads. This fake hair was perhaps bought from wigmakers or collected from brushes every time a lady brushed. Wigmakers also often doubled up as tooth-drawers and they would buy hair and teeth from poorer people, who would be forced to sell these in an attempt to stave off starvation. It is not unlike the storyline of *Les Misérables*, where Fantine is forced through desperation to sell her teeth and beautiful long hair.

The very fact Hester shaved her own hair off and wore a turban suggests that she no longer cared what others thought of her nor for the expectations that had been forced on to her sex. She did not do this out of desperation or great need, like the fictional Fantine, as money had never been a particular problem.

It is doubtful that she ever showed her bald head in public, but it was still very subversive for a woman to be without her locks. Perhaps Hester chose to do this for convenience as it would have been quite useful to have a shaved head in hotter, more humid climates. Turbans were fashionable in Georgian England towards the end of the eighteenth century when she was a little girl, but they would have almost always been worn with some hair showing at the sides of the turban, perhaps even curls escaping to the sides to frame the face. Whatever the reason for shaving her head, whether to be intentionally subversive or merely more practical reasons, she certainly made a statement wherever she went and people spoke about her in hushed tones.

Over the next two years, she travelled all over the Middle East and further into the Mediterranean, visiting Gibraltar, Malta, the Ionian Islands, Palestine, Lebanon, and Syria. She seems to have missed England very little during her travels and soaked up the cultures and customs as she went, studying them like the social butterfly that she was. However, she did not always follow the customs, once again refusing to wear a veil even in the deeply religious city of Damascus. In some Muslim countries women are still required to veil their head and face in certain buildings and in public. By refusing to wear a veil, Hester was perhaps asserting her identity rather than intentionally slighting the faith of the locals. She did not seem to be reprimanded for not wearing a veil, quite the opposite seems to be the case. In Jerusalem, the Church of the Holy Sepulchre was cleared of its faithful and reopened for her alone. This was perhaps to allow her to visit the church without her veil and at the same time keep her dignity by keeping eyes off her. It was very kind of them to allow her this privilege, but if she had worn a veil, the faithful would not have had to exit the church for her. No one seems to have approached her about this quite serious faux pas.

During her stay in the Middle East, Hester visited a fortune teller and mystic who foretold that she would marry the next messiah. This sounds like an oddly specific prediction, but she did not seem to find it strange. She began wooing and offering her hand in marriage to a powerful man Saud bin Abdulaziz Al Saud.[6] He would annex Medina and Mecca from the Ottoman Empire, allowing him to be the first to hold the title 'Servant of the Two Holy Cities' and was referred to as Saud Al Kabeer or Saud the Great. Hester might have put some hope in the words of the fortune teller, but sadly, marriage would not be in her future.

Hester's physician and companion on their trip abroad was

also a collector of her stories and adventures. Charles Meryon wrote down their conversations and would later publish her many tales and anecdotes of her travels after her death. Reading like a *Boy's Own* adventure story, it is in these recollections that Meryon mentions that Hester stumbled across a medieval Italian manuscript that had been kept hidden away in a little monastery in Syria. In this manuscript, she read that there were unimaginable treasures concealed beneath a 600-year-old mosque in the port town of Tel Ashkelon. On the strength of this medieval document, Hester set off to find the treasure in 1815, making her way through the ruins of Ashkelon on the Mediterranean coast, just north of the area of Gaza. She managed to persuade Ottoman authorities that the site needed to be excavated and was granted permission as long as the governor of Jaffa, Muhammad Abu Nabbut, accompanied her. This would be seen as the first archaeological dig in Palestine.

The treasure she found there was not gold or silver, but a seven-foot-tall finely-carved marble statue of a figure without a head. Perhaps the statue was beheaded intentionally in the past to destroy the memory of that important person, as often happened in Ancient Egypt. When the new pharoah came to power after violence, he or she would often destroy the statues of the previous ruler, scratching off their names from the bases of statues and tablets. A stunning find such as this today would be a newsworthy story that would take the archaeological world by storm. Heartbreakingly, Hester ordered that this statue be smashed into 'a thousand pieces' and thrown into the sea.[7] This awful action was done before the heat of the sun could warm the stone. In modern times this would seem like desecration, but at the time she did this as a gesture of goodwill to the Ottoman government. As strange as it sounds, she wanted to show the government that her archaeological dig was intended to find treasures for the Ottomans, not to sell their cultural history back to Europe. It was during this time that many wealthy Europeans were excavating historically and culturally significant artefacts and claiming them for the many collectors abroad. Even today, there are heated discussions about many artefacts being returned to their place of origin and the descendants of those who created them. Many collectors and museums more than a century on are still reluctant to return the items, but some have started to be restored to their countries of origin, paving the way for more talks and artefacts finding their way home. With technology being as advanced as it is, it will not be long before we could have exact copies of these beautiful ancient artefacts projected in European museums.

Although her methods of archaeology leave a lot to be desired by today's standards, Hester was in many ways the first 'modern' archaeologist. The destruction of the statue aside, she saw her work as important and for the good of the country she called home. Many so-called archaeologists of the time were essentially graverobbers and looters, there to steal what they could to bolster their own reputations and bank accounts. They cared little for the culture or heritage of the places they dug and did not accurately record where artefacts were found. This shoddy administration of past excavations has affected our understanding of certain ancient sites as there are no records of exactly where and how deep below the surface items were found, thus affecting the dating of artefacts. Any human remains found were often cast aside or torn apart to find treasures on the body. This is what happened to many Ancient

Egyptian artefacts. When a mummy was found deep inside a silent and ancient tomb, its bandages were unceremoniously torn and ripped from the remains of the bodies to find the sacred amulets and precious and semi-precious stones placed amongst the linen, to sell or perhaps keep for themselves. The skeletal remains of the mummies were sometimes just thrown away or ground up for rich and very strange Europeans to drink down as a bizarre health tonic. It is impossible to calculate how many irreplaceable cultural artefacts have been lost to these early robberies and how many have been quietly kept in private collections miles from their original home.

Hester was not like those graverobbers and instead worked more like the way archaeologists work today. She made copious notes on the site and marked where and at what depth important artefacts were found, unprecedented for the time. Anything of value she found was passed to the Ottoman government, but not before it was sketched and recorded carefully. Her impact was such that she inspired further excavations at the site and tourism began to the Middle East.[8] Travellers started going to visit the ancient site and to see what Hester's group had found there, also raising awareness of the country and its long rich history.

Hester finally ended her itinerant lifestyle in her later years, settling in Sidon, a Mediterranean town in what is now Lebanon. She seemed to enjoy living in former monasteries, despite her own apathy towards religion, living in three in her quieter years. She lived with her companion Miss Williams and her ever faithful Dr Charles Meryon for many years. Miss Williams passed away in 1828 and Meryon left in 1831. When she was alone, her companions all gone, she retired to another former monastery at Joun, close to Sidon.

Meryon would join her during the summer of 1837 for a year at this address. It would be the last time he would see her.

Hester seems to have become embroiled in the religious and Druze inter-clan wars in the area, giving sanctuary to potentially hundreds of refugees. She was even visited by emir Bashir Shihab II, the ruler of the area. She found herself with a strange power over the locals, who seemed to have an affection for her. Some locals even thought her capable of divination[9] and sought her opinion and advice. She became a local legend, a curiosity, who drew visitors from far and wide, flocking to her for her company and wisdom. She was a strange English gentlewoman, with a shaven head and a turban, who spoke with such knowledge and wit, people travelled miles to see her. She became a celebrity of sorts, her commanding personality drawing strangers from all over the Middle East to see her.

As time passed, she seemed to withdraw from public life. Perhaps the influx of strangers and visitors had become too much for her. She was seen out in public less and less, until she stopped going out entirely. It got to the point where she even stopped welcoming visitors. She found herself in massive debt. This could have been due to her helping the many charity cases who knocked on her door over the years. Without any income she found that she had to rely on her English pension to pay off her creditors. Some of her servants stole from her which is heartbreaking, considering how much she was seemingly loved by locals.

Something undoubtedly was happening to her during these last years and it has been suggested that she was suffering from severe depression. She avoided people entirely, which seemed to be very unlike the social creature she had previously been. The few visitors she received would only be seen in the darkness of her room, where only her face and hands were visible. She became a recluse, living in the shadows and avoiding people wherever possible. Few got to see her in person, though rumours and stories about her were whispered throughout the local area. This withdrawal from society certainly seems to tie in with the diagnosis of depression.

Some have suggested that she was suffering with the early stages of senility or dementia. Perhaps her hiding in the dark when visitors were permitted to enter the house backs this notion. She may perhaps have wanted to minimize the number of people she spoke to. Perhaps she knew she was losing her grip on language and memory and wanted to conceal this from the world.

Hester died in her sleep in 1839. She would die penniless. According to Robert Murray M'Cheyne and Andrew Bonar, who visited Joun some weeks after her death, 'not a para of money was found in the house'.[10] A para was the now former currency used across the Ottoman Empire. Perhaps she frittered her money away, perhaps she spent it or lost it, perhaps she had given it away to worthy causes, but it is sad that she died without a penny to her name, especially as most of her life was spent in comfort and plenty.

Lady Hester Stanhope was a pioneer. She was not only the first modern archaeologist, but a traveller, a writer, and had the single-mindedness to wear the clothes she wanted to wear, all during a time with strict social cues. She lived her life the way she wanted to and did not conform to the expectations of the rigid Georgian society.

ELIZABETH FRY

The Angel of Prisoners

❧

Elizabeth Fry is probably best known for her revolutionary work in reforming the appalling conditions of prisons in the early nineteenth century. She was also instrumental for bringing about the 1823 Gaols Act which separated male and female prisoners and promoted the employment of female guards which massively reduced sexual assault and rape amongst female prisoners. She was posthumously rewarded by her likeness being printed on the Bank of England's £5 note from 2002 to 2017.

Elizabeth Gurney was born on 21 May 1780 in Gurney Court, Norwich. The Gurneys were so rich their name is mentioned in a W.S. Gilbert comedy opera *Trial by Jury*, first produced 25 March 1875 in London, where a character sings that they are 'as rich as the Gurneys'.[1] The family were obviously very well-known as a reference to them would not have been made in a Gilbert and Sullivan musical unless it would be recognised by the audience. They were a prominent Quaker family in Norwich and helped make the city what it is today.

Her childhood home was at Earlham Hall which now makes up part of the University of East Anglia. Her father was John

Gurney, a founder of Gurney Bank, and her mother Catherine Barclay, whose family had founded Barclay's Bank. Elizabeth's mother died when she was only twelve years old, and it must have been a difficult time for the family. As the eldest child, the education and well-being of her younger siblings fell to her. With Elizabeth's influence, her younger brother Joseph John Gurney would go on to help his sister tackle the terrible conditions in prisons and their younger sister Louisa Gurney Hoare would spend her life devoted to improving the quality of education for children of poorer families. Her sisters were all reported to have a fiery passion for moving against the grain of society. Janet Witney, in her book about Elizabeth Fry,[2] paints a vivid picture of the sisters wearing their red hoods and linking arms across the road to hold up a gentleman's carriage. The passenger in the carriage was a wealthy local businessman who owned much of the land in the area. She mentions how the sisters did not break their line, even when the horses were urged forwards into a gallop. The girls then paired together, and danced around the carriage, much to the confusion and delight of the coachman and the gentleman in the carriage. It is such a vibrant image of Elizabeth and her sisters, showing her strength of mind from a young age, pushing away from the expectations that society attempted to impose on her. It would be a sign of how Elizabeth would live her life: bright, bold, and unbeholden to anyone.

Elizabeth married Joseph Fry on 19 August 1800 in Norwich Goat Lane Friends Meeting House. The couple would have a whopping eleven children, five sons and six daughters. It was of a time when large families were the norm and having multiple children the done thing, given the lack of contraception, sex education and high child-mortality rate.

All but one of their children lived long enough to marry and have families of their own. Little Betsy Fry, born in 1811, died not long after her fifth birthday. She was the seventh child and died while her mother was heavily pregnant with their tenth child, Samuel. It was all too common to lose children to disease and infection. It is thought by some that parents lost so many children that they were almost immune to the horror and sadness, but I do not think that is true. A parent who has loved and lost their child grieves deeply. I'm sure countless tears were shed by all those who lost their babies, no matter how many times it happened. Elizabeth, her husband, and the remaining children will have all mourned the passing of little Betsy.

Perhaps their faith helped them to cope with her loss? Both Elizabeth and her husband were Quakers and she was known locally as a minister as early as 1811. Joseph was a distant cousin, a tea merchant, and a struggling banker. His uncle, confusingly also called Joseph Fry, was a very successful merchant and had set up J.S. Fry & Sons in Bristol which made the first solid chocolate bars in the UK in 1847. The company merged with Cadbury's in 1919, but continued to be famous in its own right for many years following the merger.

Elizabeth and her siblings were avid writers of journals, and they kept meticulous records of their daily lives, with the exception of John, the eldest boy.[3] It was fashionable and downright irresistible to a large section of the middle to upper classes to keep a diary, pouring into it all their innermost thoughts and feelings, and writing the words they dare not say out loud. The Gurney diaries have for the most part been published and give us a clear insight into the daily lives of the family, and importantly, what they really thought of the people and places around them. It is fascinating to read those innermost thoughts. In a society determined to be polite and follow etiquette, words were left unsaid many times and it would have been difficult for many to keep their sense of calm without some sort of outlet. Writing down their thoughts, anger, and frustrations would have helped a great deal of people remain polite to those around them and allowed society to retain its well-mannered and courteous façade.

It is Elizabeth's diary entries that tell us that she was the most religious and devout of her sisters. Her sisters disliked spending their Sunday mornings in church and tired of the preacher's voice. According to J. Witney, the family would often write in their journals about their 'long and dismal two-hour long meeting in the Friends' Meeting House'.[4] Their journals perhaps gave them the opportunity to be truthful about their feelings, whilst to the outside world they smiled and bore the discomfort of attending church. Elizabeth continued to go to church into adulthood and became a preacher herself. She was in contact with many Quakers around the world and became friends with William Savery, an American Quaker preacher who was an abolitionist and advocated for the rights of the Native American people. Perhaps moved by Savery's passion for the wronged and forgotten of society, when she was invited by a family friend Stephen Grellet to visit Newgate Prison in 1813, Elizabeth did not hesitate. She was eager to step into the fray and help her fellow man. She had preached about helping people every Sunday, but now saw an opportunity to do something on a practical level.

Elizabeth was horrified by the conditions she saw at Newgate, overcrowded to the extreme with women and their children who had been there weeks, some without trial. The men and women were not segregated, with sexual assaults and rape being commonplace by other prisoners and even guards. They slept on straw on the ground with the rats and were expected to do their own cooking and washing of their clothes. It was clear that some did not feed themselves or wash. Most were in rags and their thin, half-starved bodies dirty with grime from months or even years locked up without access to running water, licking moisture from the damp stone walls of their communal cells. For some prisoners, Newgate was the last stop before deportation to Australia. When Elizabeth inspected the ships in 1814, she said the conditions on board were no better than a slave ship, suggesting that changes needed to happen quickly. Sadly, it would be another twenty years until the abolition of slavery finally happened.

Elizabeth returned to Newgate the following day with clothes and food for some of the prisoners who had struck her as most needy. Many of the inmates had been there for years, and their clothing was little more than rags, no match for the draughty damp cells in which they spent much of their time. She began to compile a list of fundamental items needed by the prisoners.

Elizabeth soon noticed that the prisoners were hungry and that malnutrition was the root cause of many of their ailments, some of which were long-term and potentially life-threatening.

Due to family financial difficulties, Elizabeth would be unable to return to the prison for two years. As soon as their family finances had been secured, she revisited the prison only to find conditions had not improved at all in her almost two-year absence. Her vision for the prison seems very modern, with its focus on rehabilitation instead of punishment, reformation instead of retribution. Prisons had always been a way of keeping the criminals off the streets. They were to be punished, hurt, and kept incarcerated until the time of their trial, where they would be executed, sentenced to hard labour abroad or released. They were in prison to be disciplined instead of providing them with support and skills to enable them to avoid returning to crime when they were released. Instead of stripping the criminal of their humanity in prison, she attempted to provide them with both physical and emotional nourishment and encouragement to make better choices. She led to a switch in the way people viewed criminals, in a way which is still the core of the justice system today.

According to Witney, Elizabeth's first impression of Newgate Prison's exterior was one of 'orderly beauty'.[5] The outside of the building was beautiful and symmetrical and pleased her. The second impression upon entering was 'one of gloom and bad smells',[6] and her third and more lasting impression of the prison was 'most overwhelming' and 'pandemonium'.[7] As she walked the corridors of Newgate, she realised the true horror. The smell must have been an assault on the nostrils and must have been eye-wateringly awful with the amount of human waste, sweat, and damp lying around. An overall feeling of sadness struck her and the 'pandemonium' of the place she realised was created by the lack of basic care for the prisoners. The noise of the place must have been awful, what with prisoners screaming, shouting, and crying, trapped in the cells all day every day, along with other human noises of vomiting and coughing due to the general ill-health of the population. The mental health of prisoners would have been at risk.

In 1816, Elizabeth began her work. She set up an in-prison school for the children of the female prisoners, whose education had been disrupted through no fault of their own. She disagreed with punishing the prisoners, and instead asked them to come up with a list of rules to agree on. They then took a diplomatic vote on the rules and this list was then made universal throughout the prison. The fact that she considered involving the prisoners in their rulemaking was revolutionary. Prisoners' voices had not been heard before, as they were deemed unworthy and inferior to voice their opinions.

In 1817 she helped to establish the Association for the Reformation of Female Prisoners in Newgate, which focused on providing the female prisoners with help and support, teaching them skills that would help them make money on the outside of the prison walls. Money would be needed upon their release to pay for rent, food, and to look after any children they had. The government provided no financial support for anyone, so it was important to be able to be financially independent. They were provided with materials and learned how to patchwork, sew, and other forms of needlework.[8] These were calming activities which reduced fighting and arguing, but were also very useful skills that not only provided potential money-earning opportunities for them, and would help them run their households when they did return home. They were invaluable skills.

Elizabeth's book *Prisons in Scotland and the North of England* discussed the fact that she had stayed the night in some of the prisons and what she had found there. She later invited some members of the nobility to stay in a prison, too, so they could get a truer impression of what it is like to be in a cell. It is safe to say that they were less than impressed with the conditions there. Thomas Fowell Buxton, Elizabeth's brother-in-law and fellow social reformer, was elected as Member of Parliament for Weymouth. Buxton encouraged his associates in parliament to listen to Elizabeth. On 27 February 1818 she was invited to meet with a House of Commons committee to speak about her findings about prisons and the reforms she felt were needed.[9] She would be the first woman to give evidence to the House of Commons. Her words shocked and appalled the members there who had lived incredibly sheltered and privileged lives.

Elizabeth's method of providing usable skills to the prisoners was adopted by other prisons in the south of England and led to the establishment of the British Ladies' Society for Promoting the Reformation of Female Prisoners in 1821. It would roll out further to other prisons over the years and the idea of rehabilitation instead of punishment came to be the accepted norm.

The meeting with the House of Commons committee led to the passing of the Gaols Act in 1823. The Act was successful in that it separated male and female prisoners, therefore cutting down the number of sexual assault and rape cases in prisons. However, the Act did not cover those in town gaols or in debtors' prisons, which were often privately run by wealthy individuals who ran these establishments as businesses, making money off their inmates by outrageously charging for their cell, food, clothes, visitors, and even certain 'freedoms' to move around the yard and prison. As always, this system benefitted the rich inmates, who paid for the relative luxury of a single cell, and had their favourite fine hot food and wine brought in. They could even have a cell with a fireplace, to be lit and stoked at their request. There are references to some rich inmates having their wives and children present in their cell and a servant serving their meals as if they were in a tavern. The rich saw out their time in ease, as prison life to them was not unlike home. The poorer inmates, however, could not afford any such luxuries. They were left in shared cells with violent strangers, hungry, cold, and unable to see their loved ones as they could not afford the fees to provide them with these creature comforts.

The 1823 Gaol Act allowed no provision to inspect the gaols to ensure that changes had been made. The gaols were very much left to their own authority, without watchdogs checking on the welfare of prisoners, conditions or building safety. Elizabeth was unhappy about the shortcomings of the Act and gave a talk to a select committee where she shared her concerns about its flaws. It would not be until the 1835 Prison Act that all prisons came under central authority prison inspectors who would routinely visit prisons to make sure that all followed the rules regarding their inmates.[10] That is twelve years of campaigning until her concerns were finally listened to. It was a great step forward for the justice system.

It was common for prisoners to suffer execution or transportation for even minor offences, such as stealing small food items from street vendors. Stealing food reflected how desperate times had become for some people, due to lack of work, poor harvests, and poor pay for those who could find work. The prisoners would be taken in chains, huddled together in an open cart through the streets of London, often to jeers and shouts from the crowds gathered at the side of the road. They would often be spat at or have rotten vegetables and human or animal waste thrown at them as a final indignity along their journey. Carrying out this passage on an open top cart was to intentionally humiliate the prisoners, to take away their humanity and make the very people they lived alongside, their friends, and neighbours, laugh at them, belittle them and assault them. It was not uncommon for the prisoners to riot the night before this journey because it was so upsetting and traumatic. It was perhaps a last desperate attempt to avoid the terrible ordeal they faced. Elizabeth would sit with the women mostly, and some male prisoners on occasion, and talk to them about their lives, ask them questions, and calm their nerves. She would write to the governor of the prison to request that the women were taken on this journey in a closed carriage to at least minimize the indignity of the last ride through the streets. They were of course not usually treated with any dignity, so her intervening here was revolutionary, treating downtrodden working-class women as if they were well-born ladies. As a lot of these women's stories would end in transportation, their closed carriage would take them to the dockside where they were to board a ship to a new life in Australia. Although this sounds like a holiday to a modern reader, this would have been anything but a pleasant experience. The passage there itself would kill some and leave others weak and close to death. Disease was rife as the people on board were shackled and sat in their own waste, without enough drinking water or food to sustain them. They were often kept hungry intentionally to keep them weak, and therefore if a mutiny should happen, the prisoners would not put up too much of a fight and could be easily quelled. Those that survived, would end up in the sun-scorched outback, with few trees or shelter, away from everyone they ever loved. The Westerners who found themselves there struggled with the heat and found life incredibly difficult, as it was their job to

Georgian Feminists

begin to build a colony, mainly doing physically demanding jobs. Between 1788 and 1868, around 162,000 prisoners were transported to Australia for their crimes in Britain and Ireland.

Prior to its setting sail, Elizabeth would approach the captain of the transportation ship and asked him to bring supplies on board such as needles, thread, and fabric so that the women could make quilts and sew so that they had useful skills to use when they arrived at their destination. Having these skills would also help them day to day, sewing for themselves and often their child, who were transported with them. Elizabeth also included a care package of sorts [11] including food, drink, a Bible, a sharp hunting knife, and string that could be used for various traps, tents, and mending various items they had managed to take with them. Elizabeth was accompanied on her mission by several other leading women desperate to help the female convicts. The women included Hannah Bevan, Elizabeth Hanbury, Katherine Fry, and Elizabeth Pryor, all of whom, like Elizabeth, strove for a level of comfort for the convicts, and wanted to provide them with useful skills to help them make a wage when they arrived in Australia, and to ensure their children were educated and could at the very least read, write, and do basic mathematics.

The female convicts were often transported to New South Wales and Van Diemen's Land, renamed Tasmania in 1856 to remove the unpleasant link with the convicts and the 'demon' connotation. The people chose to name the island after the explorer Abel Tasman, the first European to visit the island back in the early seventeenth century.

Even after the women she had got to know at the prison had been transported abroad, Elizabeth did not stop trying to make conditions better for those who came after. It was personal for her. She continued to campaign and fight for better conditions for the female prisoners throughout her life and was still visiting transportation ships until 1843.[12] She and the women who visited the prisons worked together and campaigned for the abolition of transportation, which finally came about in 1868.

Elizabeth would also later visit prisons in Belfast, Ireland and in France. She was accompanied by her husband, as well as Lydia Irving, a British philanthropist, and fellow Religious Society of Friends abolitionists William Allen and Josiah Forster. They perhaps decided to visit these locations to compare conditions between the different prisons. They found dreadful conditions wherever they went and saw it was a time for a change.

Elizabeth was also concerned with the welfare of those outside the prisons. She helped the homeless in London, of which there were many thousands. She was perhaps spurred on to do this because she witnessed seeing the body of a young boy on the streets in the freezing winter of 1819-1820. Seeing a child frozen to death would have certainly haunted anyone who witnessed it, and it drove her to do more. This would lead her to set up a 'nightly shelter' to allow the homeless a safe and warm place to sleep, leading to a vast improvement in the lives of many unfortunate souls on the London streets. It is her example that led to homeless shelters being founded, saving countless lives from misery and death. In 1824, after visiting Brighton, she set up the Brighton District Visiting Society[13] which facilitated volunteers visiting homes of the poorest in the area, to offer a friendly ear, food, money, and other essentials. The scheme was so successful, it was rolled out to other districts throughout Britain. A lot of poorer families were too proud to ask for help, but once volunteers had seen what was needed, they could provide food and coal for the fire without embarrassing the families struggling as winter drew closer.

Her good work continued. In 1840 she opened the first ever nursing school. Although she had no formal training herself, she saw the importance of the profession and her support was given freely to those who wished to help. Florence Nightingale took a team of Elizabeth's nurses to the Crimean War. Nightingale was responsible for saving countless lives of soldiers in Crimea and her advances in cleanliness changed the face of nursing.

Elizabeth felt strongly about many social issues and the next injustice she tackled was slavery. Although the Slavery Abolition Act was passed in 1833 in the United Kingdom and much of the British Empire, many places still enslaved people. She once again teamed up with her brother-in-law Thomas Fowell Buxton, leader of the abolitionist movement, and focused her efforts on the enslaved people of the Dutch colonies.[14]

She became a celebrity of sorts during her own lifetime. Young Princess Victoria, before becoming Queen, met with Elizabeth several times, and discussed her concerns about the enslaved people abroad. After Princess Victoria's uncle King William IV died, she found herself Queen on 20 June 1837, as she was the only living relative of the late king. The eighteen-year-old queen was a big fan of Elizabeth and she donated to her prison cause. Another fan was the politician Robert Peel who had been won over by Elizabeth's evidence and it was he who passed several reforms to prisons, including the Gaols Act in 1823.

Fredrick William IV of Prussia was also enamoured by Elizabeth and her work having followed it for many years and had met her several times previously all over Europe. The King of Prussia was so invested in her social reform, he demanded that plans were made for him to visit Newgate prison with her during his short stay in England. Despite the King's advisers being very much against such a visit, the king did indeed meet with Elizabeth at Newgate.[15] It seems incredible and wonderful that so many prominent figures were eager to listen to Elizabeth and take on board her worries.

She passed away on 12 October 1845 after suffering a stroke. Her remains are buried at the Friend's Burial Grounds at Barking, East London. The seamen of Ramsgate Coast Guard flew their flag at half-mast when they learnt she had passed away. This is usually done only after the death of someone of royal blood, so it is a sign of how highly they respected Elizabeth.[16] She was after all, the focus of more than one royal in Europe and drew respect from whoever she met. More than a thousand people waited in sombre silence while her remains were being interred. It is a true mark of respect.

It was decided that Elizabeth needed a proper memorial to mark her remarkable life. A meeting was held the summer following her death to determine which form this memorial should take. Some suggested a statue to be placed in either Westminster Abbey or in St Paul's Cathedral. This would have been a lovely gesture, but not one that Elizabeth would have approved of. A statue served no purpose. Instead, it was agreed that a practical memorial would be more fitting. Lord Ashley, along with a group of prominent reformers and admirers of Elizabeth, spoke in favour of this option. This was said to properly show the gratitude and 'the sympathy they entertain for her righteous endeavours'.[17]

The practical memorial was supported by the general public,

who were excited to see this fitting dedication. A fine eighteenth century townhouse was purchased at 195 Mare Street in Hackney, London. The first Elizabeth Fry Refuge opened its doors in 1849. It was a home for women when they left prison and did not have somewhere to live. If no one had paid the rent on their home while they were in prison, then they would lose their home, a common occurrence. It provided a home for vulnerable women who in many cases did not have anyone to turn to. They were sent to prison, often for petty crimes such as stealing food or a coin from a silk purse and given tough sentences. When they were released, often with their young child in tow, many found that they had lost their homes as well as their jobs. The Elizabeth Fry Refuge was funded through subscriptions and donations from some London-based companies and wealthy individuals and supplemented by the work done by inmates, such as prisoners' laundry services and sewing.

The refuge moved to larger premises during the 1950s, such was the need for the establishment, and remains there today, feeding the hungry and providing beds for the most vulnerable in society. Who knows how many women this wonderful refuge has saved from starvation, violence, dangerous situations or even death.

Elizabeth is remembered today as a force of change, an ally of the poor and mistreated, and friend to many of society's outcasts. She has been featured on the £5 note, plaques adorn the walls of buildings she was connected to, appeared on stamps, and even has a road in Johannesburg, South Africa named after her.

It really is impossible to calculate how many people's lives were saved because of Elizabeth. Her improvements in prisons and the prisoners' lives, her involvement in the abolition movement, her influence in transportation to Australia, and the work done in her honour after her death. She was an angel of goodness and change.

She not only worked hard to improve the lives of the less fortunate, but she inspired others to do the same, such as Robert Peel passing legislation to protect prisoners and Florence Nightingale to take a team of her nurses abroad to heal and save the lives of the soldiers in the Crimea.

Her influence changed the face of prisons and the way that the inmates were viewed. No longer were they in prison to be punished, condemned to terrible damp conditions, close to starvation, and wearing little but rags. They were in prison to be rehabilitated, to be nurtured and treated with humanity, to be educated and to be taught useful skills they could use once their time in prison was served.

She was a beacon of compassion and devotion to people who had mostly been forgotten about or marginalised, the prisoners, the enslaved people, and the poor. It is a testament to how important Elizabeth's work was, that we still have charities set up in her honour. Her memorial is not a piece of cold carved stone standing in a town square. Her memorial is a living, breathing community providing warmth, food, and protection to help women at the lowest time in their lives. This sanctuary opens its doors to this day and continues to help women make a fresh start and move on with their lives.

Elizabeth Fry lived a selfless life, devoted to helping other people. She saved countless lives deemed by many to be worthless. She saw value in the most desperate and desolate in society and handed them back their humanity.

MARY FILDES

A Peterloo Survivor

❦

Mary Fildes' name is perhaps one that is less familiar in this book. She was not born into a wealthy family, nor did she marry a lord and live in a grand house. Her children did not inherit grand estates and have titles. She was an ordinary working-class woman who fought for what she believed was right, putting herself into mortal danger to do so.

She was born Mary Pritchard in Cork, Ireland, although her family connections were Welsh. Her family were perhaps visiting friends or holidaying in Ireland when she was born unexpectedly.[1] Her birth date is educated guesswork and was at some point between 1789 and 1792. It was given as both these dates at different periods in her life. The upper classes often had their birth dates recorded in church registers, but usually working-class births went unmentioned. It was common for a baptism to be recorded within days of the child's birth, however meticulous records were not always kept. Mary's actual birthdate then is an educated guess, based on other events in her life, rather than existing records. She was after all, a working-class woman, without 'important' connections nor a prestigious family name.

Little is known of her early life. She seems to have lived

quietly in and around the Manchester area of England. Aged around nineteen, she married William Fildes on 18 March 1808 in Stockport. Her new husband was a reed maker, making weaving reeds for cloth manufacture. The reeds were a comb-like device for beating the weft of the thread into place as the shuttle of the loom passed over it. The Industrial Revolution was well under way by this point and now many jobs involved maintaining the machines that were becoming commonplace. Hundreds of thousands of people flocked to the cities to find work in the many mills, factories, mines, and warehouses that were dotted around those once quiet communities. The industrialized cities were becoming larger by the day, as the population swelled. Cities like Manchester became the equivalent to 'The American Dream', the place where people thought their lives would be easier, the streets although perhaps not paved with gold, but where a decent living could be made. Instead, what many found in the overpopulated cities was pollution, poor pay, overcrowding, and disease. A far cry from the idyll they had dreamt of upon moving to the city.

Mary and her husband would go on to have eight children who lived. James was born in 1808, Samuel 1809, George 1810, Robert 1815, Thomas 1818, Henry 1819, and John 1821. As there was almost a four-to-five-year gap between George and Robert, it is relatively safe to assume that she had either a miscarriage or a stillborn baby in that gap. It was common to have children every year or two, so a gap like this in the births of children would normally indicate a tragedy had occurred during this time. A miscarriage or stillborn is more likely than a death in infancy, as there are no records of a named child around this time.

Mary's last three sons were named after political activists.[2]

John was named after John Cartwright, a prominent campaigner for parliamentary reform. Thomas was named after Thomas Paine, an American founding father who was a political theorist, philosopher, and activist. Finally, Henry was named after Henry Hunt, a radical speaker and activist, pivotal to the chartist movement which led to the repeal of the corn laws and a man she would work alongside. The naming of her children after reformers and activists shows that she had strong political feelings and admired those who acted on their principles and perhaps she secretly hoped that her sons would grow up to be a force for good in the world like their namesakes.

The fateful day that Mary is remembered for is the Peterloo Massacre on 16 August 1819. The massacre was a savage and entirely avoidable slaughter. A cruel attack on innocent men, women, and even children. A vast group of peaceful protesters amassed at St Peter's Field, which was at the time just on the outskirts of Manchester. A group of Manchester women protesters accompanied the carriage containing the guest speaker at the rally, Henry Hunt. Mary rode at the front of the procession with the carriage waving a white flag, certainly not a flag of surrender, but a flag of peace and hope. The colour white could also mean a new start, simplicity, perfection, and even perhaps optimism. Some say, she simply waved a white embroidered handkerchief and not a flag at all. It drew attention to her as the carriage rolled through the crowds. She mounted the stage with her fellow protesters Elizabeth Gaunt and Sarah Hargreaves as they dismounted Hunt's carriage.[3]

Richard Carlile, a London-based radical journalist, described Mary at the protest as a heroic figure and wrote a prominent article about her in his piece on the protest, *To Henry Hunt*

Esquire.[4] Carlile must have seen how much Mary stood out in the crowd to comment on her personally. Perhaps she stood tall and proud in the crowd on that stage, or perhaps she caught his eye because of how eloquently she spoke. Whatever it was, she certainly seems to have made an impression on Carlile.

Mary was to present the male participants of the protest with a 'cap of liberty' or 'phrygian cap'. They were (and still are to a great extent) a symbol of liberty and defiance against oppression. They were used in the wars of American Independence and in the French Revolution as the 'bonnet rouge' or the 'red caps'. The cap itself could be argued to date back as far as ancient times and can be found referenced in Greek, Iranian, and Roman culture. Enslaved people would often be awarded a cap when they were made freedmen and this in turn became a symbol of freedom itself. By Mary awarding the men this cap, she was perhaps symbolically gifting them the freedom to vote, as had often been denied to them. Mary also gave Hunt the 'colours' of the Manchester Female Reform Society. William Cobbert, a journalist, had rather cruelly equated the contribution of the women protesters to that of a queen giving her knights a token of luck before a tournament or battle.[5] It is unfair to suggest this, as many queens have inspired the fiercest loyalty and devotion, and arguably outdone the kings for diplomacy and peacekeeping in centuries past. Mary herself was also in the thick of the protest, not merely handing over tokens of gratitude and commitment as a medieval queen would have done. The comment also dismisses Mary's role and that of all other women at the protest as being one of symbolism rather than recognising their important place amongst the protesters. Cobbert diminishes women's roles in the protest to one of mere bystanders, watching on the sidelines as the big strong men did the important work. He is also perhaps suggesting that women had no place in politics and therefore their attendance on that day was merely lip service, letting the women feel like they were part of the day.

Or perhaps if she was a queen, like Elizabeth I, giving her speech at Tilbury before the big battle commenced. She was wearing her proverbial armour and galloping along the front of the soldiers ready to do battle herself.

On the podium, Mary gave Hunt the scroll on which the main speech was written. The address ends: 'May our flag never be unfurled but in the case of peace and reform! And then may a female's curse pursue the coward who deserts the standard!'[6] The 'female curse' is perhaps a clever reference to the Pendle Hill witches in Lancashire in 1612, a place just forty miles from St Peter's Field. Ten women and girls and two men were accused of causing the deaths of ten people in the area. While there was real evidence against them, they were charged with witchcraft after a two-day 'trial'. Out of the twelve, ten were found guilty and hanged on the gallows. One woman died awaiting trial. It is a tourist hotspot that sometimes makes light of the witch trials, but there is still a sense of injustice about the terrible senseless loss of life. Even to this day, there are superstitions and stories about witchcraft and supernatural occurrences in and around Pendle Hill.

The St Peter's Field protest was planned to be a peaceful and just march and chant. It is understandable why they wanted to protest. The Napoleonic Wars had led to a massive economic slump which in turn led to mass unemployment. 1816 had been dubbed 'The Year Without a Summer' as a freakishly cold climate seemed to envelop the planet that year. This led to terrible harvests made worse by the corn laws keeping the price of bread high. Families were hungry and desperate. At this time only around eleven per cent of the population could vote, as the voter had to be both male and a homeowner. This overall percentage was even lower in the industrial north, where poverty and unemployment were felt even more acutely. Without a vote, the poorer working man did not have a voice, and without a voice, bad policies would keep getting made, making their lives potentially even harder than they already were.

The solution to this was seen as radical political reform, nothing less than a total reformation of the way voting took place. A massive campaign began to take shape for manhood suffrage. A petition was sent to parliament with three quarters of a million signatures on it, all wanting 'one man, one vote' regardless of class, money, or home ownership in 1817. It seemed a fair, simple, and just protest. The system that was in place was an unfair one that only benefitted the wealthy men of the country. Despite the huge support for this reform, the petition was unsurprisingly rejected by the House of Commons as it was of course no benefit to the wealthy and privileged of the Commons. A lot of people in the working-class north-west felt that they had no choice but to mobilize a march to further demonstrate the strong feeling about their decision to disenfranchise the poor once again. Their voice needed to be heard and they would shout louder until they were listened to.

The Manchester Patriotic Union organised the march and around 60,000 working-class people went to St Peter's Field to show their support for the petition. The women, men, and children who worked at the mills, factories, pits, and warehouses all culminated there. The people stood shoulder-to-shoulder in union, shoulder-to-shoulder in support of each other, together in a cause. They waited in anticipation of the speeches. The sheer numbers proved how strongly the locals felt about their cause.

These numbers frightened the local magistrate and in a terrified panic, he called upon the Manchester and Salford Yeomanry to arrest Hunt, who was giving a stirring speech to the crowd to cheers and applause. The paranoia of this local magistrate led him to make this dreadful decision, and this is when it went very wrong. The order was given and the yeomen charged the crowds, some of which were mounted on horseback. The first murder happened almost straight away, when a yeoman knocked over a woman, trampling her and her young son under his horse, killing him instantly. The boy was two-year-old William Fildes, no relation to Mary as it was a common surname in the area. The mounted cavalry did not stop and continued to charge the crowds of unsuspecting protesters. Amidst screaming, people were desperately trying to get up off the ground as more people were knocked off their feet and trampled under the hooves of the horses. The confused people nursed broken bones, half crushed to death by the terrified crowd and falling over the bodies lying dead and lifeless on the ground. The ones who fell and did not get crushed, struggled to get back up and the crowds frantically tried to escape. The yeomen attacked the group, and it was easy to be trodden underfoot in the rush of the alarmed and broken people trying desperately to escape the carnage. The cavalry arrested Hunt, dragging him from the stage, much to the outrage of those in the crowd still able to realize what was happening. William Hulton, a Cheshire magistrate and landowner demanded that the 15th company of The King's Hussars, a regiment of the British Army, disperse the crowd. Historian Robert Reid refers to Hulton as a 'young and insecure man'[7] showing his self-doubt and how he was clearly out of his depth in the situation. Hulton was not from a military background and had no experience of commanding the men, but gave orders anyway. Perhaps he felt he had to try to prove his worth by taking charge of the situation, instead of asking for advice or deferring to others who had experience in dealing with social disorders. Had the crowd been left alone to have their speeches, it would have peacefully dispersed.

The Hussars were joined by the Manchester Special Constabulary, Cheshire Yeomanry, and British Army Regulars. Three military groups brought in to add to The King's Hussars, already slicing their way through the group. They charged at the situation as if they were on a battlefield, not a town square. They mowed the crowd down, slashing at the shoulders, necks and faces of anyone they could reach with their sabres, and trampling on anyone who fell, as if they were reliving a Napoleonic battlefield. Perhaps they were suffering from what we would now recognize as post-traumatic stress from the horrors of the battlefield. This perhaps made them forget where they were, making them slash at the throats of what they thought were French soldiers. Their 'enemies' though were not foreign soldiers who were wanting to kill them. The crowd was made up of working-class women, children, and men. None were armed with more than flags and hope. It was a bloodbath. A slaughter of the innocent, enacted by bloodthirsty soldiers fresh from war on the ill-advised orders of clueless and paranoid men in power.

The protesters were forced to defend themselves with sticks and bricks and anything else that they could find lying around. They threw stones at the horses and those who rode them. It was a survival tactic for the crowd who did their best to run away from St Peter's Field that fateful day. Whole families ran for their lives, and barely got out alive. Captain Hugh Birley of the Manchester and Salford Yeomanry claimed that his men's erratic behaviour stemmed from the fact that their well-trained horses were frightened of the crowds. A poor excuse as the highly-trained war horses used in Peterloo would have been used to noise and crowds having been on the battlefields of the Napoleonic Wars where there would have been guns and cannon firing, shouting, and screaming. It could be argued that a crowd of around 60,000 people could not possibly be as loud as an entire battlefield of at least 140,000 soldiers at the Battle of Waterloo, with the musket and rifle fire, cannon fire, the slicing of swords, pounding of hooves, and shouts and screams of the men there. It is unlikely that the horses would be frightened of sticks, stones, and bricks, and a crowd of protesters. In some eyewitness accounts of the time, it is suggested that the cavalrymen at Peterloo were drunk. This perhaps explains, but certainly does not excuse the erratic behaviour of the cavalrymen that day. If they were intoxicated, they may have been more aggressive and violent, imagining themselves at war against the enemy and did not think of the consequences of their actions.

Up to 700 of the crowd were injured that day, and eighteen people died, including that little two-year-old boy and his mother, who died trying to protect him. Peterloo got its name as St Peter's Field that day became Waterloo, the bloody battle which had claimed at least 50,000 lives. Historian Robert Poole suggests that had vowed to capture the colours of the Manchester Female Reform Society after humiliating failures at meetings elsewhere',[8] after feeling humiliated at previous meetings, where perhaps they had been unable to dispel the crowds. Or they might not have been allowed to act at all and felt emasculated and dishonoured. When called upon this time, they felt compelled to push hard, using excessive force as the case turned out to be.

As Mary had been on the cart at the beginning, she was initially targeted for arrest along with Hunt. Reid states Mary was still stood at the cart as the three women were getting charged by the cavalry on horseback with their sabres slashing at them.[9] Mary was seen as a ringleader of the protest, a woman who dared to push a political ideal, a woman who dared to want her voice heard. Perhaps she was a target because she was a woman, a woman who was showing herself to be an equal to the men on the podium. Her fellow protesters, Elizabeth Gaunt and Sarah Hargreaves, were mistaken for Mary when the violence began and were badly beaten, arrested, and left in jail for many days without charge. Mary herself was knocked to the ground by the truncheon of a special constable, who had tried to snatch the flag from her hands, and it was later stated that she narrowly avoided being slashed with a sabre. She did well to escape with just a head wound, when so many others died or were seriously injured. Mary escaped from the carnage and laid low for two weeks at a friend's house. No one could blame her given the horror of that day. She would need time to recover physically and emotionally after such a traumatic event.

Mary would later get to know a novelist and like-minded woman by the name of Isabella Banks. Fascinated by Mary's story, Banks would include details of that fateful day in her novel *The Manchester Man*. She wrote: 'Mrs Fildes [was] hanging suspended by a nail on the platform of the carriage [that] had caught her white dress. She was slashed across her exposed body by an officer of the cavalry.'[10] This is a far more graphic and violent account than what actually happened to Mary, but it does highlight the worst of what occurred on that terrible day. Perhaps Banks wanted to use Mary as an example of the horrors of the massacre. People were slashed across the stomach and chest, people were snagged on nails and trapped in the crowd, only to be mown down because they could not escape. The press was immediately on the side of the victims. News of the overzealous response to a peaceful protest soon spread to national and international newspapers. Banks' novel was published some years later and it cemented this horrific day in the minds of the British public forever.

The Peterloo Massacre would later be said to be 'the bloodiest political event of the nineteenth century on English soil'.[11] The daughters and granddaughters of the women at Peterloo would go on to fight for women's right to vote. They would put themselves in danger, throwing themselves in front of the king's horse, going on hunger strike, and chaining themselves to railings just to be heard. They would not be silent and their voices were heard, leading to equal voting rights for men and women, regardless of class, home-ownership or how much money someone had.

There was a controversial blue plaque at St Peter's Fields where the massacre took place. The plaque stated in a rather matter of fact tone: 'The site of St Peter's Fields where on the 16 August 1819, Henry Hunt, Radical Orator addressed an assembly of about 60,000 people. Their subsequent dispersal by the military is remembered as Peterloo.' Many people were outraged by the wording and quite rightly so as it gave no indication that the so-called 'dispersal by the military' was bloody and murderous. After a public outcry and considerable time, the plaque was replaced by a new, more accurate red plaque, that remains to this day that reads: 'On 16 August 1819 a peaceful rally of 60,000 pro-democracy reformers, men, women and children, was attacked by armed cavalry resulting in fifteen deaths and over 600 injuries.' Despite the death toll being wrong, as eighteen people were killed, the new plaque gives a better reflection of what happened that fateful day, although again does not fully convey the true horror. There was even a campaign to change the name of Manchester's famous Piccadilly train station to Peterloo to mark the 200th anniversary of the massacre in 2019.

Although many women would follow Mary's strong political example, she never expressed any feminist leanings herself, at least not in public. She did believe, like many women of her time, that women should fight and protest alongside men. It was a highly unfair system which banned a huge section of men and all women from voting. People of the working classes were often forgotten about and had no way to be heard as they were not allowed to vote. Members of Parliament came from privilege and wealth and knew nothing of the ordinary lives of the working men and women they were meant to represent. Mary felt strongly that her voice should support the working men, to allow them to vote, which would in turn help the whole family unit. She was part of that same poorer working community, one who had known hardship, hunger and pain, and strove to put right the wrongs she saw around her.

When Francis Place, an avid early supporter of birth control, approached her for support, Mary declined. Perhaps she had a strong religious conviction which stopped her agreeing to contraception on principle. The church had long stood against contraception, believing that sex between heterosexual couples should be for procreation alone, and the introduction of birth control would encourage potentially immoral behaviour. In a time of terrible poverty, disease, and overcrowding, it is easy to see how birth control would help alleviate these problems. Large families were the norm, and few families could afford houses big enough to accommodate their many children. Their poverty often meant they lived in close quarters with not just other members of their own family, but strangers too, all in one house, sharing floor space and mattresses. This in turn led to disease, which quickly spread throughout the overcrowded damp streets. Place sent Mary a package of birth control pamphlets to distribute, possibly mistaking her for a midwife relation of her husband's. Perhaps he addressed the pamphlets to the right woman after all. It is possible that due to her forward-thinking political views, she would also have liberal views on other aspects of her life. He was sadly mistaken though and was given a sharp reply. Her response was 'as a woman, a wife, and a mother' she had to denounce 'this infamous handbill'.[12] She was clearly offended by being asked to support this pamphlet.

Mary would continue her political life, giving various talks to unions and protest groups for the many years that followed

Peterloo. She gave a talk in Heywood in Lancashire in 1833 to launch a branch of the Female Political Union.[13] A mention of her appeared in an obscure penny weekly newspaper which focused on the 'one man one vote' principle with which Mary unequivocally agreed. She also gave a series of lectures on war to a group in Chorlton near Manchester in 1843,[14] as advertised in the local newspaper the *Northern Star*. These talks were well attended, as more women became involved in politics and Mary's reputation as a powerful speaker began to grow. Her sons James and John were making their own waves in the Chartist movement in Salford.[15] Clearly her wish for her children to be involved in politics had started to come true.

After Mary's husband died, she moved to Chester and possibly became the landlady of the Shrewsbury Arms, a pub in Frodsham Street. However, it is entirely possible that she simply rented out her basement to the pub. It was common for cellars to be rented out for the use of a distiller and at this time the property she lived at was referred to as a 'spirit vault'. The census records only show a few words of what was really happening at a particular address.

In around 1854, she went to live with her son James, his wife, and their eleven-year-old son Luke near Chester. She would later manage to pay for her talented grandson to attend the well-known Warrington School of Art, where he would hone his skills and go on to become one of the greatest portrait artists of the Victorian period, painting the great and the good of the upper echelons of the era. His works include the coronation portraits of King Edward VII and Queen Alexandra, George V, along with the many unknown beautiful and interesting faces he brought to life on canvas. Without the help of his grandmother, the world would never have known the work of this iconic painter of the Victorian era.

In her late eighties, Mary died of complications due to bronchitis on 3 April 1876 back at home in Manchester.

It was not uncommon for someone to live well into their eighties and beyond, but it mostly depended on the social class someone belonged to. It is no surprise that the richer people lived longer than the poorer people. The wealthier the person was, the more disposable money they had to spend on themselves. A poor person of course had to spend what little money they had on essentials such as food and rent. Doctors and medicine cost more than most ordinary people could afford so they turned to what many would consider 'old wives' tales' and home remedies to heal the sick. The rich would also have warm homes that they could afford to heat, food in their bellies, and were able to avoid working in any dangerous jobs that so many poorer people had to endure. Mary was unusual in the fact that she lived so long, considering her poorer background.

Mary was buried in a quiet corner of St Luke's churchyard in Manchester. Sadly, the grave has been lost, as have many others over the years. Perhaps the cemetery of St Luke's was reorganised during the late Victorian period, as many graveyards were, to make room for more graves. However, St Luke's is now sadly derelict and what graves remain are badly over-grown and abandoned. Perhaps her grave is still there somewhere, beneath the deep undergrowth, just waiting to be found.

Mary Fildes' life was spent in battle, fighting against inequality and injustice. She might not have seen herself as a feminist, but did protest and speak up against unfairness. She stood up alongside the men, wrote and gave stirring speeches, and faced violence against her. She did not shy away from doing what she felt was right even if this meant moving away from the social norms and expectations of the time.

ANNE LISTER

The First Modern Lesbian

❧

Anne Lister has in recent years shot to historical fame due to the book *Gentleman Jack* by Sally Wainwright and the subsequent spin off BBC television series of the same name, starring the very talented Suranne Jones as Anne. The book and television show have taken some minor liberties with the truth, but in many ways have been very faithful to events, people, and moments in her life. She was a writer, a landowner, and a lover.

Anne did not seem to have a particularly auspicious start in life. She was born the second child and the eldest daughter of Captain Jeremy Lister, who had long served with the British 10th Regiment of Foot and fought at the Battle of Lexington and Concord during the American War of Independence.[1] He had been wounded in the elbow during an expedition to Concord and North Bridge in Massachusetts. In the television series, when the captain, wonderfully played by the brilliant Timothy West, begins to stamp his authority with his family and remind his daughter that he was in the war of independence in America, she reminds him that he fought on the losing side.

Their relationship is shown to be strained to say the least. It is not loving or even affectionate and the two argue and fight a great deal. Despite this, there is a mutual respect of sorts between the two headstrong people. He seems to have the desire for a quiet life, perhaps having spent most of his adult years in the army. Anne's need for adventure and travel are in many ways in opposition to her father's quieter twilight years. It is Captain Lister, however, who seems to be more forward thinking. He recognises reform is slowly creeping towards the industrialised north, whereas his eldest daughter does not seem to see this. The Industrial Revolution was steadily taking hold of many towns throughout the country. The younger of the two did not seem to realize what was happening regarding the increasingly modern world. This perhaps turns on its head the usual notion that the younger generations are more in tune with current affairs.

Captain Lister met and married a local girl Rebecca Battle in 1788. Despite him being eighteen years her senior, the couple would have a large family and seemed to get on well. Their first son, John, sadly died the same year he was born. Anne was born in Halifax on 3 April 1791 and when she was three, the family moved to an estate called Skelfler House, a fine estate with a lot of land in East Riding, Yorkshire. A second son, Samuel was born the year they arrived at Skelfler and he and Anne would be very close. In total, Captain Lister and his wife would have a total of four sons and three daughters, but tragically only Anne and her younger sister, Marian, born 13 October 1798, would survive beyond the age of twenty.[2] The childhood mortality rate was very high, due to diseases such as smallpox, polio, measles, rabies, syphilis-related conditions, typhus, tetanus, influenza, cholera, scarlet fever, the tragic list goes on. There was a long way to go before these diseases were controlled by vaccines, inoculations, and antibiotics. Anne would have only been five years old when Edward Jenner created the first vaccine for smallpox. It would be a long time until they became accepted and routine vaccines were given to babies and children.

Anne had an eclectic education. When she was seven years old in 1798, she attended a prestigious school run by a Mrs Hagues and a Mrs Chettle in Ripon, Yorkshire. Between the ages of ten and thirteen, she was educated at home by Reverend George Skelding, the vicar of Market Weighton, in East Riding, Yorkshire. She also had lessons from a Miss Mellin when she visited her aunt Anne and uncle James at their fine home Shibden Hall. This would become her home in later life, and she would lavish much love on the building. It is easy to imagine how Anne walked the rooms of Shibden Hall and remembered how she used to run down those corridors, noticed her old hiding places and spotted her favourite window seat. Did young Anne ever dream that she would live there one day?

It could be argued that Anne's very first love was reading. Her education, particularly at home, had left her with a passionate love of reading, particularly classical literature. She had always felt at home amongst the old bound copies in the library at home. She added to her library and had a considerable collection by the time she inherited Shibden Hall. In a letter she wrote to her aunt dated 3 February 1803, Lister explains that 'my library is my greatest pleasure'.[3]

Anne was an intelligent woman and enjoyed learning. As she grew, she widened her genres of reading. She discovered that she loved to read about medicine, mathematics, and landscaping, but also about the more industrial subjects of mining, canals, and railways, which were at their height during this period, increasing transportation and industrialisation like never before. It was not just an outward interest in those subjects she read about, but the inner workings of the railways, the cogs, and engines, the mechanics of pumping water from the mines, how much coal was needed to drive the steam train. Engineering is often considered a more masculine vocation rather than a feminine one, but Anne was fascinated by it all and read in depth about these subjects.

In around 1804, aged thirteen, Anne was sent to a private school, the Manor House School in the King's Manor buildings in York. It was an elite boarding school for girls, with expensive fees. It was here where Anne met her first love, a young lady known as Eliza Raine.[4] The same age as Anne, Eliza was willowy and pretty and caught her eye immediately. It was young love, but also the first intense relationship that Anne, and possibly Eliza, had ever had. An illegitimate daughter of an East India Company surgeon in Madras, Eliza had been sent to the Manor School after her father's death and was set to inherit a great deal of money.[5] It is perhaps cynical to suggest that this is what attracted Anne to Eliza, but the money certainly turned her head and perhaps got her attention initially, although she would also have found her physically attractive and pleasant company.

The two shared an attic room at the Manor School, which was nicknamed 'the slope', probably due to the low-pitched roof above their heads. Their little attic room made their union an easy one and Anne was eager to experience physical love for the first time. After two years at the school, Anne was asked to leave. While it is unclear why, perhaps the two had been witnessed during one of their many sexual encounters. It is also possible that rumours had circulated about the pair, given that their love affair had been going on for almost all that time. They would have perhaps considered their actions private in their small attic room, although perhaps they were not as private as they thought. Even after Anne left the school, Eliza thought about her as she was under the impression that they would move in together as adults and continue their affair. They had perhaps talked about their future together whilst tucked up in their tiny garret room. However, after Anne left the school, she seemed less interested in a committed relationship than Eliza and started to have a string of affairs with many women. Two names that are known are Isabella Norcliffe and Mariana Belcombe. Their relationship obviously meant more to Eliza than it did to Anne, who felt it reasonable to see other people during their time together.

Eliza, sensitive and madly in love, could not stand that Anne had had other relationships so easily when she could not move on from her time with Anne. Eliza fell into deep despair and ended up as a patient at the Clifton House Asylum.[6] To add insult to injury for poor Eliza, the asylum was run by the father of one of Anne's lovers, Mariana Belcombe. William ran the asylum from 1814, the year that Eliza was admitted. Eliza would later be transferred to Terrace House in Osbaldwick. Perhaps she was deemed better and sent away from the asylum, or maybe the staff there knew her end was close and discharged her, unable to help her anymore. On 31 January 1860, while at Terrace House, Eliza Raine passed away, aged around sixty-nine. She was buried in the churchyard across the road from where she had spent the last years of her life.[7] It is tragic to think about Eliza's life spent pining for Anne, literally driving herself mad because of her unrequited love. It was not a healthy love, but rather bitter and obsessive.

Four years after leaving the Manor School in around 1810, Anne met another pretty face, Isabella Norcliffe, nicknamed 'Tib' or 'Tibs'. She was the eldest child of a wealthy landowner Lieutenant Colonel Thomas Norcliffe Dalton and his wife Anne, of Langton Hall near Malton, Yorkshire. Isabella had three sisters, Charlotte, Mary, and Emily, and two brothers, Norcliffe and Thomas. Anne was immediately struck by Norciffe's wealth, effortless style, and sophistication. The Norcliffe Dalton family had newly arrived in the area and reeked of self-assurance, confidence, and glamour. Isabella was the kind of person that Anne wanted to be and to be with as she was ambitious and wanted to move in the same circles as her wealthy and fascinating new friend. Anne perhaps thought the best way to infiltrate this circle was to court someone already rubbing shoulders with these people. Isabella was only six years older than Anne, but seemed much more worldly-wise, mature, and experienced, especially compared to the immature and naïve Eliza. Isabella was as equally impressed with Anne and was even perhaps a little star-struck by her big personality. Isabella might had had all the breeding and class, but Anne had all the confidence and self-assurance. They remained friends and occasional lovers throughout Anne's life. Although they were happy when they were together, they did not have a continuous long-term relationship. Despite Anne's infatuation with Isabella, or rather, her lifestyle, Anne was not interested in continuing the relationship beyond their occasional flings. Perhaps Anne wanted to see other women and not be tied to one relationship. Isabella was heartbroken by Anne's rejection of her as a life partner, so much so that she never married or got engaged. It seems as if Isabella was more invested in the two of them, than Anne was. Perhaps like Eliza, she became strongly infatuated with Anne, arguably to an unhealthy level of obsession. Isabella perhaps cursed herself for the moment she introduced Anne to her friend Mariana Belcombe as the two would become very close. Perhaps it was Isabella's heavy drinking that Anne disapproved of, or perhaps Anne could never see much of a long-term relationship with her. It is interesting to question at what point Isabella began her heavy drinking as it is possible that she fell into alcoholism after Anne began breaking away from their relationship. It could have been Isabella's coping strategy to deal with the way she felt wronged by Anne. Isabella died in 1846, at the age of sixty-one. She never had any other relationships beyond Anne, instead she remained a loyal puppy, waiting for its master to return.

Lister had always been close to her aunt Anne and uncle James. When he passed away in 1826, Anne inherited the beautiful Shibden Hall, the place she had visited so often as a child. She controlled part of the estate until the deaths of her father and aunt in 1836, when their shares, incomes, and moneys were left to her, giving her the majority shares and control over the estate and making her a very wealthy woman. This allowed her a certain level of power and freedom due to the additional income as she no longer relied on the sum brought to her through others.

She began refurbishing the historic Shibden Hall, which dates back to around 1420. Aptly, the exterior of the house itself was used as Anne's home on the television show *Gentleman Jack*. Watched by almost 6,000,000 viewers each week, visits to the house rocketed so much so that Calderdale Council had to extend its opening hours. The house was also featured in the film *Peterloo*. Anne planned, built, and decorated the tower which stands to the back of the property. She wanted a purpose-built wing to house her library, which would provide storage and solitude for her to enjoy her vast collection of books, some of which she had loved since she was a child.

After her vast inheritance, she could have sat back and enjoyed her money and lived an easy life. However, this was not her. She liked to exercise her brain and started to get involved in various financial ventures. With a keen businesslike mind, she soon built up an impressive portfolio of properties and investments. As well as her inherited agricultural tenancies, she soon took on ownership of several properties in town. She also bought shares in the canal and railway, as well as investments in mining and stone quarries. She continued to use this considerable fortune to finance her two passions, renovating her now home of Shibden Hall and European travel.[8]

Anne thoroughly enjoyed travelling. She made her first trip to continental Europe in 1819 when she was twenty-eight years old. She travelled with her fifty-four-year-old aunt Anne, visiting France for two months.[9] It was unusual for two women to travel alone and travelling abroad was still only something that the wealthy could do as it was out of the financial reach of the majority of people in Britain at the time.

In 1824, Anne went to Paris, which soon became a favourite place of hers, staying until the following year.[10] She visited Paris again with her aunt in 1826, having been home for only a few months. Whilst in the French capital again, she resumed her affair with Maria Barlow, a brief but intense love affair she had

had when there in 1824. Anne succeeded in winning Maria's affections after flirtations over many visits. Maria, a widow, was not a rich woman, having only a moderate income from her late husband's pension. Perhaps Maria had fallen in love with Anne, or perhaps she wanted to use Anne to help her rise though the social ranks. It was a role reversal for Anne, as it had always previously been her who wished for social mobility. As a result, she was not fully committed to a relationship with Maria and continued her long-time affair with Mariana Lawton during her sometime fraternisation with Maria.[11]

In 1827, Anne set off from Paris with Maria and her aunt Anne to do a tour of northern Italy and Switzerland. She returned to Shibden Hall the following year, parting ways with both ladies. Perhaps as a change of scenery in 1828, Anne travelled around Scotland with a new lover, Sibella Maclean, the aristocratic daughter of the 15th Laird of Coll of the Inner Hebrides. In her book *Gentleman Jack: A Biography of Anne Lister, Regency Landowner, Seducer and Secret Diarist*, Angela Steidele mentions the couple's visit to Scotland. She suggests that only a very edited part of Anne's diary about the Scottish visit was ever published.[12] It is very tantalizing to think what rather juicy and scandalous details are missing from public knowledge due to the heavy Georgian editing. The Georgians liked a little scandal, but not too much, so perhaps a businesswoman lesbian's diary that mentions her love affairs was too much for the readers to cope with.

Anne was often described by her contemporaries as dressing in a very masculine way. Contrary to women's fashion of the period, she wore long riding coats, tailored in a very masculine way, without frills and lace, but with simple classic lines. On the show *Gentleman Jack*, Suranne Jones' wardrobe is extremely well thought out and beautifully designed, very masculine, right down to her wearing a waistcoat and pocket watch. She even wears a top hat. Anne's friend commented that she would look better if she 'wore bonnets'. Her look softened, though, as in 1840, Anne herself writes an inventory of her wardrobe and lists six bonnets and four caps,[13] but they are all black, not the traditional colour expected. She wore her hair in tight uniform curls around her face, with the rest of her hair tied low down on the back of her head to allow her top hat to sit correctly.

Mariana Belcombe, who was later Lawton, had a relationship with Anne for almost twenty years in total, even after she was married. Her husband had become resigned to the fact that his wife had another lover,[14] but Anne did not like her being married and considered it an infidelity. Mariana's marriage would also have other consequences as in 1820, her husband Charles contracted a venereal disease, apparently from a servant he was having an affair with. Anne then contracted it from Mariana, an incurable venereal disease, probably hepatitis B, human papillomavirus (HPV) or herpes simplex virus (HSV), all of which would be rather painful to live with. Anne probably blamed Mariana for this infection and it would have implications for her love life moving forward. Cracks in their relationship began to show.

Mariana was increasingly ashamed to be seen in public with Anne because of her appearance. When walking together, Anne was often the subject of many comments and criticisms regarding the way she was dressed. While she did not seem to care about the opinions of others, Mariana was mortified by them.

It is during this earlier period of her life that she acquired her nickname 'Gentleman Jack'.[15] On one of her trips to Europe, she took the opportunity to test her own physical strength and endurance. She became the first woman to climb Spain's Monte Perdido which stands at 11 007ft (3,355m),[16] the third highest peak in the Pyrenees. She also made the first 'official' ascent of the Vignemale, the highest peak in the French Pyrenees which stands at 10,820ft (3,298m). This would have required a ten-hour hike to reach the top and a little over seven hours to descend, showing that she had a real adventurous streak. These feats of endurance would have been easier for Anne, as she was dressed in clothing more suitable to climbing and walking. Her flatter riding boots, closely-tailored sleeves, and her breeches made striding, clambering over rocks, and scaling mountains a much easier venture. Men's tailoring was very different to that of women's, with sleek lines, form-fitting breeches, and long-line coats. They were flattering, fitted and businesslike, much more suited to physical activity. Had she worn the satin or leather slipper shoes, voluminous hooped skirts, padded gigot sleeves, and petticoats that were the fashion of the 1830s, then hiking and climbing would have been much more of a challenge. They were heavy and unwieldy, and a gentle stroll on the flat would have sufficed for most, given the huge strength needed to carry the many layers. It is easy to see that women's clothing limited their movement and made a lot of physical exertion difficult and tiring. Anne's choice of garment, therefore, although made her much talked about, helped her to achieve her goals.

Like a lot of adults living at home with a parent after a period of independence, Anne found life difficult back home on her return in 1831 from her travels abroad.[17] She found life at Shibden Hall very trying, with her father and sister Marian possibly imposing on her strict curfews and disapproving of her lifestyle. It is possible that she felt uncomfortable back at home after her many years travelling and doing what she wanted. She was not home for more than a few weeks until she left the house again, this time for the Netherlands with her long-time on and off lover Mariana Lawton.[18] According to a biography of Anne written by Steidele, between 1826 and 1832 Anne only spent a very small amount of time at Shibden Hall. She was home for perhaps weeks, or months, then would go abroad for the rest of the year, climbing mountains to stand on the peak alone, showing her extreme need for solitude. These were indeed extreme lengths to avoid her homelife.[19] It is also perhaps a need for solitude. She was an intelligent woman, and perhaps needed this seclusion and quiet time.

The love of Anne's life was without doubt Ann Walker. The two had met from time to time, and when Anne inherited Shibden Hall in 1815, they spent more time together. By the early 1830s, they were lovers. Ann and her sister Elizabeth had recently become joint heiresses of the expansive Crow Nest Estate, which made the sisters very wealthy indeed.

The couple soon felt that marriage was the next natural step. There is a beautiful romantic story about their marriage, the first ever lesbian marriage to take place in Britain. The couple exchanged vows on 10 February 1834 and then rings on 27 February the same year.[20] The two met by candlelight at Holy Trinity Church, at Goodramgate in York on the night of Easter Sunday, 30 March 1834. They took Holy Communion together, promising their love to each other. It conjures up such a beautifully romantic image, the two of them holding hands by candlelight, making their marriage vows that night. They

Georgian Feminists

were in each other's eyes now married, but sadly, not legally. Their marriage was in secret and done without paperwork. Their exchange of vows was sadly not enough to call each other wife in the nineteenth century, but their vows would have been enough in the centuries before them.

I'm sure it was not groundbreaking to them what they did that night. They were just two people avowing their love to each other in church as many hundreds of thousands of heterosexual couples had done before them. It was however, the first gay wedding in Britain, a staggering leap forward, something that would not be legalized until shockingly and shamefully late in our history with the Marriage (Same Sex Couples) Act on 17 July 2013. In 2018, a rainbow plaque on the wall of Holy Trinity Church was unveiled commemorating this momentous occasion.[21] The plaque originally read 'gender non-conforming', the word 'lesbian' very much avoided and the focus on her not conforming to the norm of the time. The York Civic Trust apologised and changed the plaque in 2019 to more appropriately describe Anne as 'Lesbian and Diarist'.

They each changed their wills to include the other and Ann gave up her family home to move into Shibden Hall only weeks after their marriage. It shows that they were deeply in love, not only Ann moving from her home, but also for them both to act as the other's sole heir. There is also a level of trust there too, to allow each other that level of openness with money and possessions. It would have no doubt had tongues wagging in the local vicinity , with neighbours possibly talking about how the two were now living together. Maybe some more naïve locals dismissed the pair as merely best friends.

The longest and most epic of Anne's trips came in 1839. It was also her last. She left Shibden Hall with Ann and two servants. They boarded their own carriage and travelled through Europe, visiting France, Denmark, Sweden, then leaving Europe to Russia. They arrived in St Petersburg in September 1839 and went on to Moscow in October.[22] Anne was excited to travel in Russia, but Ann was a lot less enthusiastic about being so far from home. She did not enjoy travelling and had always been most content at home. Perhaps she only agreed to go on this journey so she could spend time with her wife. It shows how much she loved her that she wanted to do what made her wife happy, even if what she wanted to do, made her miserable. They wrapped up warm and left Moscow in a different carriage in February 1840.[23] They travelled south, along the frozen river Volga towards the Caucasus, a region between the Black Sea and the Caspian Sea. Few Western Europeans had ventured to snowy Russia, let alone western women alone. Part of the reason why many westerners never ventured to Russia at this time, was due to the civil unrest there. Revolting against the tsarist regime,[24] the locals had attempted to limit the tsar's powers during the abortive Decembrist Revolt in 1825 and this unrest would continue rumbling on until the Russian Revolution of 1917. It was not a safe place to be for Westerners, let alone two English women alone.

The couple were the source of much curiosity and even required a military escort for certain legs of their journey. The locals who saw them were shocked and intrigued by the couple as so few visitors came to the country being far from the tourist traps of Europe where most wealthy travellers went. Anne noted in her diary that 'the people coming in to look at us if we were some strange animals such as they had not seen the like before'.[25] It is like the couple were animals in a zoo as they passed through. The locals came out to watch them in their carriage as they passed in the countryside. It appears that even Anne, who cared little for gossip or other people's opinions, was made to feel quite uncomfortable by the level of attention she and her wife received. Perhaps she felt more uncomfortable during this period because it was not just her that they were staring at, but also her wife. She may have felt quite awkward and singled-out on her wife's behalf. Anne knew that her wife was not used to the stares and whispered voices around them. Ann felt particularly alien, as someone who had always conformed before. Her wardrobe was always fashionable and conventional for those in her upper middle class. Perhaps Anne felt guilty that her wife was being subjected to this gawking. They must have felt like novelties as they travelled thorough the little villages along the way.

Anne kept detailed diaries throughout her adult life, totalling around 5,000,000 words that she started to write in 1806, after first meeting Eliza Raine until her death in 1840, in a total of twenty-six quarto volumes, a considerable series of documents. To put this figure into perspective, Samuel Pepys' diaries, which are considered an epic overview of the seventeenth century, run to only 1,250,000 words. Her diaries dwarfed that of Pepys in volume, although her diaries are not as well known. When historians and publishers came to read her diaries, they discovered some problems with the text as her handwriting is difficult to decipher.[26] Perhaps she wrote in a rush, scribbled in quieter moments of her day or night, or perhaps she intentionally made her writing difficult to read. There is also a large amount of the diary that is encrypted using a secret code. This code is quite simple, combining letters from the Greek alphabet, mathematical symbols, zodiac signs, and punctuation marks.[27] She believed, quite wrongly as it turned out, that her diaries were indecipherable to strangers. In the diary, Anne writes her innermost thoughts about her identity as a lesbian, her feelings, the women she slept with, and her methods of seduction. The diary does not only focus on details about her sexuality and her sexual encounters, but also her thoughts on current affairs, national and international news, her business ventures, who she disliked working with, what she planned to do in her following ventures in business and in love, and even mundane thoughts about the weather. Her diaries are a window into the Georgian world, of the political, social, and economic events of the day. It is a fascinating glimpse of the streets she walked, the faces she saw, the trades and industries she did business with, and the news that rocked the society she lived in.

The cypher was cracked by the last inhabitant of Shibden Hall, John Lister, a distant relative of Anne and a Bradford-based antiquarian, with the help of a friend called Arthur Burrell. Upon realising the salacious contents of the diaries, Burrell strongly suggested that Lister burn the papers. He thought that the world was not ready for reading such scandalous detail. Lister agreed with his friend, but then secretly kept the diaries in a boarded-up panel of Shibden Hall. These papers were then picked up by Lister's son, also called John. John junior was also an antiquarian and made the first serious attempt to present the now infamous Anne Lister. He thought that information about his great-great-aunt would be well received and published twenty-one instalments of her diaries in the *Halifax Guardian*. He did not publish any of the more explicit moments of her life, but included aspects of social, political, and historical importance to the good people of Halifax. Perhaps he thought that the more detailed passages about Anne's sex life was to be kept private, her relationships were her private life after all, and perhaps society was not ready for such details.

In 2011, Anne's diaries were added to the register of the UNESCO Memory of the World Programme. The register comments that while the diaries make a valuable account of the Georgian period, it was the 'comprehensive and painfully honest account of lesbian life and reflections on her nature, however which have made these diaries unique. They have shaped and continue to shape the direction of UK Gender Studies and Women's History'.[28] It is so fortunate that these diaries were not burned as suggested. It would have been a great loss to women's history and our understanding of the earlier part of the nineteenth century had they been destroyed.

Anne is not the only woman at Shibden Hall to have kept a diary during this period. In 2020, Anne Walker's diary was discovered. A fortunate find, given that it was hidden for almost 200 years, it was a diary she kept for a year between 1834 and 1835.[29] Although brief, the newly-found diary covered a pivotal time in Ann's life, and it is possible to find corresponding moments in Anne's diaries. It is the only diary found of Ann's. Perhaps she only wrote very infrequently, perhaps she destroyed diaries as and when they were completed, or perhaps other diaries are tantalisingly hidden away behind a panel at her childhood home or Shibden Hall. It would be wonderful to find more of her innermost thoughts. It is possible of course, that Ann kept this particular diary due to the period of time it covers. Perhaps it reminded Ann of happy times with Anne, a holiday maybe, or a period of contentment. When sorting through her possessions, she perhaps set aside this one volume while the rest were destroyed. She perhaps placed it behind a secret panel, and in the quiet hours, when missing Anne, took out this volume and thumbed the pages and smiled. Perhaps she even slept with the volume clasped in her hands.

Between 1988 and 1992, Helena Whitbread published some of Anne's diaries in two volumes. When they were first published, many believed they were a hoax, due to their graphic nature, but evidence has proven their authenticity.[30] There seems to be a misconception that the LGBTQ+ community is a modern concept, and it is perhaps this strange misunderstanding of human nature that led some to wrongly assume that the diaries were fake. There is also an assumption that people in the past were always very well behaved, and sex was something done in private behind closed doors and never spoken about in polite society. It would perhaps seem scandalous that a Georgian woman would not only have enjoyed sex, but wrote about it in detail. It would have been seen as shocking to their sensibilities to discuss such things. The publication of the diaries would have shaken the polite façade of the Georgian society.

Anne passed away on 22 September 1840, aged only forty-nine. She had caught a fever on her final travels with Ann.[31] The word 'fever' was used to describe any number of infections which raised the body's temperature. Without antibiotics, these infections would often result in death. It was perhaps a quick death, as there is no reference to a lingering sickness. She died in Koutais, know called Kutaisi in Georgia, a small country in Eastern Europe and West Asia. Ann had her wife's body brought back to Britain and buried in Halifax Minster on 29 April 1841,[32] only around a twenty-minute walk from their former home of Shibden Hall. It would have taken quite some time to bring her body back to England, via long sea voyages, over many weeks. Her tombstone was lost for some years, having been covered in 1879 by the laying of flooring.[33] The Victorians rarely cared for the architecture that came before them, and simply covered the older graves up, regardless of who they were. It was luckily rediscovered in 2000 when said flooring was pulled up. It was a great find and brought this influential woman's name back into the public domain.

Upon reading Anne's will, it was discovered that she left the estate to her father's cousins. However, Ann was not forgotten, and given 'life interest' meaning that she was allowed to stay on at Shibden Hall as long as she wished to live there, or until her death. It was proof that Anne must have thought a great deal of her wife to leave her her home, a place that she had always loved and put so much work in to renovating.

It appears that Ann never recovered from Anne's death. She was never the same again and was soon declared to be of 'unsound mind'. This is a legal definition and refers to someone who no longer has the capacity to comprehend the passing of time and inability to make decisions for his or herself. It is an impairment or disturbance of the brain and cognitive function. She was more than likely suffering from deep depression following the death of her wife. Perhaps she was overcome with grief and had no way to deal with those feelings.

This incapacity seems to have come upon her shortly after Anne's death, so it is very likely that it was in fact grief and not an unrelated mental breakdown. This helplessness could have been brought on because Ann was so reliant on Anne in her everyday life. She perhaps allowed Anne to do the organising, planning, and bill paying of their daily lives. Anne being independent and strong-willed, probably happily took on the dominant role. When Anne passed away, Ann mourned not only her wife, but also the organisation and the order that Anne had brought to her life. Perhaps Ann had always needed someone like Anne to care for her, to take over those everyday annoyances like paperwork and travel plans, unable to make those plans herself. Equally, Anne was perhaps the kind of person who needed to be in control and enjoyed taking care of Ann. From what we know of Anne, this certainly seems to be the case. Their relationship had worked, but once Anne had died, Ann found herself distraught and struggling to function. They were puzzle pieces that completed each other, they were two sides of the same coin. In brief, they had been perfect for each other.

Ann worried her friends and family so much that it was agreed that she would move in with relatives at Terrace House, a private home in Osbaldwick for some weeks. There she was monitored closely for any changes in her mood, having been told of her fragile condition. For some reason, she was only there a short time. Perhaps she disapproved of the close observation, or perhaps the relatives there were concerned for her health and well-being. Whatever the reason, she soon moved in with her sister and brother-in-law in London. She perhaps could not stand to be at Shibden Hall alone. The place was haunted by the memory of Anne after all the time they had spent there together. She did return there in 1845, after almost five long years away. It is easy to imagine Ann slowly walking around Shibden Hall, the place she had once called home, the place she had lived with Anne for so many years. Perhaps Ann silently wandered around the house with tears in her eyes, gently touching her wife's portrait, stroking the half-read volume on the table, sitting in her favourite chair staring out at the gardens that were so familiar.

Ann stayed there for only a short time. Maybe the feeling of emptiness never left her there. It seems as if she could not settle anywhere anymore. Perhaps she felt displaced by the loss of Anne and nowhere felt like home anymore. After some time there, Ann collected her clothes and possessions from Shibden Hall and locking the door, said goodbye to the place forever. She never again returned to the house. After leaving her former home in 1848, she decided to rejoin her family at their estate in Lightcliffe in West Yorkshire, where she had grown up.

Ann avoided the fate of Eliza Raine and others who had suffered having been left by Anne. Perhaps she avoided this because Anne had been faithful to her, as far as we can tell. Perhaps if Anne had been unfaithful as she had been in previous relationships, Ann would have reacted differently. She avoided being admitted into an asylum, but she was left bereft by the loss of her wife, as many are having lost the love of their life.

Ann would die at her childhood home at Lightcliffe on 25 February 1854. Her death certificate stated that she died of a 'congestion of the brain, effusion'. The congestion of the brain was an umbrella term which meant a number of issues including but not limited to a blockage of blood vessels. Effusion was the discharge of blood or any other bodily fluid into a cavity. A modern working hypothesis for her death is that she had an internal cerebral haemorrhage or stroke. This could change if more information comes to light, but at the moment, this is the most prevalent theory.

Without a doubt, Anne Lister was a most singular person. She was often referred to as being 'masculine' as if to insult her because of the way she dressed and to some extent, her behaviour. She was single-minded, businesslike, and had relationships with a string of women, and this was deemed as a masculine way to behave. What society saw was a woman who did not conform to its rules. She dressed how she wanted, took lovers, was a successful businesswoman, and above all was true to her own feelings and wants, regardless of expectations. She recorded her thoughts about the political landscape and the major historical events of the time. Her diaries are a direct link to the past and what it was like to be a woman and a lesbian in the Georgian period. Her innermost thoughts when read are almost as if she is speaking to us in a private conversation. We feel like we are in on a secret that few are party to.

Her diaries have acted as a beacon of hope through the years to the LGBTQ+ community. Anne proved that someone's sexuality and gender are no barrier to being successful in business and life in general. She was an incredibly successful businesswoman and carried on her various deals and ventures with men who underestimated her to their peril.

MARY ANNING

The Palaeontological Pioneer

❧

We have all heard the children's rhyme and tongue-twister *She Sells Seashells On The Sea Shore*, but did you realize this rhyme is about the palaeontological pioneer Mary Anning? The seashells were in fact fossils, and she not only sold them, but found and categorised them herself. She was the first to ever do so. She did often sell her finds to wealthy collectors and museums both from her family's shop and through friends and was often found wandering along the windswept beach beneath the cliffs to find the treasures.

Although Mary is now recognized as a pioneer of palaeontology and a leader of the science, she did not gain the recognition she so clearly deserved because of her sex and the era she was born. Her knowledge was sought by the men in her field, but then her name missed from their research papers after they were submitted. They did not dismiss her outright, but with some audacity asked for her help, only to leave out any mention of her contributions to their papers when they were published in distinguished periodicals and research papers. She single-handedly discovered and categorised many species of prehistoric animals and risked her life to do so.

She was born on 21 May 1799 in the town of Lyme Regis, on a stretch of coast that is now known as the Jurassic Coast due to the frequency of fossils found there. She occupies a unique period of history, as her childhood was Georgian, her later adult life was during the reign of Queen Victoria. Mary was the daughter of Richard Anning, a local cabinetmaker, who often supplemented his meagre income by digging around the cliffs on the beach and selling the strange rocks he found there to tourists passing through the town. Their house not only overlooked the wild sea, but was dangerously close to the waves, and there are stories, perhaps apocryphal, that the storms that battered the coastline and uncovered the fossils they loved so much, also sometimes flooded the family home. Allegedly, on one particularly stormy and terrifying night this happened to such a degree that the family were forced to crawl out of a bedroom window onto the slopes above the house to escape drowning.[1]

Mary's mother, also Mary, but sometimes called Molly, gave birth to ten children. Mary was named after both her mother and her older sister, who died in a freak accident, aged four, when her dress caught fire in the family home. The incident was reported in the *Bath Chronicle* on 27 December 1798.[2] It was a tragedy that happened all too often during this period. Every home had at least one open fire, and embers or coal often fell from the grate as the fire burned. The fashion for long dresses, even for children, led to many horrific accidents when these embers or perhaps a flame leapt close to the child as they danced around the room. The fabrics were not flame retardant as they are today, and the skirts of women and children would quickly be engulfed by flames, leaving little chance of survival.

The famous Mary was born only months after her older sister's death, and it was not uncommon to name babies after their dead siblings, although rather uncomfortable to our modern sensibilities. Of the ten Anning children, only Mary and her brother Joseph survived until adulthood, the others living only for a year or two after their birth.[3]

By this time, the Industrial Revolution was in full swing. Many people still flocked to the towns and cities from the countryside for work and to seek their fortunes, only to be faced with over-crowding, poverty, and poor living conditions. The city environment did little for the health of the people who lived there, and diseases such as smallpox, typhoid, and cholera attacked the weakest and youngest in society.[4] Food shortages began to cripple poorer families with the French Revolutionary War and the Napoleonic Wars not helping matters as French blockades prevented food being imported into Britain. The price of grain tripled within the first twelve years of Anning's life while working wages remained almost unchanged, leading to widespread hunger and unrest.[5] Anning's father, Richard, being astute and aware of the plight of families affected by these shortages, organised a peaceful protest against this inequality. He knew all too well how poor families like theirs struggled to feed and clothe their children and how little the government was doing to alleviate the suffering of the many thousands of families living hand-to-mouth. Richard must have felt very strongly for him to be the one to organize the protest, but many others must have agreed with him for the protest to go ahead.

The family's poverty only became worse after Richard's death in 1810. He had suffered a fall when trying to climb to reach a specimen high on the cliff face, perhaps desperate to reach the specimen to bring the family more money. By risking his life this way, he had put his whole family's welfare in jeopardy. Whilst recovering from this terrible fall, he contracted tuberculosis and would pass away, aged only forty-four. His death left the family in massive debt and without savings, and in a time before national social welfare, life became incredibly difficult for his widow and children. Richard's wage as a cabinetmaker had never been overly lucrative, but without this or the supplement of selling fossils he found on the beach, the family were forced to apply for poor relief, often given through the church. As a proud woman, the mother Mary did not want to apply for this relief. She, like many others in her position, had always strived to be independent, looking after her family without external help. Sadly, after her husband's death and the loss of his income, she was forced to admit that she needed help to feed herself and her two remining children. The Poor Law enabled the church to provide financial assistance at a local level. This money was levied from the taxes on the richest in the parish. A representative would visit the house and assess whether or not the claimant was 'worthy' of the aid. If they were seen as a worthwhile case, the family would get money or if the parish was unable to provide funds for the needy family, relief would come in the form of clothing, fuel in the winter months, and food, mostly bread. It was not much, but it provided essential help to those in desperate need and was quite literally the difference between life and death to those who sought poor relief. Without organisations such as this, many families would have starved or frozen during the bitterly cold and relentless winters.

When Mary was a child, her parents used to run a little fossil shop from their home. Many people would run shops from their front rooms to avoid overheads of renting a separate premises to sell their goods. People sold any number of items from their homes, even running cafes and pubs. Running a fossil shop was not common, but it was in the entrepreneurial spirit that many had. Any opportunity to make money was taken and it was a small price to pay having strangers in and out of their homes.

Richard would discover the specimens on the beach, the mother Mary would clean them, and the children, Mary and Joseph, would help to sell them. Richard would often take the children onto the beach at Lyme and taught them how to spot fossils in the stone and shale. He taught them to recognize the texture of the fossils and how it differed from the texture of stone. Perhaps Richard showed the children techniques to determine bone from stone, one of which is to touch it to one's tongue. If it was bone, it would stick to the tongue, due to the honeycomb texture left behind by the series of holes that once ran the nerves and blood vessels for the animals. He taught them not only how to recognize the bones and other specimens but also other practical tips, such as what sold well in their shop and what items would bring a good price. He told them what fossils were the most rare and lucrative and told them to keep their eyes peeled for these special items.

Scrambling around cliffs was not a ladylike way to spend time for a young Georgian girl, but it is fortuitous that Richard encouraged his children equally in their interests. Many fathers would not have allowed their daughters to climb and get dirty clambering up the cliffs, digging in the sand and shale to find fossils. Many Georgian girls would be expected to stay indoors and read, sing, play music, embroider, and other 'ladylike' tasks, and poorer girls would be expected to learn to run a house and look after their younger siblings or perhaps even work to make money to contribute to the family. Mary did not have younger siblings to looks after, as it was only herself and Joseph. This freed her to not be stuck at home with little brothers and sisters, but be outdoors with her father and brother. She seemed to enjoy being outdoors and walked several times daily. If she had belonged to a wealthier family, perhaps she would not have had the opportunity to do this. Wealthier parents would have made her stay home and learn the skills to make her a desirable wife. While she lacked the wealth of the upper classes, she had the rare freedom to pursue her interests.

There is a tragic story attached to Mary when she was an infant. One stormy night in August 1800, when she was only fifteen months old, an event took place that passed into legend. Three local women stood beneath a tree watching a travelling company of horsemen. A family friend and neighbour, Elizabeth Haskings, was holding the infant Mary as they enjoyed the show. In a moment, a beautiful scene quickly turned to tragedy and horror. Thunder rolled across the sky and the sea bowled violently into shore. The sky suddenly turned black and threatening. Lightning struck the tree the women were standing beneath, bringing it down upon all four. The tree fell in a second, killing all three adults,[6] and knocking the infant Mary out of Hasking's arms and to the ground. The baby Mary was knocked unconscious immediately, where she remained for some hours. She was rushed home and revived with a hot bath.[7] Amazingly, Mary seemed not only unharmed, but her health improved. She was reported as having always been a sickly baby before the accident, but afterwards seemed to thrive. For many years to come, the community she called home attributed her curious nature and intelligence to this terrible incident.[8] It proves how poor the family must have been not to take their sick and then injured daughter to see the doctor and it is sad to think how many parents were forced to make a difficult decision about their children's health because of their poverty. Visiting the doctor cost a great deal of money and as the family were poor, they were strongarmed into taking baby Mary home and hoping their home remedies of hot baths, cuddles, and prayers were enough to revive their little one.

Mary's education was very basic and reflected the norm of the time for girls from lower earning families. She attended Sunday School that followed the Congregationalist doctrine, a branch of the Church of England that fully supported education of the poor. Her learning was mostly reading and writing, woven with scripture and prayer, as expected. Her most prized possession was a leather-bound volume of the Dissenters' *Theological Magazine and Review*. This publication contained two essays by their family pastor, Reverend James Wheaton. In one essay, he discussed the importance of believing that God created the world in six days, and resting on the sabbath, and in the second, he promotes the new science of geology and insists that Dissenters study the subject.[9] It is interesting to think that both essays were published by the same man within the same publication, when their ideologies are so diametrically opposite. Geology would of course continue to be of interest to Mary as she studied, questioned, and evaluated items she found on that lonely beach.

By the late nineteenth century, many tourists were flocking to seaside towns such as Lyme Regis, as the French

Revolutionary War and the Napoleonic Wars made much of Europe a frightening and unsuitable holiday destination.[10] The aristocracy and well-to-do had frequented Lyme Regis for quite some time and it was common for 'curios' to be sold. These 'curios' were given wonderful nicknames such as 'snakestones', 'Devil's fingers', and 'vertaberries' known to us today as ammonites, belemnites, and vertebrae. They were sold not only as weird and wonderful novelties, but also endorsed as having magical properties.[11]

One story regarding snakestones is found in Whitby. The Saxon Abbess Saint Hilda, who lived between 614 and 680, was tasked with founding the stunning Abbey on the clifftops of Whitby. She first had to get rid of the snake infestation there. Snakes had often been associated with the Devil, due to the Bible story in Genesis where the snake tempts Eve in the Garden of Eden. It was seen as important for St Hilda to remove these much-maligned creatures from the site before the first foundation stone of the Abbey was laid. Saint Hilda then cast a spell upon the land and all the snakes there curled up and turned to stone. She then threw them down from the clifftops to the beaches below. This story of the magical Saint Hilda was so prevalent that snake heads were often carved onto the snakestones, not realising what they had actually found, and how special the fossil was without carving.

Mary would spend a lot of time walking along the beach of Lyme Regis, particularly along the Blue Lias, a laminated rock formation that contained a rich plethora of fossils from the Jurassic period. It has been referred to as the richest fossil location in Britain.[12]

She was around twelve years old in 1811, when she and

her brother Joseph went along the cliffs, as they always did. After a storm the previous night, Joseph spotted an unusual shape sticking out of the rock and the pair spent many hours uncovering what turned out to be an impressive 4ft-long ichthyosaur skull. A few months later, Mary would find the rest of the ichthyosaur skeleton, which would turn out to be 5.2m long and the first complete specimen to be found anywhere in the world. The family initially sold the skull for £23,[13] just under £2,000 in today's terms. This amount would have been a great boost to the family's coffers, and the children no doubt were congratulated for their wonderful find. It is not as much money as an equivalent find would bring today. The skull was labelled incorrectly as 'Crocodile in Fossil State'. It was sold through various collectors and would eventually be sold on in 1819 to Charles Konig of the British Museum. Konig would go on to give the creature its name we now know it by, which means 'fish-lizard' though it is neither fish, nor lizard.[14]

The family were still in dire financial straits, despite their poor relief and the sales they had made of the fossils found by the Anning children. Their biggest customer, who bought several large pieces off the family, was Lieutenant-Colonel Thomas James Birch, a wealthy collector from Lincolnshire. He was saddened by the Anning family's poverty and offered to help them by selling the pieces he had already bought at auction. Birch wrote to his colleague Gideon Mantell about the matter, telling him that the auction would be 'for the benefit of a poor woman and her son and daughter in Lyme' and that 'I may never again possess what I am about to part with, yet in doing it, I shall have the satisfaction of knowing that the money is well applied'. He seems aware of how special the specimens were, but was happy to sell them on to help the Anning family. It was very kind of Birch to do this for them. The auction was held at the London-based Bullocks Auction House on 15 May 1820 and raised £400, worth just over an impressive £31,000 in today's money.[15] It is unclear exactly how much of this amount the family were given by Birch, but it was enough to help them live more comfortably. Birch not only improved the lives of the Anning family, but he brought worldwide attention to Mary Anning and her keen scientific eye.[16] They saw the young Mary for what she was: an intelligent, keen-eyed scientist, who knew these fossils better than her contemporaries.

The local newspaper *The Bristol Mirror* in 1823 referred to Mary as a 'persevering female' and discussed the life-threatening ordeals she had to go through to find the fossils.[17] The cliffs were incredibly dangerous after heavy rain as the fragile layers became loose and would tumble down onto the beach below, but it was for this reason that Mary and her brother would walk there regularly after bad weather. Precious specimens could be found in the freshly revealed rock. Tragically, her trusty companion, a little black and white terrier, Trey, who often walked the beaches with her was crushed one day with one such collapse. She wrote to a friend and claimed that 'it was but a moment between me and such a fate'.[18] So committed was she to fossil finding, she continued to risk her life alone, without the companionship of her loyal pup. This tragic event must have served as a horrible reminder of just how dangerous her fossil-hunting was, and how quickly her life could be ended by the very rocks she searched every day.

Her confidence in her own ability grew with each find and identification. She even wrote a letter to the highly acclaimed

Magazine of Natural History pointing out an error in one of their articles that claimed that the newly discovered Hybodus, a long-extinct sharklike creature, was a new genus. Mary knew that this creature was not a new species, as she herself had found many examples of it with both straight and hooked teeth many years before. This would be the only time she would be published in a scientific journal, perhaps she felt she had to write to the magazine to prevent any confusion regarding the supposed new species of Hybodus.[19] It is shocking to think that she was only published to correct an error, and never had the opportunity to write her own published article or scientific paper.

Her expertise was sought by the gentlemen geologists, but they failed to mention her name or her contributions when their work was published, understandably leaving her to feel bitter and resentful. She was approached from far and wide for her scientific expertise in her field. At the time Mary was making her amazing discoveries, women were not allowed to vote, attend university, or hold any sort of public office. The newly-founded but increasingly influential Geological Society of London did not permit women to become members there or even allow women into attend the lectures.

Anna Pinney, a young woman who had begun to accompany Mary on her excursions to the beach, wrote: 'she[Anning] says the world has used her ill ... these men of learning have sucked her brains, and made a great deal of publishing works, of which she furnished the contents, while she derived none of the advantages.'[20] It is so unfair that these men had used Mary's expertise to make themselves respected and left her name out of their published articles and research papers.

She herself once wrote: 'The world has used me so unkindly, I fear it has made me suspicious of everyone.'[21] She contributed to scientific advancement and was sought by influential fellows from various geological and palaeontological groups for her knowledge and proficiency in prehistoric specimens. These were the same men who barred her from being a member of their groups, or even attending lectures there, despite her being far more knowledgeable and arguably more worthy than any of the members at the Geological Society.

Mary was not only female, but working class, which possibly led her to be further seen as an outsider to the scientific community. Quarrymen, sailors, and construction workers would often find interesting specimens during their work and sell them to wealthy collectors, who often claimed to have found the fossil themselves, leaving out the real eagle-eyed discoverer. The original finders never got the credit they deserved for their discoveries.[22]

Some were far from dismissive of Mary. William Buckland, a Doctor of Divinity and a Fellow of the Royal Society, often accompanied Mary on her fossil finding missions. A respected lecturer of geology at the University of Oxford, it was to him that Mary would prove that the strange irregular-shaped objects that were often referred to 'bezaur stones' were in fact coprolites, fossilized faeces, specifically from plesiosaurs and ichthyosaurs. [23]

An English fossil collector and dealer Thomas Hawkins also joined Mary one year to unearth ichthyosaur skeletons along the beach at Lyme. Hawkins had a rather dubious reputation amongst his fellow fossil finders and would later be exposed as a fraud as he had added unrelated bones to some ichthyosaur skeletons, some which he found with Mary, to make them seem more complete.[24] He sold these almost fully complete skeletons for a great deal of money, even selling some to the government for inclusion in the British Museum.

By 1830, Mary was facing financial difficulty once more. The country's economy had not improved and as a result, fewer people had money to spend of non-essential items such as fossils. As well as this, larger finds were few and far between, leaving large gaps in between payments. Mary's good friend and geologist Henry De la Beche kindly stepped in, realising her impending poverty. He commissioned the water colourist and lithographer Georg Scharf to create the *Duria Antiquior*, which was a depiction of the prehistoric animals in their early Devonshire landscape, showing the creatures Mary had discovered. De la Beche sold many copies of this beautiful lithograph to the wealthy collectors and geologists in his acquaintance, which helped to keep her financially stable.[25] Luckily around this time she also discovered and identified an almost complete skeleton of a new species of plesiosaur, which she sold for £200,[26] the equivalent of almost £18,500 in today's money.

Mary's old friend, William Buckland would once again extend a hand of friendship to her. He wrote to the British Association for the Advancement of Science and to the British government, requesting that they award Mary a life annuity, a regular sum of money for the rest of her life, in recognition of her continued contribution to science. They agreed and rewarded Mary with an annual sum of £25 per annum, the equivalent of around £1,700, which was enough to keep her head above water financially.[27]

Her palaeontological work took place during a time in which

many Christians still believed in a literal interpretation of the Bible, particularly Genesis. They believed the creation story, that the world was created in six days, with God resting on the seventh day. It was thought by the majority of believers that the world was only around 6,000 years old, created by God. It was a story told without the inclusion of dinosaurs or any other prehistoric animals. They perhaps thought of these unusual specimens as creatures from far off countries they had never seen before, rather than long dead creatures. Although Georges Cuvier had recently introduced the theory of extinction, Charles Darwin would not publish *The Origin of Species* until 1859, almost twelve years after Mary's death. The fossil records opposed the biblical view of the history of the world, showing the planet to be millions, not thousands of years old and this upset many religious people of the time. It's interesting to think about what Mary's opinion would have been about the publication of Darwin's work. Would she have felt vindicated?

Mary passed away in 1847. She died of breast cancer aged only forty-seven. She was in a lot of pain and regularly took laudanum, a mixture of alcohol and opium to ease her agony. She kept quiet about her illness and rumours began that she was an alcoholic, seen less and less as her sickness took hold.[28] It was a tragic end to her life, with upsetting rumours about substance abuse. It is awful that it was assumed by some locals that she was abusing substances and avoiding her rather than checking on her welfare.

The Geological Society had a stained-glass window dedicated to her memory at St Michael's Church. The inscription on the window is dedicated to her 'usefulness in furthering the science of geology and also of her benevolence of heart and integrity of life'.[29] The stained-glass window shows that she was well-liked and respected for her work and as a person. It is telling that the Geological Society paid for the memorial, showing that they perhaps finally recognised her contribution to the fields of geology and palaeontology. The Society did not accept female members until 1919, so sadly Mary was never allowed into the very society that honoured her with the window. It was the first official recognition of her professional work that sadly came posthumously, too late for her to appreciate it.

Her legacy is immortal, stretching back millennia and far reaching in our understanding of our world. It is difficult to underestimate how significant Mary was to the world of geology and palaeontology. She was used by the male geologists in her field whilst being excluded from joining their societies and not given the credit for her work. After many years, she now has the recognition she deserves and there is even a statue of her and her little dog in Lyme Regis, overlooking the spot she frequented so often. It is a beautiful statue and one which shows her mid stride as if she was walking towards the beach for another fossil-finding session.

She opened the eyes of people to a whole ancient world of creatures. She unearthed the bones of long-dead animals and brought attention to them from not just the scientific world, but also the general public.

ADA LOVELACE

The Enchantress of Number

❧

Ada Lovelace was born into the nobility and had a wonderful start in life. She grew to be one of the most influential people in mathematics. She revolutionised the subject like no other had done before and her legacy is seen all around us today. She had a wonderfully scientific and mathematical mind and was the mother of computing as we know it.

The Right Honourable Augusta Ada Byron was born on 10 December 1815. She was the daughter of Lord George Gordon Byron, the Romantic poet and peer, and Lady Anne Isabella Noel Byron, a highly-intelligent noble woman.

It was never a secret that her father had wanted a 'glorious boy' and was disappointed at the birth of a girl. It had always been the case that baby boys were longed for whilst baby girls were seen as less desirable. Boys would automatically inherit their father's fortune and girls would be married off with a dowry provided by their families, thus costing them money.

The baby girl was named after her father's half-sister, Augusta Leigh, with whom Lady Byron often suspected her husband was having an incestuous affair. Lord Byron had a reputation as a wastrel, a womanizer, and a narcissist and the latter was proven without doubt when he demanded his wife and daughter leave their family home without knowing where they would go. Lady Byron had no choice but to go to her mother's house with the infant Ada, who was only five weeks old. Lord Byron made no attempt to gain custody of his daughter, despite the English law usually granting custody to the father in cases where a separation took place, regardless of who was to blame for the marriage breakdown. Lord Byron didn't care for his daughter or for his wife. He had had his fun with Lady Byron, and now he found himself bored of her company. He never seemed to be paternal in any way, and his only concern in life seemed to feed his own hedonist lifestyle doing whatever pleased him, oblivious to any adult responsibilities. He seemed to act like a spoilt boy half his age, rather than a lord and a man. He did request that his sister keep him informed of any news about Ada, but never saw her in person again and did not seem to miss or think about her. It is a little odd that Lord Byron requested his sister report back on his child and not the mother of his child. It is almost as if he had forgotten about Lady Byron's existence by this point.

Lord Byron left England, never to return after signing a separation order from his wife. He wrote a poem to Lady Byron upon his leaving the country. He wrote: 'And when thou would'st solace gather/when our child's first accents flow/Wilt thou teach her to say 'father'/Though his care she must forgo.'[1] It is heartbreaking to think of this poem being penned, and difficult to understand how he could leave his infant daughter before she even spoke her first words. The last line quoted here suggests that he knew he would never return to see her, but it also insinuates that Lord Byron would have provided 'care' to her. He was never a fatherly figure and only managed to stay in her life for five weeks, hardly the actions of a caring father. The line of the poem which reads 'when our child's first accents flow/wilt thou teach her to say "father"', is obviously a question aimed at Lady Byron. Would she have talked to her daughter about the man who had abandoned them? Her anger at her former husband would surely lead to her omitting him from conversation and any mention of the man would have understandably made her very angry and hurt. Would Ada even learn what the word 'father' meant, given that she had never really had any paternal figure in her life? He is perhaps questioning whether his former wife would tell Ada about him when she was older, the man who would not even stay for more than five weeks. A baby's hearing and vision is only being developed around this time, so it is possible that little Ada did hear and see her father before he pushed them out the door, although she would not have remembered this encounter at all. The last line of the poem, 'Though his care she must forgo', suggests that Lord Byron never intended to return to see his wife and daughter again. She would have to 'forgo' his company and grow up fatherless, however, an absent father is better than a close toxic father.

Lady Byron and her daughter carried on living their lives without him, but she continued to feel bitter about her husband's cruel and selfish behaviour. This separation and her father's behaviour would follow Ada around, linking her to scandal throughout her life. Lord Byron's shadow loomed large over her, despite her never knowing him. It was assumed like father like daughter.

Lord Byron died of a fever in Greece on 19 April 1824, aged

only thirty-six. How many shed tears over his death when he treated people so badly? Did he have many mourners at his funeral? His body was taken back to England where the Dean of Westminster Abbey refused to have his remains buried at the Abbey due to his monstrous reputation, and he was buried at St Mary Magdalene Church, in Hucknall Torkard, Nottingham. It would be much later, 8 May 1969, when a memorial stone was laid for him in Poet's Corner in Westminster Abbey. His memorial plaque lies alongside much-loved wordsmiths as Lewis Carroll, D.H. Lawrence, and Dylan Thomas. It is possible that his poetry by this point had taken over his caddish reputation in people's minds.

Was Byron missed by those around him? It is possible that people missed the beautiful poetry that would not now be written, however, Lord Byron was not missed by those who knew his cruelty and self-centred nature well.

Ada was only eight years old when her father died. Although by this age many children have a true sense of love and belonging, she never felt close to either parent. Her cold and emotionally distant mother unsurprisingly rarely spoke of the man who had discarded them both when she was only a baby. Lady Byron only showed her daughter a portrait of her father when she was an adult, showing the life-long resentment and anger towards her late husband. It is intriguing to think about how Lady Byron felt about hearing of her former husband's death. Was she deeply saddened by the news, relieved, or was she unaffected given the many years they had spent apart? It is also interesting to think about how Ada responded to seeing the portrait of her father. Had her mother stayed silent all those years without a single mention of the man? Had her mother told her young daughter that her father had died? Had Ada known who her father was through rumours and gossip? Did she look at that portrait and see a part of herself there, perhaps the same crooked smile, the same twinkle in the eyes? Was that portrait then kept in her possession or once again hidden away with the same seething anger as her mother felt?

Ada had a half-sister, Allegra, whom she never met. Allegra was the result of her father's affair with Claire Clairmont, who would become the stepsister of the gothic writer Mary Shelley. Despite the best efforts of the nuns who attended her, little Allegra died in 1822, aged only five years old, within the Papal States in Italy. Some biographers have suggested that she died of typhus fever. There were rumours that Lord Byron had also fathered a child with his half-sister, Augusta Leigh. It is entirely possible given his tendency to have many affairs. The rumours about Lord Byron and his half-sister had been persistent for many years. Ada did have some contact with her would-be half-sister Elizabeth Medora Leigh, but the two never got on and their relationship was cold at best. Lady Bryon would later confirm to Ada, that Elizabeth was indeed her half-sister, something that she had always suspected. This further confirmed to Ada her father's character, how he had never been truly faithful to any of the women in his life, fathering at least two, perhaps more children, only to abandon them and their mothers.

It must have been a difficult life for Ada growing up. Her father had abandoned her and her mother when she was a baby and she never saw him again. Her mother was uncaring and saw her daughter as an inconvenience at best, a burden at worst. She left the motherly duties to her maternal grandmother,

Judith, the Right Honourable Lady Milbank, who adored the girl and doted on her as a mother should. However, to keep up the pretence of being a good mother to a judgemental society, Lady Byron sent regular letters to Lady Milbank enquiring about her daughter's welfare. Sending a child to live with relatives was common enough and would not raise too many eyebrows, but it was expected that regular correspondence took place between the adults involved. Lady Byron would ask in a cover note that the letters were kept in case she needed to 'prove' her motherly adoration.[2] Perhaps if a nosy neighbour were to become suspicious and ask too many questions, Lady Byron could produce the letters to Lady Milbank and provide evidence that she really was a caring mother. However, this plan had a major flaw. The contents of the letters showed a complete disregard for her young daughter. In one letter Lady Byron refers to Ada as 'it', showing a terrible contempt for her. She seems to reject her, not only as her daughter, but even as a human being. The word 'it' is debasing, and it degrades the girl. It seems to point to her being little more than an inanimate object or perhaps animal that she has no feelings for. It is a very strange way to write about her only daughter. She wrote: 'I talk to it for your satisfaction, not my own, and shall be very glad when you have it under your own.'[3] Here she also shows that she wishes to be released from even the most meagre of parental duties, the writing of the letters. She writes because society expects it, and Lady Milbank also perhaps demands a level of involvement from the girl's mother. The line that she 'shall be very glad when you [Lady Milbank] have it under your own' suggests that Lady Byron is looking forward to relinquishing all maternal responsibilities as soon as possible, leaving her daughter to be brought up entirely by her grandmother.

As Ada got older, Lady Byron would for some reason become involved with her daughter once more, having washed her hands of the girl many years earlier. Lady Byron would spy on her daughter through friends and extended family members and demanded reports on any moral deviation, behaviour Lady Byron deemed unfeminine, depraved, or unacceptable. Her mother went from one extreme to another. When Ada was a child, her mother took great measures to distance herself from her parental duties just as her father had done. Then when Ada was a teenager, her mother voluntarily sneaked around and spied on her daughter behind her back, wanting to control her every move. It seems strange that Lady Byron wanted to spend less time with her as a child, but as an adult, she interferes in the girl's life when she could have had much less contact with her. Later Ada would complain that these 'spies' exaggerated and even made up their reports to her mother, making her sound like she was living a life of debauchery.[4] The friends of her mother would suggest that Ada was out late each night, meeting multiple lovers in the dark and dancing until dawn. She was made to sound like a feminine version of her father, living a life of wickedness and depravity, drinking, using drugs, and sleeping with an army of lovers. It must have angered Ada to be described this way. She must have prided herself on not being like her father and being compared to him would have hurt, especially as the stories about her were exaggerated or completely fictitious.

She was in fact a sickly child, suffering from terrible headaches which often debilitated her to the point she could not even see. These headaches were likely to be migraines, brought on by perhaps stress, anxiety, diet or too much exercise or too little rest. When she was around eight years old in 1829, she contracted measles, which left her paralyzed. This must have had a profound effect on Ada throughout her entire life, both physically and psychologically. She was kept in bed for an entire year, which perhaps exacerbated her migraines due to the stress and frustration of being kept indoors so long. It would be almost two years before she was able to walk with crutches and even then she struggled to move further than the four walls of her house. As she was confined to her room for a long time, she could do very little but think and she continued using her inquisitive mind. She would sit, trapped in her bed, and read and imagine about the natural and scientific world.

She was also a studious and very serious child. As a twelve-year-old, she dreamt of flying. Perhaps she watched the birds flutter around the window beside her bed. It is easy to imagine the young girl, desperate to escape the confines of her bed, looking out of the window at the world she could not yet step in to. One day, she began designing wings, which could be worn on the arms and flapped like a bird's. Perhaps she felt as if by designing these wings, she could escape her bed. These wings did not need her legs to work, and she could maybe one day fly away into the blue sky she longingly looked at. She threw herself into this work, becoming obsessed by the notion of flight. She tested the flexibility of various materials and began making prototypes with wire, oil-silk, paper, and feathers to test the durability of each. She had incredible focus and passion in this quest, studying the anatomy of birds and working out mathematically the correlation of wing length and body weight. Her need to get away was overwhelming. She could perhaps fly away from that room, and her overbearing and judgemental mother.

She decided to write down her findings on flight in a book she called *Flyology*. In this book she outlined the concepts of flying, and her findings regarding flight from her experiments. She listed the items she would need to achieve her goal, including a compass to 'cut across the country by the most direct route' so she could navigate over mountains and valleys and wide-open oceans. Her final flourish to add to her flying apparatus was to add steam.[5] It is quite telling that even as a twelve-year-old, she was full of passion and logic, and had such an analytical mind that she would approach a childlike idea with such an intellectual determination. Many children dream of flying, but few go so far as to design a steam-powered apparatus to do so.

She showed an amazing skill with numbers from an early age. This is perhaps because her mother was so determined to keep her daughter busy with learning and stretching her mind. Lady Byron had often accused her estranged husband of being insane, and did not want her daughter given space to develop such an affliction. Keeping her mind busy would perhaps dispel any of her father's madness that dwelt there. Ada certainly had an addictive personality like her father, but chose to focus it on her work rather than living her life like him. Her father was addicted to laudanum and alcohol, but his daughter's addictions seemed to be mathematics, numbers, and invention.

Ada filled her time with various mathematical obsessions. That is not to say that her life was all work and no play. She had a short but passionate affair with her tutor in 1833, aged eighteen. They planned to elope, but the friends and spies of Lady Byron found out and told her mother about the relationship. It is quite sad that her first real romantic relationship was ended by her mother's interference. Whether it was a passing infatuation or whether it could have been more, she would never find out because of her mother's network of spies and informants. Any mention of the affair was quickly hushed up to prevent a public scandal.[6] She was technically an adult at this time, but it did not stop Lady Byron interfering and preventing the couple from continuing their budding relationship.

Ada rubbed shoulders with the most renowned scientists, mathematicians, and writers of her day. She knew Charles Dickens, the famous writer; Andrew Crosse and Michael Faraday, both noted for their work on electricity; Sir David Brewster and Charles Wheatstone, both inventors and prominent in their respective fields. Two who she became particularly close to were Mary Somerville and Charles Babbage. She shared a close personal friendship with Somerville, who was a fellow scientist, writer, polymath, astronomer, and mathematician, and was one of only two women admitted as Honorary Members of the Royal Astronomical Society. The two remained close, sharing letters for the rest of their lives. Perhaps they felt close being in such a minority of female mathematicians. They were few and far between so were kindred spirits, keeping close together. Charles Babbage was a polymath, an inventor, a mathematician, inventor, philosopher, and mechanical engineer. He is the inventor of the first programmable computer.

Ada was presented at court when she was only seventeen and became a popular 'belle of the ball' for her 'brilliant mind'.[7] She was not only very intelligent, but beautiful and danced with many eligible bachelors at the balls and parties she attended. One man, however, a friend of Lord Byron, John Hobhouse called her a 'large, coarse-skinned young woman, but with something of my friend's features, particularly the mouth'.[8] This cruel comment was made as Ada had just rejected him loudly within earshot of others at the ball, and he perhaps lashed out with a hurt ego. Ada was always inclined to dislike those who had got on well with her father, given their non-existent and yet still toxic relationship. She was perhaps particularly upset because Hobhouse commented that she had a resemblance to her father. She cannot have liked to be told that she looked like him in any way. It was perhaps the same pain she felt when her mother had assumed that her behaviour was like that of her father. Ada and Hobhouse would later strike up friendship, despite this less than auspicious start.

She would marry William, 8th Baron King, Earl of Lovelace and he would later become Lord King. Ada herself had descended from the then extinct Barons Lovelace line through her father, but in 1838, William would be made Earl of Lovelace, meaning that she would become the Countess of Lovelace.

They had three grand residences: Ockham Park in Surrey; a house in London; and a Scottish estate on Loch Torridon in Ross-shire. They had their honeymoon at Worthy Manor in Ashley Combe, near Somerset. It was built in 1799 in the mock Tudor style known as Tudor revival and was extended and refurbished according to Ada's own designs.

They had three children: Byron in 1836: Anne Isabella, nicknamed Annabella, born 1837: and Ralph Gordon, born 1839. Lady Byron, perhaps strangely transformed by becoming a grandmother for the first time, or perhaps seeing another chance to control her daughter's life, stepped in and organised a tutor for the children. She had had little to do with her daughter for many years, but upon having the children, Lady Byron once again loudly gave her opinions. The tutor was William Benjamin Carpenter, a Fellow of the Royal Society, physician, invertebrate zoologist, and physiologist and came highly recommended. He was employed to be the children's 'moral instructor' as well as an academic tutor.[9] Carpenter quickly became infatuated with Ada. Perhaps it was her beauty or her intelligence, or perhaps the unique combination of the two. He flirted with her, and she tolerated it for a short time perhaps out of politeness. However, when he became more forceful and asked her to express her presumed suppressed feelings for him, she dismissed him and left him with no doubt that his feelings would not be reciprocated.[10] It is an all too familiar experience for many women to politely play along with unwanted flirting, fearing the consequences of saying 'no'. Having endured Carpenter's undesirable company over the many meetings between them, she was forced to be candid with him and told him she did not like him and did not want to be in his company. He did not like being rejected and expressed his displeasure at being rejected by her.

This is not to say that she was always faithful to her husband. She flirted and possibly had several affairs with various men.[11] This was seen as scandalous behaviour in Georgian society. A married man of the aristocracy or royalty having an affair with a string of mistresses was not only accepted but expected of them. King George IV had many high-profile mistresses whilst being married to Queen Caroline, and these affairs continued throughout their marriage, without secrecy or apology. Queen Caroline was expected to be faithful and turn a nonchalant blind eye away from her royal husband and his string of mistresses and potentially several illegitimate children. It was unforgivable for married women, of any class, to conduct extramarital affairs. Ada's affairs shocked and scandalised Georgian society. She was a wife and a mother, and her husband and children were expected to be her main priority. Indeed, her only priority. She was expected to give up any thought or need of her own and wait upon her family. By having an affair, she was putting her own needs first, very unlike the traditional woman was expected to be. Ada continued to flirt and lived her life as she wished, regardless of the fine ladies whispering about her behind their lace-gloved hands over their polite afternoon tea.

Ada would later have a shadowy affair with her friend Andrew Crosse's son, John, from around 1844 for about a year. There is strong enough evidence that their relationship was physical at some point. The pair wrote steamy letters to each other, and John would burn the letters as requested. Very little information is known about their relationship, other than that it was brief and intense. After her death she left him a great many of the heirlooms she had inherited from her father.[12] On her deathbed, she wanted John to visit,[13] but he did not. Perhaps visiting her would have brought their relationship to the attention of others in their respective families. It is possible that he had moved on and did not want to revisit their time together.

Ada also caused scandal though her gambling. Gambling itself was not seen as shocking in the Georgian period, but the vast sums of money involved in Ada's case were astonishing. Eyebrows were raised by the sheer volume of bets she placed and the amounts. Gambling was more of a high society pastime, perhaps because the poorer people had little to bet with and could not afford to lose what little they had. It was common in gentlemen's clubs and parties to have games of cards, played for high stakes. Both men and women played at these tables and was generally accepted as long as fortunes were not lost in their entirety. It appears there was a limit to the acceptance of the amounts gambled away. It could be a very lucrative venture, and some well-off ladies 'with no other income sometimes allowed their houses to be turned into gambling houses'.[14] The Prince Regent, later George IV, loved gambling and frittered away great amounts of the vast royal fortune. It is one of the many reasons he was generally despised by his subjects, spending, gambling, and his ample 50-inch waist whilst many of his subjects went hungry. Whig politician Charles Fox was a compulsive gambler, and over the course of a particularly wild week-long gambling bender, found himself in debt for a whopping £140,000, over £12,000,000 in today's terms. Luckily Charles' father, Lord Fox, paid off his son's debts, with the alternative being debtor's prison, such as Marshalsea in London, where Charles Dicken's father was sent in 1824 for non-payment of debts. A place where many suffered and died whilst their families struggled to scrape together money to pay off the debts of their loved ones.

Ada's gambling was nowhere near that of Fox's addictive level or the Prince's carelessness, but she still lost a huge amount of money. During the 1840s, it is estimated that she lost around £3,000 on horseracing bets, the modern equivalent being £246,000, a massive sum. There was even a racing horse named after Ada, due to her love for betting. She formed a syndicate with some of her male friends and in 1851 she set about creating a mathematical model on which to place successful bets.

Finding a betting formula that worked every time proved to be impossible, as many avid gamblers have discovered, and Ada found herself in debt for thousands of pounds to her syndicate. It was so much money that she was forced to tell her husband.[15] She had up to this point managed to keep her gambling a secret, but could do so no longer, given her mounting debt. She had been forced to secretly sell her family diamonds to cover her debts.

It was unusual for the time for Ada to have a gambling syndicate at all, but to have a syndicate with a group of men was even more rare. It was still a period when a woman was not to be alone with a man unsupervised until they were married and chaperoned if they were unmarried. Ada had male company that she called friends, not uncommon today, but very atypical of the Georgian period. She met with these men, as she would a group of female friends, and discussed gambling, money, and the next best bet, whether card games or various events on which bets could be made. There seemed to be no thought of gender norms or social constraints crossing her mind when meeting with her friends. They were not men, they were friends, regardless of gender.

Throughout her life, she was interested in numbers and mathematics, including some of those rather odd 'sciences' such as phrenology and mesmerism. Phrenology is the study of the lumps and bumps on a person's head and how that determines their personality and perhaps state of mind. Mesmerism is the art of hypnotism, putting someone into a trance or deep sleep-like state where they become susceptible to suggestion. Both have been dismissed as any form of science now.

Her interest in the human brain was one that perhaps

stemmed from her mother's preoccupation with Lord Byron's fragile mental state. She would attempt to understand and create a mathematical model of how the brain gives rise to thoughts and how nerves work in relation to feelings. Perhaps she believed that if she found how the brain works and where madness stems from, she could understand a little better the father she had never known. She perhaps even thought that by learning about the brain, she would learn if the way her father lived his life and treated people was through choice or because of the way his brain worked. It could be that she needed to know whether she could forgive him for what he had done to her and her mother all those years before. She never achieved her goal of mapping out the human mind, but it was an extremely ambitious undertaking.

She first met Charles Babbage in June 1833, through their mutual friend and fellow scientist and mathematician Mary Somerville. Babbage invited Ada to see his invention, the Difference Engine, an automatic mechanical calculator, capable of tabulating polynomial functions. Ada was enthralled by the machine and asked her friend Somerville to take her to speak with Babbage regularly. The machine seemed to spark her interest and she was immediately transfixed by it and equally fond of Babbage. He was likewise equally fond of her, astounded by her intellect, passion, and analytical questioning. He would refer to her as 'The Enchantress of Number'.

Between 1842 and 1843, Ada began translating the Italian mathematician, and future Prime Minister of Italy, Luigi Menabrea's article on Babbage's newest invention, the Analytical Engine, which was a simpler and more refined successor to the Difference Engine.[16] In her translation, she explained how the

Analytical Engine was distinctive from the Difference Engine,[17] and added detailed notes, explaining Babbage's new machine. It was a difficult task, as many of their contemporary great and good could not understand the complex theories behind the machine. She not only understood it completely, but also had a talent for explaining the machine simply in a way that others could understand. Although many could not understand either the purpose or the workings of the new machine, Ada still had support. Michael Faraday, a leading contributor in the study of electromagnetism, described himself as a fan of Ada's work.[18] Faraday was a prominent physicist of the time, held in esteem for his work with magnetism, electromagnetism, the principles of induction, and the laws of electrolysis.

Her notes on the machine are around three times longer than the article itself and go into great detail about the machine and its capabilities.[19] The article also includes a method of using the machine to calculate Bernoulli numbers, a sequence of rational numbers which occur frequently in analysis. Sadly, the Analytical Engine remained on paper alone, a pipe dream that was never built. Ada was sure it would have worked had it been built.

Due to her detailed work on both the Difference and Analytical Engines, Ada is often considered the world's first computer programmer. Others dispute this as some of Babbage's early work could be thought of as computer programmes. However, although her work was based on the principles that Babbage theorised, Ada took it a step further, writing a programme with practical uses to problem solve. To Babbage, the Analytical Engine was about numbers, but to Ada, she saw a world of possibilities in those numbers. She saw musical notes and letters, she saw so many possibilities, developing the machine into so much more than a mere calculator. In her mind, the machine's power could be harnessed into many everyday practical purposes, 'translating' the numbers into gadgets, tools, and instruments that could make people's lives easier and better. She could see how this machine could be used in the future, seeing the many potential uses of this unique contraption.

In her translation and notes on Menabrea's article, often referred to as 'Note G', she dismisses the notion of Artificial Intelligence, stating that a computer can 'follow analysis, but it has no power of anticipating any analytical relations or truths'.[20] She suggests here that computers will follow instruction alone and will have no independent thought. Her comment about AI has led to much debate, especially as technology has come so far from those early days of Babbage and Ada's partnership. Alan Turing, the undisputed 'father of modern computer science', would later write his article on AI titled 'Computing Machinery and Intelligence'[21] in which he challenged Ada's notes. He suggested that perhaps there is no simple answer to give on this debate. Turing states in his paper that when Ada comments that the computer can do 'nothing new', he argues that 'there is nothing new under the sun' and perhaps humans themselves even on a subconscious level never have a unique or original thought. It is a very deep philosophical idea, one which I'm sure Ada would have debated with glee with Turing had their genius minds met.

Babbage became upset with Ada when her paper was published, because of her wording in the unsigned preface, which she wrote without Babbage having read it. Babbage was concerned that Ada had written negatively about the British government's lack of support for Babbage's machine. As it was unsigned, he worried that the preface and therefore the criticism of the government would be laid at his door. He demanded that Ada withdraw her paper and edit it to contain her own signature at the foot of the preface. It was a few sentences, but Babbage was upset about this and wanted the changes made, given how uncertain his relationship was with the British government.

Ada died aged only thirty-six, due to what was probably uterine cancer, on 27 November 1852. She and Babbage kept in touch via letters throughout her fight with the disease. Annabella, her daughter, kept her friends and other family members away from the house for the several months her mother was ill. She had asked Babbage to become executor of her will, but nothing was formalised, and her daughter stepped in to overtake this duty.[22] Annabella was deeply religious and persuaded her mother to repent her former conduct in life and find God. On 30 August, Ada confessed something to her husband that made him leave her bedside and never return.[23] Whatever secret she shared, was not something that her husband wanted to hear from his wife. Perhaps she had confessed to an affair with a lover or two, perhaps she admitted to losing another fortune at the gambling table. Whatever the confession, Ada was left alone to face her fate in her final months. He walked out of that room and never returned. Did she regret telling him the secret? Did she die in peace knowing she had finally come clean to her husband?

At the request of the Byron family, she was buried next to her father in the Byron family vault in the cemetery of the Church of St Mary Magdalene in small town of Hucknall in Nottinghamshire. It is odd that she was placed next to her father for all eternity, a man she had spent five weeks with her entire life. Would Ada have approved of being buried in her father's family plot? The church still stands to this day, and their names are carved there.

Ada may have had some regrets as she lay in her sickbed in the final months of her life, but she lived her life as full as she could. She defied Georgian norms of ladylike behaviour, taking many lovers, and gambling as she wished. Her intelligence was legendary and rivalled any scientific and mathematical mind of her time, writing unapologetic notes and articles on subjects she was passionate about. As a countess, she could have just sat back and enjoyed her days in leisure, she could have sat in the grounds of one of her beautiful estates, drinking tea and catching up with the gossip of the area in tranquillity. Perhaps this life would have been rather boring to her. Her mind would have vegetated not being allowed to stretch her brain. Instead, however, she worked on computer programmes and algorithms, when technology was in its infancy and fought for her voice to be heard about the subjects she loved. Without her, we would not have the technology we have today.

Her work and determination would pave the way for women in science, technology, mathematics, and engineering, breaking into subjects that were dominated by men.

Her work would lead to the likes of physicist Pearl L. Young becoming the first woman to be hired by the National Advisory Committee for Aeronautics (NACA), the agency that would go on to become the National Aeronautics and Space Administration (NASA). Doctor Harriet Jenkins who worked for NASA as part of the Equal Opportunities Programme, pursued her career there and completed her doctorate and became a Fellow. Doctor Sally Ride was a successful astronaut candidate and flew for the first time in 1983. After retiring, she joined the University of California at San Diego as a professor and started an organisation called Sally Ride Science which encouraged girls to enter science, maths, engineering, and technology fields.

Ada's work led to the creation of the Electronic Numerical Integrator and Computer (ENIAC), the first programmable general purpose digital computer, first completed in 1945. Other computers had been built, but this was the first of its kind, including the best elements of its predecessors. It was first designed by John Mauchly and J. Presper Eckhert to calculate artillery firing tables for the United States Army's Ballistic Research Laboratory. It was not a lightweight machine, weighing in at twenty-seven tons. The computer was a lot more advanced than the machines that Ada had used herself, but still so far away from the handheld user-friendly devices we are used to today.

ENIAC's primary programmers were all women, something that had never happened before. They were Kay McNulty, Betty Jennings, Betty Snyder, Marlyn Wescoff, Ruth Lichterman, and Fran Bilas. They learned not only how to input the ENIAC programmes, but also developed an understanding of the computer's workings. They were even able to narrow down bugs to a single line of code or individual failed tube, so it could be replaced by a technician.

It is impossible to tell how many women and girls have been inspired by Ada's work. Without her, young women would not have had the opportunity to enter the fields of science, technology, engineering, and mathematics. She was the inspiration for those budding STEM women who came after her. Each generation of amazing women looking back to the previous generation of genius women, but she was the first to take that step forward into subjects that had previously been dominated by men.

It is amazing to think that without Ada Lovelace, we would not have had the advancements in computing we have.

Notes

Introduction

1. Jane Austen, *Pride and Prejudice*, Chapter 8
2. Ibid, Chapter 8
3. Ibid, Chapter 8
4. Ibid, Chapter 8
5. Ibid, Chapter 1
6. Madeleine Luckel, *Why It's Time to Revisit the Handheld Fan – And Its Secret Language*, Vogue, April 24 2018
7. Ibid
8. Exodus 1:16, Bible
9. Genesis 2:7, Bible
10. Lucy Ellis, *The Art of Dressing: Shaping Fashion in Georgian England*, 2023, www.artuk.org/discover/stories
11. www.artuk.org/discover/stories/the-art-of-dressing-shaping-fashion-in-georgian-england
12. Ibid. www.artuk.org/discover/stories/the-art-of-dressing-shaping-fashion-in-georgian-england

Sarah Pennington

1. John Pennington (1737–1813), Member biographies, www.historyofparliamentonline.org
2. Obtaining a Divorce, UK Parliament website, www.parliament.uk/about/living/divorce
3. Lorna Sage, *The Cambridge Guide to Women's Writing in English*, Cambrige University Press, 1999, p. 494
4. Ghislaine McDayter and John Hunter, *Flirtation and Courtship in Nineteenth-Century British Culture*, London: J. Walter, 1784, pp. 1-14, 111-117
5. Ibid, pp. 2-14
6. Ibid, pp. 2-14
7. Ibid, pp. 111-117
8. Lady Sarah Pennington, 'An Unfortunate Mother's Advice To Her Absent Daughters', In *A Letter to Miss Pennington*, A. Millar, W. Law and R. Cater, 1761, p. 7

9. Ibid, pp. 7-8
10. Ghislaine McDayter and John Hunter, *Flirtation and Courtship in Nineteenth-Century British Culture*, London: J. Walter, 1784, pp. 1-14, 111-117
11. Ibid, pp. 112-117
12. Lady Sarah Pennington, 'An Unfortunate Mother's Advice To Her Absent Daughters', In *A Letter to Miss Pennington*, A. Millar, W. Law and R. Cater, 1761, p. 8
13. Ibid, p. 19
14. Ibid. p. 114
15. Ibid. p. 114
16. Ibid. p. 151
17. Ibid. pp. 151-152
18. Ibid. p. 152
19. *The Gentleman's Magazine, 1783*, Historical Journals on microfilm, Open Court Publishing Co. Volume 53, Issue 9
20. Lorna Sage, *The Cambridge Guide to Women's Writing in English*, Cambridge University Press, 1999, p. 494

Mary Wollstonecraft: The First of a New Genus
1. Mary Wollstonecraft: Discovering Literature, The British Library, www.britishlibrary.uk
2. Emma Raymond, *Mary Wollstonecraft, East End Women's Museum*, 2021, www.eastendwomensmuseum.org
3. Janet Todd, *Mary Wollstonecraft: A Revolutionary Life (Lives in Letters)*, Orion, 2000, p. 11
4. Claire Tomalin, *The Life and Death of Mary Wollstonecraft*, Penguin, 2012, pp. 34-43
5. Mary Wollstonecraft, *East End Women's Museum*, 2021, www.eastendwomensmuseum.org
6. Emily W Sustein, *A Different Face: The Face of Mary Wollstonecraft*, Little Brown & Co., 1975, pp. 22-25
7. Janet Todd, *Mary Wollstonecraft: A Revolutionary Life (Lives in Letters)*, Orion, 2000, pp. 22-24
8. Ralph Martin Wardle, *Mary Wollstonecraft: A Critical Biography*, University of Kansas, 1951, pp. 12-18

Notes

9. Janet Todd, *Mary Wollstonecraft: A Revolutionary Life (Lives in Letters)*, Orion, 2000, p. 62
10. Emily W. Sustein, *A Different Face: The Face of Mary Wollstonecraft*, Little Brown & Co., 1975, pp. 103-106
11. Ralph Martin Wardle, *Mary Wollstonecraft: A Critical Biography*, University of Kansas, 1951, pp. 100-120
12. Janet Todd, *Mary Wollstonecraft: A Revolutionary Life (Lives in Letters)*, Orion, 2000, pp. 106-107
13. Ibid. p. 116
14. Claire Tomalin, *The Life and Death of Mary Wollstonecraft*, Penguin, 2012, pp. 64-88
15. Janet Todd (ed.), *The Collected Letters of Mary Wollstonecraft*, Allen Lane, 2003, p. 139
16. Emily W Sustein, *A Different Face: The Face of Mary Wollstonecraft*, Little Brown & Co., 1975, pp. 151-155
17. Janet Todd, *Mary Wollstonecraft: A Revolutionary Life (Lives in Letters)*, Orion, 2000, pp. 134-135
18. M. D'Ezio, *Hester Lynch Thrale Piozzi: A Taste for Eccentricity*, Cambridge Scholars Publishing, 2010, pp. 35-37
19. Janet Todd, *Mary Wollstonecraft: A Revolutionary Life (Lives in Letters)*, Orion, 2000, p. 153
20. Claire Tomalin, *The Life and Death of Mary Wollstonecraft*, Penguin, 2012, pp. 151-152
21. Tom Furniss, *Mary Wollstonecraft's French Revolution*, Cambridge University Press, 2006, p. 60
22. Ibid. p. 61
23. Ibid. p. 61
24. Ibid. p. 61
25. Ibid. p. 64
26. Ibid. p. 65
27. Ibid. p. 65
28. Ibid. p. 68
29. Claire Tomalin, *The Life and Death of Mary Wollstonecraft*, Penguin, 2012, p. 218
30. Ralph Martin Wardle, *Mary Wollstonecraft: A Critical Biography*, University of Kansas, 1951, p. 202

31. Emily W. Sustein, *A Different Face: The Face of Mary Wollstonecraft*, Little Brown & Co., 1975, pp. 254-255
32. Janet Todd, *Mary Wollstonecraft: A Revolutionary Life (Lives in Letters)*, Orion, 2000, pp. 286-287
33. Claire Tomalin, *The Life and Death of Mary Wollstonecraft*, Penguin, 2012, pp. 225-231
34. Janet Todd (ed.), *The Collected Letters of Mary Wollstonecraft*, Columbia University Press, 2004, pp. 326-327
35. Ralph Martin Wardle, *Mary Wollstonecraft: A Critical Biography*, University of Kansas, 1951, pp. 245-246
36. William St. Clair, *The Godwins and the Shelleys: A Biography of the Family*, Faber and Faber, 1989, pp. 164-169
37. William Godwin, 'Godwin on Wollstonecraft: The Life of Mary Wollstonecraft', *Classical Biographies* edited by Richard Holmes, Harper Perennial, 2011, p. 95.
38. Ralph Martin Wardle, *Mary Wollstonecraft: A Critical Biography*, University of Kansas, 1951, pp. 286-292
39. Claire Tomalin, *The Life and Death of Mary Wollstonecraft*, Penguin, 2012, pp. 275-283.
40. C. Kegan Paul, *William Godwin: His Friends and Contemporaries*, Volume 1, Henry S. King & Co, London, 1876, pp. 272-292.
41. Janet Todd, *Mary Wollstonecraft: A Revolutionary Life (Lives in Letters)*, Orion, 2000, p. 457
42. Lyndall Gordon, *Vindication: A Life of Mary Wollstonecraft*, Virago, 2006, p. 446
43. Emily W. Sustein, *A Different Face: The Face of Mary Wollstonecraft*, Little Brown & Co., 1975, pp. 349-351
44. Robert Southey, *A Memoir of the Life and Writings of William Taylor of Norwich*. Ed. J. W. Robberds. Volume 2, London: John Murray, 1824, 1:504

Dido Elizabeth Belle: Spark of the Abolitionist Movement

1. Historic England website, Slavery and Justice Exhibition at Kenwood House, 14 June 2014, www.historicengland.org.uk
2. English Heritage Website, Women in History: Dido Elizabeth Belle, www.english-heritage.org.uk
3. Historic England website, Slavery and Justice Exhibition at Kenwood House, 14 June 2014, www.historicengland.org.uk

Notes

4. Gene Adams, *Dido Elizabeth Belle – A Black Girl at Kenwood: An Account of a protegee of the 1st Lord Mansfield*, Camden History Review, Volume 12, Internet Archive, 28 June 2014

5. English Heritage Website, Women in History: Dido Elizabeth Belle, www.english-heritage.org.uk

6. Slavery and Justice at Kenwood House, Part 1, Internet Archive: Historic England, 14 June 2015, www.historicengland.org.uk

7. English Heritage Website, Women in History: Dido Elizabeth Belle, www.english-heritage.org.uk

8. Nisha Lilia Diu, 'Dido Belle: Britain's First Black Aristocrat', *The Telegraph*, 6 June 2014, www.telegraph.co.uk

9. Ibid. www.telegraph.co.uk

10. Ibid. www.telegraph.co.uk

11. Jacob F. Field, 'Domestic Service, Gender, and Wages in Rural England, c 1700-1860', *The Economic History Review*, Issue 66, pp. 249-272

12. Sarah Murden, 'Dido Elizabeth Belle: Questions and Answers', *All Things Georgian*, 29 April 2020, www.georgianera.wordpress.com

13. Bob Mullan and Gary Marvin, *Zoo Culture: The Book About Watching People Watch Animals*, University of Illinois Press Urbana, Illinois, Second Edition, 1998, p. 98

14. Nisha Lilia Diu, 'Dido Belle: Britain's First Black Aristocrat', *The Telegraph*, 6 June 2014, www.telegraph.co.uk

15. James Walvin, *Black Ivory*, Fontana, 1993, pp. 12-16

16. English Heritage Website, Women in History: Dido Elizabeth Belle, www.english-heritage.org.uk

17. Sarah Murden, 'Dido Elizabeth Belle: Questions and Answers', *All Things Georgian*, 29 April 2020, www.georgianera.wordpress.com

18. Sarah Murden, 'Dido Elizabeth Belle and John Daniniere, what became of them?' 10 July 2018, www.georgianera.wordpress.com

19. Ibid. www.georgianera.wordpress.com

20. Ibid. www.georgianera.wordpress.com

21. Sarah Murden, 'The Descendants of Dido Elizabeth Belle', *All Things Georgian*, 21 July 2021. www.georgianera.wordpress.com

22. Parbury's Oriental Herald and Colonial Intelligencer, Government Notifications: Madras, London 1837, pp. 59 and 117

Jane Austen: A Hopeful Romantic

1. Janet Todd, *The Cambridge Introduction to Jane Austen* (2nd Edition), Cambridge University Press, 2015, p. 2
2. Deirdre Le Faye, *Jane Austen: The World of Her Novels*, Frances Lincoln, 2004, p. 11
3. Park Honan, *Jane Austen: Her Life*, 1st Edition, St Martin's Press, New York, 1987, pp. 211-212
4. Deirdre Le Faye, *Jane Austen: The World of Her Novels*, Frances Lincoln, 2004, p. 29
5. Ibid. p. 29
6. Irene Collins, *Jane Austen: The Parson's Daughter*, Bloomsbury Continuum (New Edition), 2007, pp 35, 133
7. Janet Todd, *The Cambridge Introduction to Jane Austen* (2nd Edition), Cambridge University Press, 2015, p. 3
8. Claire Tomalin, *Jane Austen: A Life*, Penguin Books, 1997, pp. 9-10, 23, 33-38
9. Irene Collins, *Jane Austen: The Parson's Daughter*, Bloomsbury Continuum (New Edition), 2007, p. 42
10. Park Honan, *Jane Austen: Her Life*, 1st Edition, St Martin's Press, New York, 1987, pp. 66-68
11. Penny Gay, *Jane Austen and the Theatre*, Cambridge University Press, 2002, pp. 4-10
12. Claire Tomalin, *Jane Austen: A Life*, Penguin Books, 1997, pp. 54-60
13. Mary Lascelles, *Jane Austen and Her Art*, Oxford University Press, 1966, pp. 106-107
14. George Holbert Tucker, 'A Goodly Heritage': *A History of Jane Austen's Family*, Sutton Publishing Ltd, 1983, pp. 2-6
15. Park Honan, *Jane Austen: Her Life*, 1st Edition, St Martin's Press, New York, 1987, pp. 61-62, 70
16. Janet Todd, *The Cambridge Introduction to Jane Austen* (2nd Edition), Cambridge University Press, 2015, p. 4
17. Abigail H Bok, *The Jane Austen Companion with A Dictionary of Austen's Life and Works*, Macmillan, New York, 1986, p. 244
18. Richard Jenkyns, 'A Fine Brush on Ivory': *An Appreciation of Jane Austen*, Oxford University Press, 2004, p. 31
19. Janet Todd, *The Cambridge Introduction to Jane Austen* (2nd Edition),

Cambridge University Press, 2015, p. 5

20. Claire Tomalin, *Jane Austen: A Life*, Penguin Books, 1997, p. 47
21. Park Honan, *Jane Austen: Her Life*, 1st Edition, St Martin's Press, New York, 1987, p. 75
22. Ibid, p. 93
23. Deirdre Le Faye (ed), *Jane Austen's Letters* (Fourth Edition), Oxford University Press, 2014, p. 1
24. Ibid. p. 1
25. John Halperin, *Jane Austen's Lovers*, Rice University, 1985, p. 721
26. Henry Fielding, *Tom Jones*, Book VII, Chapter XII
27. Deirdre Le Faye (ed), *Jane Austen's Letters* (Fourth Edition), Oxford University Press, 2014, p. 4
28. Ibid. p. 4
29. John Halperin, *Jane Austen's Lovers*, Rice University, 1985, p. 721
30. Ibid. p. 722
31. Kathryn Sutherland, *Jane Austen's Textual Lives: From Aeschylus to Bollywood*, Oxford University Press, 2005, pp. 16-18
32. Deirdre Le Faye, *Jane Austen: A Family Record*, Cambridge University Press, 2004, pp. 100, 114
33. Ibid. p. 104
34. Claire Tomalin, *Jane Austen: A Life*, Penguin Books, 1997, p. 120-121
35. Irene Collins, *Jane Austen: The Parson's Daughter*, Bloomsbury Continuum (New Edition), 2007, pp. 8-9
36. Kathryn Sutherland, *Jane Austen's Textual Lives: From Aeschylus to Bollywood*, Oxford University Press, 2005, p. 21
37. Claire Tomalin, *Jane Austen: A Life*, Penguin Books, 1997, pp. 168-175
38. Robert P. Irvine, *Jane Austen*, Routledge, 2005, pp. 4-6
39. Ibid. pp. 4
40. John Halperin, *Jane Austen's Lovers*, Rice University, 1985, p. 729
41. Deirdre Le Faye (ed), *Jane Austen's Letters* (Fourth Edition), Oxford University Press, 2014, p. 21
42. Robert P. Irvine, *Jane Austen*, Routledge, 2005, p. 3
43. Karli Hall, *Jane Austen: A Biography*, BYU, Dramaturgy blog, February 6 2014, byuprideandprejudice.wordpress.com
44. Jane Austen, *Pride and Prejudice*, Chapter 20

45. Deirdre Le Faye (ed), *Jane Austen's Letters* (Fourth Edition), Oxford University Press, 2014, Letter dated 18-20 November 1814, pp. 278-282
46. Jane Austen, *Sense and Sensibility*, Volume II, Chapter VII
47. Kathryn Sutherland, *Jane Austen's Textual Lives: From Aeschylus to Bollywood*, Oxford University Press, 2005, pp. 15, 21
48. Robert P. Irvine, *Jane Austen*, Routledge, 2005, p. 13
49. Ibid. p. 15
50. Ibid. 15
51. Park Honan, *Jane Austen: Her Life*, 1st Edition, St Martin's Press, New York, 1987, pp. 378-379
52. Janet Todd, *The Cambridge Introduction to Jane Austen* (2nd Edition), Cambridge University Press, 2015, p. 13
53. Ibid. p. 13
54. Jane Austen's epitaph, Winchester Cathedral
55. Jan Fergus and Luke J. Wood, *Jane Austen: A Literary Life*, Palgrave Macmillan, 1991, pp. 26-27
56. Devoney Looser, 'Fan Fiction or Fan Fact: An Unknown Pen Portrait of Jane Austen', *The Times Literary Supplement*, 13 December 2019

Hester Stanhope: A Non-conformist Adventurer

1. Hugh Chisolm (ed), 'Stanhope, Lady Hester Lucy', *Encyclopaedia Britannica,* Volume 25 (11th edition), Cambridge University Press, p. 775
2. Ellis Kirsten, *Star of the Morning: The Extraordinary Life of Lady Hester Stanhope*, HarperPress (first edition), 2008, pp. 100-113
3. Catherine Lucy Wilhelmina Powlett, 'Duchess of Cleveland', *Life and Letters of Lady Hester Stanhope*, Murray, London, 1914, pp. 225-239
4. Marcel Theroux, 'Lady Hester Stanhope: Meet the Trailblazing Queen of the Desert', *Guardian* article from Sunday 17 May 2020.
5. Ellis Kirsten, *Star of the Morning: The Extraordinary Life of Lady Hester Stanhope*, HarperPress (first edition), 2008, p. 131
6. Lady Hester Lucy Stanhope and Charles Lewis Meryon, *Travels of Lady Hester Stanhope*; Forming the completion of her memoirs, London, H Colburn, 1846, Volume 1, pp/ 226-239

Notes

7. Neil Asher Silberman, 'Restoring the Reputation of Lady Hester Stanhope', *Biblical Archaeology Review*, Edition 10, pp. 68-75
8. Shirley Seidler, *The Eccentric English Lady Who Introduced Archaeology to the Holy Land*, Haaretz, 21 May 2015, www.Haaretz.com
9. Hugh Chisolm (ed), 'Lady Hester Lucy Stanhope', *Encyclopaedia Britannica*, Volume 25, 11th Edition, Cambridge University Press, p. 775
10. Allan Harman (ed), 'Mission of Discovery: The beginnings of Modern Jewish Evangelism', *Christian Focus Publications*, 1996, p. 203

Elizabeth Fry: The Angel of Prisoners

1. W.S. Gilbert and A. Sullivan, *Trial By Jury*, Act I, Scene 1, Line 185
2. Janet Witney, *Elizabeth Fry*, George G. Harrap & Co Ltd, London, 1951, pp. 11–13
3. Ibid. p. 14
4. Ibid. p. 25
5. Ibid. p. 117
6. Ibid. p. 117
7. Ibid. p. 117
8. Clare Hunter, *Thread of Life: A History of the World Through the Eye of a Needle*, London: Sceptre (Hodder & Stoughton), 2019, p. 50
9. E.R. Pitman, 'Evidence before the House of Commons: Elizabeth Fry,' Boston: Robert brothers via Project Guttenberg, E-book edition, Chapter VII
10. Anne Isba, *The Excellent Mrs Fry: Unlikely Heroine*, London, Bloomsbury Academic; Continuum, 2010, pp. 139-144
11. Lucy Frost, 'Gifts of Patchwork and Visits to Whitehall: The British Ladies' Society and Female Convict Ships', Sue Thomas (ed), *Victorian Traffic: Identity, Exchange, Performance*, Newcastle, UK, Cambridge Scholars Publishing, 2008, pp. 2-18
12. Dennis Bardens, *Elizabeth Fry: Britain's Second Lady of the Five Pound Note*, London, Chanadon, 2004, pp. 50-63
13. Janet Witney, *Elizabeth Fry*, George G. Harrap &Co Ltd, London, 1951, p. 249
14. Annemieke van Drenth, *The Rise of Caring Power: Elizabeth Fry and Josephine Butler in Britain and the Netherlands*, Amsterdam University Press, 1999, p. 27

Georgian Feminists

15. Kelly Grovier, *The Gaol*, John Murray Publishers, 2009, p. 278
16. Thomas Timpson, *Memoirs of Mrs Elizabeth Fry* (2nd Edition), London, New York: Aylott and Jones: Stanford & Swords. 1847, pp. 82-99
17. Anne Isba, *The Excellent Mrs Fry: Unlikely Heroine*, Bryan B. Rasmussen (ed) Victorian Studies, Indiana University Press, Autumn 2011, Volume 54, No. 1, pp. 153-155

Mary Fildes: Peterloo Survivor

1. Robert Poole, 'Mary Fildes', *Oxford Dictionary of National Biography*, Oxford University Press
2. Ibid. p. 2
3. Robert Poole, *Peterloo: The English Uprising*, Oxford University Press, 2019, pp. 285-290, 305-307
4. Theophilia Carlile Campbell, *The Battle of the Press: As Told in the Story of the Life of Richard Carlile By His Daughter Theophilia Carlile Campbell*, A. & H.B. Bonner, London, 1899, Chapter iii
5. Micheal L. Bush, 'The Women at Peterloo: The Impact of Female Reform on the Manchester Meeting of August 16 1819', *History* Volume 94, 2006, pp. 209-232
6. James Wroe, 'Peterloo Massacre: Containing A Faithful Narrative of the Events which preceded, Accompanied, and Followed the Fatal Sixteenth of August 1819', 2nd Edition. Manchester, 1819, pp. 21-22
7. Robert Poole, 'Mary Fildes': *Oxford Dictionary of National Biography*, Oxford University Press
8. Robert Reid, *The Peterloo Massacre*, Penguin, 2018, p. 242
9. Ibid, p. 258
10. Isabella Banks, *The Manchester Man*, Manchester, Abel Heywood, 1896, Chapters 19, pp. 462
11. Robert Poole, *Peterloo: The English Uprising*, Oxford University Press, 2019, pp. 1-2
12. M.L. Bush, 'The Friends and Following of Richard Carlile': *A Study of Infidel Republicanism in Early Nineteenth-Century Britain*, Twopenny Press, 2016, pp. 128-134
13. J. Hampson, Letter to the Editor, *The Poor Man's Guardian*, 27 July 1833, H. Hetherington, 13 Kingsgate Street, Holborn, Edition 112
14. Advertisement, *Northern Star*, 14 January 1843

Notes

15. Robert Poole, 'Mary Fildes': *Oxford Dictionary of National Biography*, Oxford University Press

Anne Lister: The First Modern Lesbian

1. Sir William Dugdale, *Dugdale's Visitation of Yorkshire, with Additions*, W. Pollard & Company, 1894, p. 118
2. Ibid. p. 118
3. Helena Whitbread, 'No Priest but Love': *Excerpts From the Diaries of Anne Lister 1824-1826*, New York University Press, 1992, p. 2
4. *The Secret Diaries of Miss Anne Lister*, St Thomas' Church, Osbaldwick Lane, Osbaldwick, York, Internet Archive, 4 April 2020, www.osbaldwickandmurtonchurches.org.uk
5. Rebecca Woods, 'The Life And Loves of Anne Lister', BBC News, 3 May 2019, www.bbc.co.uk/news/resources
6. Muriel Green, *Miss Lister of Shibden Hall: Selected Letters* (1800–1840), 1992, Book Guild, pp. 7, 19
7. The Parish of St Thomas Osbaldwick with St James Murton: About the Parish of St Thomas', 6 July 2020, www.osbaldwickandmurtonchurches.org.uk
8. Jill Liddington, 'Anne Lister of Shibden Hall', Halifax (1791-1840) for Diaries and the Historians, *History Workshop Journal*, Volume 35, Issue 1, Spring 1993, pp. 45-77, www.academic.oup.com
9. Angela Steidele, *Gentleman Jack: A Biography of Anne Lister*, Regency Landowner, Seducer and Secret Diarist, Serpent's Tail, London, 2018, pp. 64-68
10. Ibid. p. 133
11. Helena Whitbread, *Anne's Lovers*, 2015, www.annelister.co.uk/annes-lovers/
12. Angela Steidele, *Gentleman Jack: A Biography of Anne Lister*, Regency Landowner, Seducer and Secret Diarist, Serpent's Tail, London, 2018, pp. 99-110
13. Anne Lister, General Inventory, January 1840, Calderdale Museums, 10 May 1824
14. Elizabeth Mavor, 'Gentleman Jack of Halifax', *London Review of Books*, London, LRB Ltd, 4 February 1988, www.lrb.co.uk
15. Rictor Norton, 'Anne lister: The First Modern Lesbian', *Gay History*

and Literature, 1 August 2003, www.rictornorton.co.uk/lister

16. Nanou Saint-Lebe, *Les Femmes a la decouverte des Pyrenees* (in French), Toulouse, Privat, 2002, pp. 60-70
17. Angela Steidele, *Gentleman Jack: A Biography of Anne Lister, Regency Landowner, Seducer and Secret Diarist*, Serpent's Tail, London, 2018, p. 179
18. Ibid, p. 179
19. Ibid, p. 186
20. Anne Chroma, *Gentleman Jack: The Real Anne lister,* Penguin Publishing, pp. 62, 182-183, 2019
21. Anne Lister: Reworded York Plaque For 'First Lesbian', 28 February 2019, www.bbc.co.uk
22. Olga Khoroshilova, *Gentleman Jack in Russia* (In Russian), Moscow, MIF, 2022, pp. 10-25
23. Angela Steidele, *Gentleman Jack: A Biography of Anne Lister*, Regency Landowner, Seducer and Secret Diarist, Serpent's Tail, London, 2018, pp. 266-267
24. Ibid. p. 291
25. Ibid, p. 273
26. Jill Liddington, *Anne Lister of Shibden Hall*, Halifax (1791-1840) for Diaries and the Historians, *History Workshop Journal*, Volume 35, Issue 1, Spring 1993, pp. 45-77, www.academic.oup.com
27. Rictor Norton, 'Anne Lister: The First Modern Lesbian', *Gay History and Literature*, 1 August 2003, www.rictornorton.co.uk/lister
28. UK Memory of the World Register, UK National Commission for UNESCO, 2011, www.UNESCO.org
29. Journal of Anne Walker, Calderdale, West Yorkshire Archive Service, WYC:1525/7/1/5/1, June 1834-February 1854
30. Rictor Norton, 'Anne Lister: The First Modern Lesbian', *Gay History and Literature*, 1 August 2003, www.rictornorton.co.uk/lister
31. David M. Lang, 'Georgia in 1840: The Lister Diaries', Bulletin of the School of Oriental and African Studies, Cambridge University Press, 1990, pp. 115-120
32. The Shibden Hall Estate, *The Leeds Times*, 22 July 1882, www.britishnewspaperarchive.co.uk
33. Explore Anne 'Gentleman Jack' Lister's Halifax, Visit Calderdale,

12 August 2021, www.visitcalderdale.com/explore-anne-gentleman-jack-listers-halifax

Mary Anning: The Palaeontological Pioneer

1. Emling, Shelley, *The Fossil Hunter: Dinosaurs, Evolution, and the Woman whose Discoveries Changed the World*, Palgrave Macmillan, 2009, pp 11-14
2. Cadbury, Deborah, *The Dinosaur Hunters: A True Story of Scientific Rivalry and the Discovery of the Prehistoric World*, Forth Estate, 2000, pp 5, 6
3. Emling, Shelley, *The Fossil Hunter: Dinosaurs, Evolution, and the Woman whose Discoveries Changed the World*, Palgrave Macmillan, 2009, pp 11-14
4. Goodhew, Thomas W., *Curious Bones: Mary Anning and the Birth of Palaeontology* (Great Scientists), Morgan Reynolds, 2002, p. 2
5. Cadbury, Deborah, *The Dinosaur Hunters: A True Story of Scientific Rivalry and the Discovery of the Prehistoric World*, Forth Estate, 2000, pp 4-5
6. Hawkes, Jaquetta, *A Land*. London: Readers United, 1953, pp 56, 57
7. Cadbury, Deborah, *The Dinosaur Hunters: A True Story of Scientific Rivalry and the Discovery of the Prehistoric World*, Forth Estate, 2000, pp 5-6
8. Emling, Shelley, *The Fossil Hunter: Dinosaurs, Evolution, and the Woman whose Discoveries Changed the World*, Palgrave Macmillan, 2009, pp 14-16
9. Ibid, p. 26
10. Cadbury, Deborah, *The Dinosaur Hunters: A True Story of Scientific Rivalry and the Discovery of the Prehistoric World*, Forth Estate, 2000, p. 4
11. Ibid, pp 6-8
12. McGowan, Christopher, *The Dragon Seekers*, Persus Publishing, 2001, pp 11-12
13. Sharpe, T., McCartney, Paul J, *The Papers of H.T. De la Beche (1796-1855)* in the National Museum of Wales, 1998, pp. 15
14. Howe S.R., Sharpe T., Torrens H.S., *Ichthyosaur: A History of Fossil 'Sea Dragons'*, National Museum of Wales, 1981, p 12
15. Bank of England Inflation Calculator for 1820-2023
16. Dean, Dennis R., *Gideon Mantell and the Discovery of Dinosaurs*,

Cambridge University Press, 2009, p. 58

17. Torrens, Hugh, 'Mary Anning (1799–1847) of Lyme: The Greatest Fossilist the World Ever Knew', *The British Journal for the History of Science*, 1995, 257-284

18. Goodhew, Thomas W., *Fossil Hunter: The Life and Times of Mary Anning*, Accademia Press LLC, 2004, p. 84

19. Emling, Shelley, *The Fossil Hunter: Dinosaurs, Evolution, and the Woman whose Discoveries Changed the World*, Palgrave Macmillan, 2009, p 172

20. Christopher McGowan, *The Dragon Seekers*, Persus Publishing, 2001. pp 203-204

21. Charles Dickens, *Mary Anning; the Fossil Finder*, Volume 13, All Year Round, 1865

22. Torrens, Hugh, 'Mary Anning (1799-1847) of Lyme: The Greatest Fossilist the World Ever Knew', *The British Journal for the History of Science*, 1995, 257-284

23. McGowan, Christopher, *The Dragon Seekers*, Persus Publishing, 2001, pp 26-27

24. Ibid, 133–148

25. Rudwick, Martin J.S., *Scenes from Deep Time: Early Pictorial Representations of the Prehistoric World*, The University of Chicago Press, 1992, pp. 42-47

26. Emling, Shelley, *The Fossil Hunter: Dinosaurs, Evolution, and the Woman whose Discoveries Changed the World*, Palgrave Macmillan, 2009, p 143

27. Ibid, 171-172

28. Brice, William, Hugh S. Torrens, History of Geology Division Award, Geological Society of America

29. McGowan, Christopher, *The Dragon Seekers*, Persus Publishing, 2001, pp pp 200-201

Ada Lovelace: The Enchantress of Number

1. George Gordon Byron, 6th Baron Byron, 'Fare Thee Well', Poem to Lady Byron, Stanza 11

2. Benjamin Wooley, *The Bride of Science, Romance, Reason and Byron's Daughter*, Pan, 2015, pp. 85-87

3. Ibid, p. 86

4. Ibid, p. 119

Notes

5. Betty Alexandra Toole, *Poetical Science: The Byron Journal*, Number 15, Liverpool University Press, 1987, pp. 55-65
6. Benjamin Wooley, *The Bride of Science, Romance, Reason and Byron's Daughter*, Pan, 2015, pp. 120-121
7. Catherine Turney, *Byron's Daughter: A Biography of Elizabeth Medora Leigh*, Scribner, 1972, p. 138
8. Ibid, pp. 138-139
9. Benjamin Wooley, *The Bride of Science, Romance, Reason and Byron's Daughter*, Pan, 2015, pp. 285-286
10. Ibid, pp. 289-296
11. Ibid, p. 302
12. Ibid, pp. 336-337
13. Ibid, p. 361
14. David G Schwartz, *Roll the Bones: The History of Gambling*, Gotham Books, 2006, p. 162
15. Benjamin Wooley, *The Bride of Science, Romance, Reason and Byron's Daughter*, Pan, 2015, pp. 340-342
16. Velma R. Huskey, Harry D. Huskey, 'Lady Lovelace and Charles Babbage', *The Annals of the History of Computing*, Volume 2, Issue 4, October-December 1980, pp. 299-329
17. Benjamin Wooley, *The Bride of Science, Romance, Reason and Byron's Daughter*, Pan, 2015, p. 267
18. Ibid. p. 307
19. Ada Augusta, Countess of Lovelace (translator and ed), L.F. Menabrea (author), A Sketch of the Analytical Engine: Invented by Charles Babbage, Bibliotheque Universelle de Geneve, 1842, No.82
20. Ada Augusta, Countess of Lovelace (translator and ed), L.F. Menabrea (author), *A Sketch of the Analytical Engine: Invented by Charles Babbage*, Bibliotheque Universelle de Geneve, 1842, No. 82
21. A.M. Turing, *Computing Machinery and Intelligence*, Mind, Oxford Academic, Volume LIX, Issue 236, October 1950, Note 6, pp. 433-460
22. Benjamin Wooley, *The Bride of Science, Romance, Reason and Byron's Daughter*, Pan, 2015, p.370
23. Ibid, p. 369

Bibliography

Adams, Gene, *Dido Elizabeth Belle – A Black Girl at Kenwood: An Account of a protegee of the 1ˢᵗ Lord Mansfield, Camden History Review*, Volume 12, Internet Archive, 28 June 2014.

Augusta, Ada, Countess of Lovelace (translator and ed), L. F. Menabrea (author), *A Sketch of the Analytical Engine: Invented by Charles Babbage*, Bibliotheque Universelle de Geneve, 1842.

Banks, Isabella, *The Manchester Man*, Manchester, Abel Heywood, 1896.

Bardens, Dennis, *Elizabeth Fry: Britain's Second Lady of the Five Pound Note*, London, Chanadon, 2004.

Bok, Abigail H., *The Jane Austen Companion with A Dictionary of Austen's Life and Works*, Macmillan, New York, 1986.

Brice, William and Torrens, Hugh S. *History of Geology Division Award*, Geological Society of America.

Bush, M. L., *The Friends and Following of Richard Carlile: a Study of Infidel Republicanism in Early Nineteenth-Century Britain*, Twopenny Press, 2016.

Bush, Micheal L., The Women at Peterloo: The Impact of Female Reform on the Manchester Meeting of August 16 1819, *History* Volume 94, 2006.

Cadbury, Deborah, *The Dinosaur Hunters: A True Story of Scientific Rivalry and the Discovery of the Prehistoric World*, Forth Estate, 2000.

Cadbury, Deborah, *The Dinosaur Hunters: A True Story of Scientific Rivalry and the Discovery of the Prehistoric World*, Forth Estate, 2000.

Campbell, Theophilia Carlile, *The Battle of the Press: As Told in the Story of the Life of Richard Carlile By His Daughter Theophilia Carlile Campbell*, A & H B Bonner, London, 1899.

Chisolm, Hugh (ed), Stanhope, *Lady Hester Lucy*, Encyclopedia Britannica, Volume 25 (11th edition), Cambridge University Press.

Chroma, Anne and Wainwright, Sally, *Gentleman Jack: The Real Anne Lister*, Penguin Publishing, 2019.

Collins, Irene, *Jane Austen: The Parson's Daughter*, Bloomsbury Continuum (New Edition), 2007.

D'Ezio, M., *Hester Lynch Thrale Piozzi: A Taste for Eccentricity*, Cambridge Scholars Publishing, 2010.

Dickens, Charles, *Mary Anning; the Fossil Finder*, Volume 13, All Year Round, 1865.

Bibliography

Diu, Nisha Lilia, *Dido Belle: Britain's First Black Aristocrat*, The Telegraph, 6 June 2014, www.telegraph.co.uk.

Dugdale, Sir William, *Dugdale's Visitation of Yorkshire, with Additions*, W. Pollard & Company, 1894.

Ellis, Lucy, *The Art of Dressing: Shaping Fashion in Georgian England*, 2023, www.artuk.org/discover/stories/the-art-of-dressing-shaping-fashion-in-georgian-england.

Emling, Shelley, *The Fossil Hunter: Dinosaurs, Evolution, and the Woman whose Discoveries Changed the World*, Palgrave Macmillan, 2009.

Emling, Shelley, *The Fossil Hunter: Dinosaurs, Evolution, and the Woman whose Discoveries Changed the World*, Palgrave Macmillan, 2009.

Fergus, Jan and Wood, Luke J., *Jane Austen: A Literary Life*, Palgrave Macmillan, 1991.

Field, Jacob F., 'Domestic Service, Gender, and Wages in Rural England, c 1700-1860', *The Economic History Review*, Issue 66.

Fielding, Henry, *Tom Jones*, Book VII, 1749.

Frost, Lucy, '*Gifts of Patchwork and Visits to Whitehall: The British Ladies' Society and Female Convict Ships*', Thomas, Sue (ed), Victorian Traffic: Identity, Exchange, Performance, Newcastle, UK, Cambridge Scholars Publishing, 2008.

Furniss, Tom, *Mary Wollstonecraft's French Revolution*, Cambridge University Press, 2006.

Gay, Penny, *Jane Austen and the Theatre*, Cambridge University Press, 2002.

Goodhew, Thomas W., *Curious Bones: Mary Anning and the Birth of Palaeontology (Great Scientists)*, Morgan Reynolds, 2002.

Goodhew, Thomas W., *Fossil Hunter: The Life and Times of Mary Anning*, Accademia Press LLC, 2004.

Gordon, Lyndall, *Vindication: A Life of Mary Wollstonecraft*, Virago, 2006.

Green, Muriel, *Miss Lister of Shibden Hall: Selected Letters (1800-1840)*, 1992, Book Guild.

Grovier, Kelly, *The Gaol*, John Murray Publishers, 2009.

Halperin, John, *Jane Austen's Lovers*, Rice University, 1985.

Hampson, J., *Letter to the Editor, The Poor Man's Guardian, 27 July 1833, H Hetherington*, 13 Kingsgate Street, Holborn, Edition 112.

Harman, Allan, (ed), *Mission of Discovery: The Beginnings of Modern Jewish*

Evangelism, Christian Focus Publications, 1996.

Hawkes, Jaquetta, *A Land*. London: Readers United, 1953.

Historic England website, *Slavery and Justice Exhibition at Kenwood House*, 14 June 2014, www.historicengland.org.uk.

Honan, Park, *Jane Austen: Her Life, 1ˢᵗ Edition*, St Martin's Press, New York, 1987.

Howe S. R., Sharpe T., and Torrens H. S., *Ichthyosaur: A History of Fossil 'Sea Dragons'*, National Museum of Wales, 1981.

Hunter, Clare, *Thread of Life: A History of the World Through the Eye of a Needle*, London: Sceptre, Hodder & Stoughton, 2019.

Huskey, Velma R., and Huskey, Harry D., 'Lady Lovelace and Charles Babbage,' *The Annals of the History of Computing*, Volume 2, Issue 4, October-December 1980.

Irvine, Robert P., *Jane Austen*, Routledge, 2005.

Isba, Anne, *The Excellent Mrs Fry: Unlikely Heroine*, London, Bloomsbury Academic; Continuum, 2010.

Jenkyns, Richard, *A Fine Brush on Ivory: An Appreciation of Jane Austen*, Oxford University Press, 2004.

Khoroshilova, Olga, *Gentleman Jack in Russia (In Russian)*, Moscow, MIF, 2022.

Kirsten, Ellis, *Star of the Morning: The Extraordinary Life of Lady Hester Stanhope*, Harper Press (first edition), 2008 .

Lascelles, Mary, *Jane Austen and Her Art*, Oxford University Press, 1966.

Le Faye, Deirdre, *Jane Austen: The World of Her Novels*, Frances Lincoln, 2004.

Liddington, Jill, *Anne Lister of Shibden Hall, Halifax (1791-1840) for Diaries and the Historians*, History Workshop Journal, Volume 35, Issue 1, Spring 1993.

Luckel, Madeline, *Why It's Time to Revisit the Handheld Fan – And It's Secret*.

McDayter, Ghislaine and Hunter, John, *Flirtation and Courtship in Nineteenth-Century British Culture*, J Walter publishers, London, 1784.

McGowan, Christopher, *The Dragon Seekers*, Persus Publishing, 2001.

Millar, A., and Law, W., *An Unfortunate Mother's Advice to Her Absent Daughters, In A Letter to Miss Pennington*. Vogue, 24 April 2018.

Mullan, Bob and Marvin, Gary, *Zoo Culture: The Book About Watching People Watch Animals*, University of Illinois Pressm Urbana, Illinois, Second Edition, 1998.

Murden, Sarah, *Dido Elizabeth Belle: Questions and Answers*, All Things Georgian, 29 April 2020, www.georgianera.wordpress.com.

Norton, Rictor, *Anne Lister: The First Modern Lesbian, Gay History and Literature*, 1 August 2003 www.rictornorton.co.uk/lister.

Parbury's Oriental Herald and Colonial Intelligencer, *Government Notifications: Madras*, London, 1837.

Paul, Charles Kegan, *William Godwin: His Friends and Contemporaries*, Volume 1, Henry S. King & Co, London, 1876.

Pennington, Lady Sarah, An and R Cater, J Towers, 1761. Pp. 5–9.

Poole, Robert, *Mary Fildes: Oxford Dictionary of National Biography*, Oxford University Press.

Poole, Robert, *Peterloo: The English Uprising*, Oxford University Press, 2019.

Powlett, Catherine Lucy Wilhelmina, Duchess of Cleveland, *Life and Letters of Lady Hester Stanhope*, Murray, London, 1914.

Reid, Robert, *The Peterloo Massacre*, Penguin, 2018.

Rudwick, Martin J. S., *Scenes from Deep Time: Early Pictorial Representations of the Prehistoric World*, The University of Chicago Press, 1992.

Sage, Lorna, *The Cambridge Guide to Women's Writing in English*, Cambridge University Press, 1999.

Saint-Lebe, Nanou, *Les Femmes a la decouverte des Pyrenees (in French)*, Toulouse, Privat, 2002.

Schwartz, David G., *Roll the Bones: The History of Gambling*, Gotham Books, 2006.

Sharpe, T., and McCartney, Paul J., *The Papers of H.T. De la Beche (1796-1855) in the National Museum of Wales*, National Museum of Wales, 1998.

Silberman, Neil Asher, *Restoring the Reputation of Lady Hester Stanhope*, Biblical Archaeology Review, Edition 10.

Southey, Robert, *A Memoir of the Life and Writings of William Taylor of Norwich*. Ed. J. W. Robberds. Volume 2, London: John Murray, 1824.

St. Clair, William, *The Godwins and the Shelleys: A Biography of the Family*, Faber and Faber, 1989.

Stanhope, Lady Hester Lucy and Meryon, Charles Lewis, *Travels of Lady Hester Stanhope*; Forming the completion of her memoirs, London, H Colburn, 1846, Volume 1.

Steidele, Angela, *Gentleman Jack: A Biography of Anne Lister*, Regency Landowner, Seducer and Secret Diarist, Serpent's Tail, London, 2018.

Sustein, Emily W., *A Different Face: The Face of Mary Wollstonecraft*, Little Brown & Co., 1975.

Sutherland, Kathryn, *Jane Austen's Textual Lives: From Aeschylus to Bollywood*, Oxford University Press, 2005.

The Parish of St Thomas Osbaldwick with St James Murton: About the Parish of St Thomas', 6 July 2020 www.osbaldwickandmurtonchurches.org.uk.

Theroux, Marcel, *Lady Hester Stanhope: Meet the Trailblazing Queen of the Desert*, The Guardian, Sunday 17 May 2020.

Timpson, Thomas, *Memoirs of Mrs Elizabeth Fry* (2nd Edition), London, New York: Aylott and Jones: Stanford & Swords. 1847.

Todd, Janet, *Mary Wollstonecraft: A Revolutionary Life (Lives in Letters)*, Orion, 2000.

Todd, Janet, *The Cambridge Introduction to Jane Austen (2nd Edition)*, Cambridge University Press, 2015.

Tomalin, Claire, *The Life and Death of Mary Wollstonecraft*, Penguin, 2012.

Toole, Betty Alexandra, *Poetical Science: The Byron Journal*, Number 15, Liverpool University Press, 1987.

Torrens, Hugh, 'Mary Anning (1799-1847) of Lyme: The Greatest Fossilist the World Ever Knew', *The British Journal for the History of Science*, 1995.

Tucker, George Holbert, *A Goodly Heritage: A History of Jane Austen's Family*, Sutton Publishing Ltd, 1983.

Turing, A. M., 'Computing Machinery and Intelligence', *Mind*, Oxford Academic, Volume LIX, Issue 236, October 1950.

Turney, Catherine, *Byron's Daughter: A Biography of Elizabeth Medora Leigh*, Scribner, 1972.

van Drenth, Annemieke, *The Rise of Caring Power: Elizabeth Fry and Josephine Butler in Britain and the Netherlands*, Amsterdam University Press, 1999.

Wardle, Ralph Martin, *Mary Wollstonecraft: A Critical Biography*, University of Kansas, 1951.

Whitbread, Helena, *No Priest but Love: Excerpts From the Diaries of Anne Lister 1824-1826*, New York University Press, 1992.

Witney, Janet, *Elizabeth Fry*, George G Harrap &Co Ltd, London, 1951.

Wooley, Benjamin, *The Bride of Science, Romance, Reason and Byron's Daughter*, Pan, 2015.

Wroe, James, *Peterloo Massacre: Containing A Faithful Narrative of the Events which preceeded, Accompained, and Followed the Fatal Sixteenth of August 1819*, 2nd Edition. Manchester, 1819.

Index

Abolition 91, 103-105
Al Saud, Saud bin Abdulaziz 144
Analytical Engine 235
Anning, Mary 204-218
Arden, Jane 60
Austen, Jane 10-13, 112-136
Austen, Reverend George
    113, 130

Babbage, Charles 234-237
Banks, Isabella 176
Battle of Waterloo 174
Belcombe, Mariana 188, 191-192
Belle, Dido Elizabeth 89-111
Belle, Maria 89
Bentley, Richard 135
Bigg-Wither, Harris 128
Blood Frances, 'Fanny' 61-68,
    80-81, 85
Blue Coat School 15, 16
Blue Stocking Club 70
Browning, Robert 86
Buckland, William 215
Burney, Frences 119
Butchart, Amber 100
Buxton, Thomas Fowell 157
Byron, Lady Anne Isabella Noel
    219-229
Byron, Lord George Gordon, 6th
    Baron Byron 140, 219-223,
    228, 237

Cadell, Thomas 123
Cartwright, John 168

Childbed Fever 23-25, 85
Childbirth 23-28
Clare, Reverend 61
Cobbert, William 169
Contraception 178-179
Corday, Charlotte 74
Crimean War 161-164
Crosse, Andrew 228, 231

Dame School 16, 17
Darwin, Charles 216
de Pompadour, Madame 36
Dickens, Charles 216,
    228, 232
Difference Engine 234-236

East India Company 184
Education 15, 16, 116
Elizabeth Fry Refuge 163-164
Elliot, George 132

Faraday, Michael 228
Fildes, Luke 179
Fildes, Mary 166-181
Fossils 210, 211
Fry, Elizabeth 150-165
Fuseli, Henry 70-71

Gambling 57, 231-233
Gaol Act 1823 150, 156-158
Gentleman Jack 191
Geological Society of London 215,
    217-218
Gilbert W. S. 150

262

Godwin, William 69-71, 76-78, 83 84, 87
Gurney, John 151

Holcroft, Thomas 85
Hulton, William 173
Hunt, Henry 168, 172, 177

Imlay, Fanny 77-79
Imlay, Gilbert 77-80
Industrial Revolution 206

Johnson, Joseph 70, 82
Juvenilia 118, 119

Kenwood House 96, 97, 102, 103
King Henry VI 39
King George IV 232
King, Margaret 65-67
King William Fredrick IV of Prussia 162
Kingsborough, Lady 67

Language of fans 20
Lefroy, Thomas Langlois 119-122
Leigh, Cassandra 113
LGBTQIA+ 196-203
Lindsay, Sir John 89-94
Lister, Anne 182-203
Lister, Captain Jeremy 182, 183
Locke, John 61
Louis XV of France 19, 36
Lovelace, Ada 219-240

Marat, Jean-Paul 74
Mental health 148

Meryon, Charles Lewis 145-148
Mikhaila, Ninya 100
Millbank, Right Honourable Lady 224
Moore, Lieutenant General Sir John 38
Muncaster Castle 39, 40
Murray, Sir William, 1st Earl of Mansfield 102-109

Napoleonic Wars 206, 210
National Advisory Committee for Aeronautics (NACA) 238
National Aeronautics and Space Administration (NASA) 238
Newgate Prison 153-155
Newington Green School 65-67, 87
Nightingale, Florence 162
Norcliffe, Isabella 187
Northanger Abbey 124, 135

Paine, Thomas 69
Peel, Robert 165
Pennington, Lady Sarah 37-54
Pennington, Sir John 39-40
Pennington, Sir Joseph 38-44, 47-48, 50
Peterloo Massacre 168-177
Pinney, Anna 214
Pitt, William, the Younger 69
Pregnancy 22-28
Pride and Prejudice 11-13, 122-123, 128, 129
Prisons in Scotland and the North of England 156

Quakers 151-153
Queen Marie Antoinette 75-76

Raine, Eliza 184-187
Rawlins, Sophia 71
Roscoe, William 86

Salzmann, Christian
  Gotthiff 69
Sense and Sensibility 124, 130
Shelley, Mary 55, 68
Shibden Hall 184-189, 192
Simpson, Elizabeth 82
Skelding, Reverend George 184
Somerset, James 103-108
Somerville, Mary 228
Smith, Charlotte 119
Stanhope, Charles, 3rd Earl
  Stanhope 137
Stanhope, Hester 137-149
Stanhope, Major Honourable
  Charles Banks 139
Stuart, Charles 102, 109-111
Swift, Johnathan 61

Taylor, Thomas, 62
The British Royal Navy 131
The French Revolution 35, 36,
  71-75, 79, 206
The Luck of Muncaster 39, 40
The Manchester Man 176
The Royal Society 215
The Slavery Abolition Act 110-111
Transportation 161
Turing, Alan 236

UNESCO Memory of the World
  Programme 196-198

Wainwright, Sally 119
Walker, Anne 193-203
Waterhouse, Harriet 100
Wesley, John 31
West, Jane 119
Wheaton, Reverend James S. 210
Wollstonecraft, Mary 55-88
Woolf, Virginia 88

Zong 107